Religion Around Virginia Woolf

RELIGION AROUND, VOL. 6

PETER IVER KAUFMAN, *Founding Editor*

Books in the Religion Around series examine the religious forces surrounding cultural icons. By bringing religious background into the foreground, these studies give readers a greater understanding of and appreciation for individual figures, their work, and their lasting influence.

RELIGION AROUND
VIRGINIA WOOLF

STEPHANIE PAULSELL

THE PENNSYLVANIA STATE UNIVERSITY PRESS
UNIVERSITY PARK, PENNSYLVANIA

Material from chapter 1 appeared in an earlier form as "Family Resemblances: Religion Around Virginia Woolf," in *Cultural Icons and Cultural Leadership*, edited by Peter Iver Kaufman and Kristin M. S. Bezio (Cheltenham: Edward Elgar Publishing, 2017), 81–102.

Library of Congress Cataloging-in-Publication Data

Names: Paulsell, Stephanie, 1962– author.
Title: Religion around Virginia Woolf / Stephanie Paulsell.
Other titles: Religion around ; v. 6.
Description: University Park, Pennsylvania : The Pennsylvania State University Press, [2019] | Series: Religion around vol. 6. | Includes bibliographical references and index.
Summary: "An exploration of the religious contexts of Virginia Woolf's life and work, her religious practices, her ideas about God, and the new forms of community she imagined"—Provided by publisher.
Identifiers: LCCN 2019025528 | ISBN 9780271084879 (cloth)
Subjects: LCSH: Woolf, Virginia, 1882–1941—Religion. | Woolf, Virginia, 1882–1941—Criticism and interpretation. | Religion and literature.
Classification: LCC PR6045.O72 P38 2019 | DDC 823/.912—dc23
LC record available at https://lccn.loc.gov/2019025528

Printed in the United States of America
Published by The Pennsylvania State University Press,
University Park, PA 16802–1003

The Pennsylvania State University Press is a member of the Association of University Presses.

It is the policy of The Pennsylvania State University Press to use acid-free paper. Publications on uncoated stock satisfy the minimum requirements of American National Standard for Information Sciences—Permanence of Paper for Printed Library Material, ANSI Z39.48–1992.

For my father, who gave me the mystics,
and my mother, who gave me Woolf.

CONTENTS

ACKNOWLEDGMENTS

I am grateful to Peter Kaufman for imagining the Religion Around series and inviting me to be a part of it. This book benefited enormously from the formal and informal conversations Peter organized among the writers of this series and from the work done in Peter's own book on religion around Shakespeare, W. Clark Gilpin's on Emily Dickinson, and Tracy Fessenden's on Billie Holiday. It is an honor to be among these scholars from whom I have learned so much.

I am also grateful to Kathryn Yahner, who edits the series at Pennsylvania State University Press, for her encouragement, her insightful comments, and her patience. Her colleagues at the press, especially Janice North, Brian Beer, Alex Ramos, Laura Reed-Morrisson, and Regina Starace, were all tremendously helpful along the way, and I am grateful for the care they took with this volume.

With his usual generosity, Kevin Madigan, my husband and first reader, believed in this project and read all of these pages with care. Two other writers I admire and adore—Amy Hollywood and René Steinke— also read the whole manuscript and offered crucial advice. I can never thank these three enough. I am also grateful to the two anonymous readers who gave me the benefit of their expertise.

My colleagues at Harvard Divinity School have kindly listened to me talk about Virginia Woolf at faculty retreats and seminars over the years, and I am grateful for their questions and their many insights into this project. Ann Braude, Catherine Brekus, Davíd Carrasco, David Hempton, Mark Jordan, Kerry Maloney, Anne Monius, Laura Nasrallah, Kimberley Patton, Matthew Potts, Mayra Rivera Rivera, Dudley Rose, and Terry Tempest Williams have been especially generous with their time and have helped me think both about the religion around Woolf and the religious dimensions of her work. Kristine Culp, Tracy Fessenden, Constance Furey, Kathryn Lofton, Amanda Madigan, Ariana Nedelman, Kay Northcutt, Diane Paulsell, Richard Rosengarten, Casper ter Kuile, Jen Werner, Mara Willard, Lauren Winner, and Vanessa Zoltan have been wise and encouraging conversation partners along the way.

I have learned a great deal from the students in my seminars on Virginia Woolf and religion in Harvard Divinity School and in the Harvard Extension School and hope that they hear echoes of our discussions in these pages. Some of these students are beginning to publish their own work on Woolf, and I look forward to reading more and more in the years to come.

Michael O'Sullivan and Bernadette Flanagan invited me to give a lecture on "The Spirituality of Virginia Woolf" at the Spirituality Institute for Research and Education in Dublin, Ireland, in 2016, where a thoughtful audience helped push my thinking forward. I am grateful to Michael and Bernadette for organizing the lecture and for their collegiality over many years.

I am grateful to Vanessa Zoltan for inviting me to be a part of her extraordinary pilgrimage project, Common Ground. The reading and walking pilgrimage she organized around *To the Lighthouse* taught me a great deal about how reading and walking can create a community out of strangers and how a book can become a portable sacred space. Thank you to our thirteen pilgrims and to Vanessa's colleagues, Julia Argy and Elizabeth Slade, for a week I will never forget.

Finally, I am grateful beyond words to my mother, Sally A. Paulsell, and my father, William O. Paulsell, whose scholarly passions, ethical commitments, and religious longings have given my aspirations their shape. This book is dedicated, with love and gratitude, to them.

INTRODUCTION

SOMETHING MORE

In his 1935 essay "Religion and Literature," T. S. Eliot outlined what he believed to be three phases in the secularization of the novel. In the first, writers like Dickens, Fielding, and Thackeray took Christian faith so much for granted that they felt no need to make it explicit in their works. In the second, religion became visible through the struggle with religious doubt that pervaded the novels of writers like George Eliot and Thomas Hardy. The third phase—that of Eliot's own day—he described as characterized by the work of novelists who "have never heard the Christian Faith spoken of as anything but an anachronism."[1]

Eliot did not name names in his description of this third phase (although he did cite James Joyce as an exception to it), but one imagines that he was thinking of his friend Virginia Woolf. The daughter of prominent Victorian agnostics, she was raised, unlike George Eliot or Thomas Hardy, without a religious faith to lose.[2] Although Woolf and Eliot were friends who admired each other's work, his belief in God and his devotion to the church mystified her. Upon hearing of his conversion to Anglo-Catholicism, Woolf wrote to her sister, Vanessa Bell: "I have had a most shameful and distressing interview with poor dear Tom Eliot, who may be called dead to us all from this day forward. He has become an Anglo-Catholic, believes in God and immortality, and goes to church. I was really shocked. A corpse would seem to me more credible than he is. I mean, there's something obscene in a living person sitting by the fire and believing in God."[3]

Woolf was often at her most hyperbolic—and wickedly funny—when writing to her sister. Eliot, though, was not only not "dead" to Woolf but remained a well-loved friend. Her hyperbole reflects what Quentin Bell, Woolf's nephew and biographer, has called her "aggressive agnosticism."[4] But when these kinds of statements are used, as they sometimes are, as the only lens through which to examine Woolf's relationship to religion, they serve to obscure her lifelong interest in it, its influence on her writing, and the religious dimensions of her own literary project.

A recent book on the history of prayer, for example, describes Woolf as someone who simply could not understand the practice, even when T. S. Eliot tried to explain it to her. "Woolf," the authors assert, "was largely devoid of religious sensibilities."[5] But even Stephen Spender, the poet whose account of Woolf's arch interrogation of Eliot about his religious practice[6] inspired that assessment, understood her novel *The Waves* as a book "about vision, prayer, poetry itself, the open and aware attention which people can pay to one another."[7] Other readers have gone further, finding in their experience of reading Woolf something akin to religious experience itself. The novelist Dale Peck has said that he reads *The Waves* every year because "it affects me like spiritual instruction. I always feel like a better person after I put it down."[8] For many readers, reading Woolf feels spiritually transformative. When we raise our eyes from any of her novels—not just *The Waves*—we find our perception has changed. We are, at least for a time, more finely attuned to the mystery of other people, more aware of each other's hidden interiority. Woolf returns our own experience to us, illuminated, and we may feel, as Woolf felt when she read Tolstoy, that "this is what I have always felt and known and desired!"[9] We sense, for a moment, the invisible connections that run between us. Her work affects us like spiritual instruction. As Alexandra Harris has put it in her biography of Woolf, "Whatever else she does, she makes one want to live more consciously and fully."[10] Her work possesses, in the words of Mark Hussey, "implications for our lived experience in the world."[11] To read Virginia Woolf is to experience her literary genius, to be challenged by her political critique and delighted by her wit, but it is also to encounter something more, something difficult to put into words, something readers often reach for the language of religion to describe.

Virginia Woolf sought that something more as a reader herself. When we read great writers, Woolf insists, "all our faculties are summoned to the task, as in the great moments of our own experience; and some consecration descends upon us from their hands which we return to life, feeling it more keenly and understanding it more deeply than before."[12] Rather than someone lacking religious sensibilities, Woolf seems to have understood a great deal about religious experience, how it can intensify and saturate the present moment and transform our relationship to it. When she writes about reading, she often uses religious language: consecration, revelation, spirit, soul. When her readers write about reading her, we often do the same.

Scholarship on Woolf sometimes acknowledges her engagement with religion and the religious quality of her work while at the same time seeming reluctant to discuss it. The feminist critic Jane Marcus both recognized Woolf's "mysticism" and reduced it to "an imaginatively fulfilling substitute for mounting the barricades."[13] A few years later, in her important study of the influence on Woolf's work of her aunt, the Quaker theologian Caroline Emelia Stephen, Marcus returned to this theme: "As a feminist critic, I had avoided the subject of Woolf's mysticism, and of *The Waves*, feeling that acknowledging her as a visionary was a trap that would allow her to be dismissed as another female crank, irrational and eccentric. I was drawn to her most anticapitalist, anti-imperialist novels, to Woolf the socialist and feminist, logical, witty, and devastating in argument."[14] The fear that exploring the religious dimensions of Woolf's work would obscure its political concerns and make it less available for political work in the present has made it difficult, at times, to think about Woolf's engagements with religion.

Despite such anxieties, it was the feminist reappraisal of Woolf in the 1970s and 1980s that opened the door to considering how various religious influences shaped her work. Feminist studies of Woolf often revealed that, rather than diminishing or obscuring Woolf's politics, studying Woolf in relation to religion illuminated her politics in new ways.[15] Woolf's encouragement to "think back through our mothers"[16] led scholars to study the range of ways in which the women who influenced her were involved with religion—her Quaker aunt, Caroline Stephen; her agnostic mother, Julia Stephen; her Christian friends, Violet Dickinson and Ethel Smyth; Jane Ellen Harrison, the scholar of ancient Greek religion; Clara Pater and Janet Case, Virginia Stephen's tutors in Greek language and literature. Feminist studies of these relationships[17] have helped clarify Woolf's own complicated engagements with religion throughout her life and prepared the way for more work on Woolf and religion, such as Pericles Lewis's study of Woolf's work in the context of the larger modernist project of rethinking the sacred,[18] James Wood's exploration of Woolf's mysticism,[19] Donna J. Lazenby's study of the cataphatic and apophatic dimensions of that mysticism,[20] Michael Lackey's celebration of Woolf as a champion of atheism,[21] and Jane de Gay's recent study of Woolf and Christian culture.[22] At the same time, books continue to be written about the many contexts that shaped Woolf's development as a writer without mentioning religion at all.[23]

The most-studied aspect of the religious dimension of Woolf's work is the mystical.[24] Although understandings of the term range widely in this scholarship, the word "mysticism" is often used to keep Woolf on the secular side of a perceived secular-religious divide. "Woolf's version of transcendental reality was hybrid, emphatically secular, yet also mystical,"[25] Andrew MacNeillie writes in a representative description. The last twenty pages of *The Waves*, James Wood has asserted, is a "pure example" of "secular mystical writing."[26] Jane Marcus found in Woolf's mysticism a religious purity "without the dogmas and disciplines of organized religion."[27]

Certainly within the Christian culture of Great Britain in the first half of the twentieth century, Virginia Woolf was an agnostic who, like her parents, had no interest in joining religious institutions and felt, as she put it, "dulled and bothered" in religious settings by "the obstacle of not believing."[28] As Bernard complains in *The Waves*, "the certainty, so sonorously repeated, of resurrection, of eternal life" was too neat, too confident, too tidy. Like Bernard, Woolf trusted "nothing neat. Nothing that comes down with all its feet on the floor." When it came to religion, she much preferred the acknowledgment of "the sadness at the back of life" that she found in ancient Greek thought and literature to "Christianity and its consolations."[29]

But is "secular" the best way to describe Woolf and her writing? Belief is not the only way to engage religion or to do religious work. "Certainly and emphatically there is no God," Woolf wrote in her autobiography, but she had learned from the scholar of ancient Greek religions Jane Ellen Harrison that religion did not require belief in a god.[30] Woolf engaged religion in a number of ways: studying the history of religions; reading the Bible; talking with friends, both religious and not, about religion; reading the letters and diaries of Christian ministers; following the debates over women's ordination in the Church of England; studying religious art and thinking about her own art in relation to it; drawing in complex ways on religious language and religious themes both in her novels and in her reflections on the practices of reading and writing; and creating a literature that did, and continues to do, a kind of religious work. For Woolf, religion was part of the life of the world, one of the "invisible presences" that shape our lives whether we are aware of it or not.[31] Woolf sought to make more of life visible in her art, and so religion, and the invisible life of the spirit, was, for her, as much the business of the novelist and essayist as love, war, peace, and family life.[32]

Although she stood purposefully outside of the religious institution most proximate to her, the Church of England, Woolf never hesitated to critique it on religious grounds. Like others of her time, influenced by Ernest Renan's studies of early Christianity, she appealed to a distinction between "the mind of the founder" of Christianity and "the mind of the church."[33] The latter she believed to be shaped less by the working-class Jesus she found in the gospels[34] and more by St. Paul, to whom she traces the church's policing of women's bodies, clothing, and behavior.[35] Her infrequent encounters with the institutional church were dispiriting. After the funeral for her friend Ottoline Morrell, she bemoaned "the lack of intensity" in the service and the ways in which symbols of British power, in the form of medals on the clergyman's robe and the presence of the Union Jack in the sanctuary, undermined the solemnity of the occasion and the sacredness of the space.

What did any of this have to do "with Ottoline, or our feelings?"[36] she asked when she reflected on the day in her diary. And when she read a bishop's empty musings on heaven in a newspaper, she despaired at how unequal the representatives of religion were to the task of articulating religious hopes and desires. "The duty of heaven-making," she wrote, needs more than a bishop can bring to it; "it needs time and concentration. It needs the imagination of a poet."[37]

Such enervating experiences were part of the religion around her. But religion entered her life in other ways as well. Some of the most significant currents of religious thought and practice that flowed through Virginia Woolf's world had been shaped by her ancestors and close relatives. Her parents' agnosticism, her Quaker aunt's "rational mysticism," and the commitment to social change of her evangelical grandparents and great-grandparents all left their mark on Woolf and her work. For example, although she did not inherit their Christian beliefs, Woolf did inherit her ancestors' conviction that one should devote oneself to a vocation that would contribute to the good of the world. She devoted herself to writing in her youth and never wavered from that devotion, believing until the end of her life that "by writing I am doing what is far more necessary than anything else."[38] Her excavation of the interior lives of her characters was an ethical, nonviolent project that stood, as she did, against war. In the last months of the First World War, she wrote in her diary that "the reason why it is easy to kill another person must be that one's imagination is too sluggish to conceive what his life means to him—the infinite possibilities of a succession of days which are furled in him."[39] Through her novels and her criticism, she helped her readers cultivate an imagination alive to the infinite possibilities of the unlived days of others.

The early influences of parents, aunt, and ancestors were crucial to the shaping of the religious dimensions of her literary project. But they were by no means the only ones. Her relationship with her pious cousin Dorothea Stephen instilled in her a life-long abhorrence of proselytizing, both intimately, within a family, and globally, in the missionizing work Dorothea grew up to advance. Woolf's reading and travel exposed her to Islam, Roman Catholicism, and ancient forms of religion, none of which could be accounted for in any of the religious options practiced within her family. As she grew into adulthood, married, and enlarged her circle of friends, other religious influences touched her life and work.

The religious dimensions of Woolf's literary project emerged, in part, from her creative reworking of such influences. Indeed, the literary problems Woolf set for herself as a writer sound very like religious problems. When she writes about so-called realistic literature, she asks the kinds of questions her parents asked of Christianity: "Is this all? And, if this is all, is it enough? Must we, then, believe this?"[40] Woolf was after something more in literature, something that "forever escapes" the attempts of the novelist to capture it.[41] This something more goes by many names in Woolf's writing—she calls it, variously, "life itself," "something in the universe one's left with," "the real." She experiences it as "something abstract; but residing in the downs or sky; beside which nothing matters; in which I shall rest & continue to exist. Reality I call it. And I fancy sometimes this is the most necessary thing to me: that which I seek."[42]

Woolf's desire for new prose forms through which to express—and seek—this something more can be traced back through the loss of faith that her parents, and many other Victorians, experienced in the face of the discoveries of modern science and the historical-critical study of the Bible. In 1880 Matthew Arnold had argued in "The Study of Poetry" that, since discredited religious facts rendered religion unable to do the work it used to do—that is, "to interpret life for us, to console us, to sustain us"—lyric poetry would now have to do that work.[43] Half a century later, Woolf would argue that poetry had itself "failed to serve us as it has served so many generations of our fathers."[44] Rather than attaching itself to discredited facts, as Arnold contended religion had done, Woolf argued that the lyric was not capacious enough to give an account of human experience in the face of the failure of religion and the "monstrous, hybrid, unmanageable emotions" that new knowledge about the world had created. Neither Arnold's religious "facts" nor the lyric poetry he proposed as a substitute were up to the task. "Life," she wrote, "is always and inevitably much richer than we who try to express it."[45] The new prose forms Woolf imagined and sought in her own writing would give her room to explore hidden, undescribed dimensions of human life:

the interior "treasure" and "the unseen part" of her characters in *Mrs. Dalloway*; Mrs. Ramsay's "wedge-shaped core of darkness"; "the unacted part" of the characters in *Between the Acts*; the moments of being that saturate ordinary life with presence; the moments in which the boundaries between one person and another, or between human beings and the natural world, become, for a moment, crossable.

None of this sounds like the secularizing program T. S. Eliot described in "Religion and Literature." It sounds, rather, like an attempt to create a literature that could do the work of religion: to gesture toward an excess presence in life that resists our attempts to communicate it, to explore the life of the spirit, to make space for the work of mourning[46] and the search for meaning, to cultivate new forms of sacred community and devotional practice, to interpret, console, and sustain.

A single scene from *Mrs. Dalloway* offers a few examples of the many engagements with religion that mark Woolf's body of work as well as the religious quality of her experiments with form. In this scene an airplane flies over London, attracting the attention of people on the ground.[47] The airplane is one of Woolf's attempts, as James Wood has put it, "to outwit narrative sequence."[48] Woolf wanted to show several people, seemingly unconnected, thinking their thoughts simultaneously. Tracing the journey of the airplane above in relation to the thoughts of the people below, Woolf attempts to excavate each character from the "beautiful caves" she has dug out behind them and bring them "to daylight at the present moment."[49] When she does, we find their thoughts are turned, in one way or another, to religion.

Mrs. Dempster, lonely and wishing for a "kiss of pity," looks up when the plane flies overhead and remembers her own longing to travel to foreign lands, perhaps to visit her missionary nephew. As she imagines the pilot in the swooping plane, it flies over "the little island of grey churches, St. Paul's and the rest" until it reaches the fields beyond London, beyond the churches, where the life of birds and snails and the "dark brown woods" goes on without reference to anything human.

In this brief passage, both the missionary nephew and the grey churches of London reflect the Christian forms that were part of the geography of Woolf's life and work. London's steepled, spired, and domed churches rise up through the landscape of this novel and others, especially St. Paul's Cathedral, "the brooding hen with spread wings," as she describes it in *The Waves*,[50] a more somber version of Gerard Manley Hopkins's description of the Holy Spirit in his 1877 poem "God's Grandeur." In this scene, the soaring airplane recalls the nephew, carried by his religious commitments away from London and into the "foreign parts" Mrs. Dempster "always longed to see." The nephew embodies some of the complex ways the religion around Woolf functioned. As a missionizing force, religion contributed to the violence of the colonial project. As a ticket out of England and into "foreign parts," it opened the possibility that one's understanding of the world could be enlarged and transformed.[51] The churches—"St. Paul's and the rest"—are points of connection to the nephew, monuments that echo his task and are united to him, wherever he is, not only by invisible filaments of shared belief and practice but also by a shared responsibility for his ministry and its effects. The airplane soaring overhead links the missionary to the churches and London to the world beyond it, enlarging both the geography of the scene and the moral claim it makes on readers.

Continuing beyond the island of grey churches, the plane flies over the fields and the woods that spread out on either side of London. Indeed, the view from the plane would show a city surrounded by another world altogether, with a humming life of its own. The contrast Woolf establishes here—between institutional religion and nature—is one that she explores repeatedly in her novels, from her first, *The Voyage Out*, where the restrained religious rituals of British tourists stand opposite the teeming life of the tropical forest, through her last, *Between the Acts*, where the rhododendron forests and mastodons of prehistoric England seem to lie just below the surface of the Christianized landscape of the present. Throughout her work, Woolf explores the idea of nature as the true home of the sacred. In her short story "A Simple Melody," written in the mid-1920s, George Carslake gazes at a landscape painting and thinks that the heath would endure while the churches would perish. "This was right," he thinks; "there was nothing sad about it."[52] In her 1922 novel *Jacob's Room*, a clergyman's wife, walking on the moors, risks "confound[ing] her God with the universal that is."[53] In *The Years*, published in 1937, Kitty can hear the land itself singing—"singing to itself, a chorus, alone."[54] Woolf portrays the natural world as a refuge from, and a challenge to, London's grey churches.

As the airplane continues its journey, Mr. Bentley, rolling out sod in Greenwich, looks up and thinks of the plane as "a symbol . . . of man's soul, of his determination . . . to get outside his body, beyond his house, by means of thought, Einstein, speculation, mathematics, the Mendelian theory."[55] With Mr. Bentley, Woolf gestures toward another response to the human desire for transcendence: the scientific response. If Mrs. Dempster believes her longing to get beyond her body, beyond her house, can be answered through travel, Mr. Bentley imagines instead an intellectual journey toward transcendence. Like the sixteenth-century religious thinker Teresa of Avila, who advised her nuns that they could take the journey toward the God who dwells within whenever they wanted without leaving their room or asking permission of their superior,[56] Mr. Bentley imagines getting "beyond his house" not by traveling to foreign lands but by way of intellectual practices worked out within the free space of the mind: mathematics, genetics, the theory of relativity.

This is a response to the human longing for transcendence that Woolf knew well. It was the response of her father and many of his contemporaries, for whom scientific discoveries and theories, especially those of Darwin, liberated them from Christian beliefs they found incapable of accounting for life as they found it. Woolf, who grew up playing with Darwin's grandchildren, recognized Darwin's intellectual authority and knew what his work had meant to her father. But she was less sanguine about science as a mode of transcendence. For Woolf, the scientific view of the world did not solve every mystery, any more than religion did. As Elizabeth G. Lambert has noted, Woolf understood both science and religion to have been co-opted by colonialism and patriarchy. Science might differ from Christianity on the origin of man, she knew, "but not on the subordination of women."[57] As Woolf would write in an essay two years after publishing *Mrs. Dalloway*: "science and religion have between them destroyed belief."[58]

The third person to have his attention arrested by the airplane is an unnamed "seedy-looking nondescript man" who hesitates on the steps of St. Paul's with a bag full of pamphlets. He imagines neither travel nor nature nor science as a mode of transcendence. He instead considers, for a moment, the power of religion to lift him from his circumstances. At the threshold of the church, the man asks himself: Why not enter?

> For within was what balm, how great a welcome, how many tombs with banners waving over them, tokens of victories not over armies, but over, he thought, that plaguy spirit of truth seeking which leaves me at present without a situation, and more than that, the cathedral offers company, he thought, invites you to membership of a society; great men belong to it; martyrs have died for it; why not enter in, he thought, put this leather bag stuffed with pamphlets before an altar, a cross, the symbol of something which has soared beyond seeking and questing and knocking of words together and has become all spirit, disembodied, ghostly—why not enter in?[59]

Why not indeed? He imagines the church offering something beyond questing and writing, a victory over "that plaguy spirit of truth seeking" that has left this man without a job and Septimus Warren Smith, the shell-shocked veteran at the heart of the novel, scribbling and suffering. It also offers company, community—the very thing Mrs. Dempster, looking up at the plane in Regents Park, longs for, and the very thing Septimus's isolated wife, Rezia, so desperately needs to find. "I am alone; I am alone!" she thinks to herself as she walks in Regents Park with her husband. "Help, help! she wanted to cry out to butchers' boys and women. Help!"[60] The unnamed man standing on the threshold of St. Paul's illuminates more than his own loneliness and uncertainty; he also helps us see more clearly the isolation of others in the novel. Woolf uses the flight of the airplane to illuminate connections that are less visible on the ground.

Standing on the threshold of the church with his bag of pamphlets, the unnamed man holds some of the fragments from which Woolf created her art—political convictions, religious possibilities. His location on the porch of the church recalls other such thresholds where new spiritualities, new religious languages, and new religious communities have been imagined. Woolf's aunt, Caroline Stephen, named her home in Cambridge "The Porch" because she imagined it as the threshold of eternity. From there she hosted Quaker meetings, welcomed students from Cambridge University, wrote her influential books, sheltered her niece when she needed a place to recover, and engaged her in lengthy conversations about religious experiences and ideas. For Caroline Stephen, the threshold was a generative place, a place of meeting where new thoughts could take shape.

George Herbert, the seventeenth-century priest and poet disdained by Woolf's father but understood by Woolf as part of England's "fountain of spiritual life,"[61] wrote "The Church Porch" as the threshold to his long work "The Temple." "A verse may find him" on the porch of the church, "who a sermon flies," Herbert wrote.[62] He anticipates Arnold, who put his faith in the power of poetry to reach those for whom religion no longer spoke meaningfully, and also Woolf, who saw the need to go beyond poetry into new forms of prose that would do poetry's—and thus religion's—work.

Thirteen years later, in *Three Guineas*, Woolf would celebrate the way young women experiment with their power by absenting themselves from church. In a twist on Milton, she writes, "those also serve who remain outside."[63] In *Mrs. Dalloway*, Woolf leaves her nameless man with his bag of pamphlets standing on the porch of St. Paul's; like her, he remains outside. The airplane continues its flight across the city and, with smoke pouring out behind it, begins to spell out an advertisement. The symbol of transcendence that stimulated so much thought within the people watching it from the ground turns out to be anchored to this world, "a commercial instrument and weapon of war," as Elyse Graham and Pericles Lewis have put it.[64] Does the banality of its purpose render ridiculous the thoughts of transcendence it inspired? Maybe not, but it does show how difficult it is for profound thoughts to deepen, or to lead anywhere, when the vehicles to which one might attach them, including religious institutions, are so compromised.

Unlike her friend T. S. Eliot, Virginia Woolf never did enter the church. She developed other forms of sacred community, both in her fiction and in her life. For Woolf, the "seeking and questing and knocking of words together" was the truer path. As a writer, Woolf assembled her fragments like the common reader for whom she wrote, "guided by an instinct to create for himself, out of whatever odds and ends he can come by, some kind of whole."[65] The creation from fragments of new wholes, new ways of describing the incommunicable aspects of life, and new experiments in living was her life work, her religious practice. Even as a young woman, before she had published a single story, she knew what she was after: "some kind of whole made of shivering fragments."[66] The ready-made whole of religion did not suffice for her as it did for T. S. Eliot. Neither did poetry as it had for Matthew Arnold. As Bernard puts it in *The Waves*: "Some people go to priests; others to poetry; I to my friends, I to my own heart, I to seek among phrases and fragments something unbroken."[67]

The drive to create new wholes from fragments suffuses Woolf's work. Mrs. Dalloway and Mrs. Ramsay bring together unlikely assortments of people from which they fashion their offerings. The painter Lily Briscoe understands the vocation of the artist to be that of making, from seemingly incongruous elements, "a globed, compacted thing over which thought lingers and love plays." In *Orlando*, Woolf urges her reader to craft "from bare hints dropped here and there the whole boundary and circumference of a living person." In her "Letter to a Young Poet," she instructs the poet of the title "to find the relation between things that seem incompatible yet have a mysterious affinity."[68] Her faith in the assembling of incongruous elements into something new is a spiritual, aesthetic faith and a political and social one that implicates institutions and communities. The university Woolf imagines in *Three Guineas* seeks "not to segregate and specialize, but to combine." In the ideal university, students and teachers should explore "the ways in which mind and body can be made to co-operate; discover what new combinations make good wholes in human life."[69]

The airplane scene in *Mrs. Dalloway* does not only solve a narrative problem for Woolf. It is also a way of struggling with a religious problem: Who are we, and how are we connected to one another? What do we owe one another, and how might the fragments of our lives be combined into "good wholes"? As the airplane flies overhead, it reveals the invisible ways in which we are already connected and illuminates the need for new forms of community that could bring those connections to life and "sustain the living," as Graham and Lewis have written, "in a real way."[70]

This book considers Virginia Woolf as a writer whose life and work were shaped, in part, by the religion around her. It is also a meditation on Woolf as a religious thinker who both engaged with the religion around her and moved beyond it, creating from fragments new possibilities for sacred community and new ways of describing her sense of that abstract reality that was "the most necessary thing to me; that which I seek." The first two chapters explore the religious forms and ideas that Woolf encountered in her family, her friendships, her travels, and her reading, especially during her childhood and young adulthood. Chapter 3 considers Woolf as a religious reader and explores how religious reading practices grounded her life and her shaped fiction. Chapter 4 examines the ideas about God that appear throughout Woolf's work and often hover in the minds of her characters. Chapter 5 reflects on the new forms of community Woolf imagined and worked for as fascism gained strength in Europe.

The work of seeking new combinations among fragments provided Woolf no victories over the "plaguy spirit of truth seeking," but it was religious work nonetheless. One of the possible roots of the word "religion" is *religare*: to bind, to connect. Woolf felt her way along the path of the permanent quest to which she was committed by binding and connecting the fragments she found within her and around her, fashioning and refashioning new combinations in art and in life. Religion provided some of those fragments, but so did much else. Binding and connecting and creating new wholes that impel both thought and love, Woolf was a religious thinker for her age, and perhaps for ours as well.

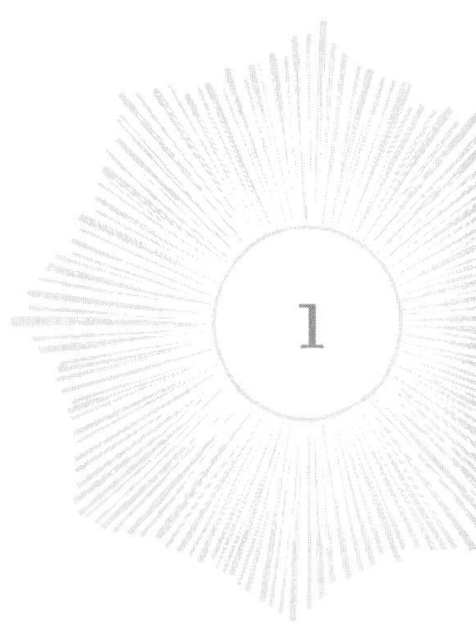

FAMILY RESEMBLANCES

Katherine Hilbery, the protagonist of Woolf's second novel, *Night and Day*, belongs to a family that passed intellectual power down through the generations "with apparent certainty that the brilliant gift will be safely caught and held by nine out of ten of the privileged race."[1] Like Katharine, Woolf was "born into a large connection"[2] so accomplished and influential that it has been described as an "intellectual aristocracy."[3] Some of its members served as "lighthouses firmly based on rock for the guidance of their generation"; others as "steady, serviceable candles, illuminating the ordinary chambers of daily life."[4] Katharine's family cultivated a sense of reverence around their family accomplishments, lending their celebrations a "semi-sacred character . . . observed as days of feasting and fasting in the Church."[5] Woolf's family drew its spiritual energy from the activist evangelical Clapham Sect and the religious restlessness of its descendants. Her family inheritance included not only "the brilliant gift" of intellect but of religious imagination as well.

The Clapham Sect, which left its mark on generations of Woolf's family, was a group of upper-middle class evangelical families in the first half of the nineteenth century whose members dedicated themselves to philanthropy, the propagation of the Christian faith, and the abolition of slavery, which they believed "revers[ed] every law of Christ."[6] Born from what Charles Taylor called a "strong surge of piety" that arose in Britain partly in reaction to the Revolutionary and Napoleonic Wars, evangelical movements like the Clapham Sect helped shape a view of civilization as British, Protestant, and devoted to "discipline and decency, freedom and benevolence" that would extend beyond the resurgence of Christian belief and practice.[7] Miss La Trobe, in Woolf's last novel, *Between the Acts*, would mock this view in her village play: "*Prosperity and respectability always go, as we know, [hand in hand]. . . . Purity our watchword; prosperity and respectability.*"[8]

Many members of the Clapham Sect lived in the Surrey village of Clapham, where they anchored their social action in practices of devotion, including the domestic worship for which they were known. Deeply critical of Christian complacency, the Claphamites led an evangelical revival within the Church of England that called on Christians to live lives of radical, sacrificial holiness.[9] Their contemporaries dryly called them "Saints." In 1807, a high-church critic of the circle, Sydney Smith, implying a certain heterodox sectarianism in their ranks, referred to them in the pages of the *Edinburgh Review* as "the Clapham church." Woolf's grandfather, in his own essay on Clapham for the same journal in 1844, transformed Smith's sneering phrase into "the Clapham sect."[10] James Stephen's appellation stuck, changing a term of derision into a badge of honor.

The central project of the Clapham Sect—the eradication of slavery—had initially drawn Woolf's great-grandfather, also named James Stephen, to the group. Stephen had witnessed the brutality of slavery and the unjust treatment of enslaved people in the courts as a lawyer in the West Indies, where he had moved to escape the humiliation of a sexual scandal.[11] Soon he began corresponding with William Wilberforce, the Clapham Sect's leading light, about the abolitionist movement. In 1794 he returned to England and moved to Clapham in order to be near Wilberforce and his circle. By this time, James Stephen had committed himself to evangelical Christianity. Following the death of his first wife, he married Wilberforce's sister, Sarah Wilberforce Clark, a woman known for giving away almost everything she owned to charity. James Stephen helped Wilberforce draft the Slave Trade Act of 1807, which ended the slave trade in the British Empire (although it did not abolish slavery itself).

James Stephen's third son and namesake, Woolf's grandfather, deepened the family's association with the Clapham Sect by marrying Jane Venn, the daughter of John Venn, a rector in Clapham and a founding member of the Church Missionary Society. James Stephen the younger became a colonial administrator and, with his essay in the *Edinburgh Review* and his two-volume *Essays in Ecclesiastical Biography*, the historian of the Clapham Sect. In 1833, he extended the work begun by his father and William Wilberforce by writing the Slavery Abolition Act that ended slavery throughout the British Empire.

In early 1897, fifteen-year-old Virginia Stephen read her grandfather's two-volume *Essays in Ecclesiastical Biography*, including his essay on the Clapham Sect. It was a slog. "The Ecclesiastical Biography gradually pulling through, poor thing," she wrote in her diary as she neared the end.[12] When she was finished, she asked her father for a volume of her godfather James Russell Lowell's literary essays, "which rejoice my heart after my grandpapa."[13]

The teenager dutifully reading her grandfather's volumes may have struggled to get through his lengthy essays on religious figures and movements, but when she became a writer, some of his literary preoccupations became her own. James Stephen's method, in his essay on the Clapham Sect, was to dip down into the lives of its members, one by one, letting their interior convictions and habits illuminate their public accomplishments. Unlike his granddaughter, for whom the "the quivering thing, the living thing"[14] that animated each person could never be wholly known or described by another, he was confident of what he would find within each Clapham figure if he could only gain access: "But the interior life of John Bowdler, if it could be faithfully written," Stephen wrote in a typical passage, "would be a record which none could read without reverence, and few without self-reproach."[15] Woolf would resist her grandfather's certainties and his pieties, but she would hold onto his conviction that external events do not tell the whole story of any life; without an account of what is happening within each person—the mind's "soliloquy in solitude"[16]—we remain at a considerable distance, she believed, from "life itself."[17]

Virginia Woolf famously derided the so-called realistic fiction of her day for offering an unreal depiction of human existence. Victorian evangelicals tended to mistrust all literary art, especially novels, on the same grounds: that it does not reflect reality. As the writer of one evangelical magazine put it, in language Leslie Stephen would later use to describe religious belief, fiction "transforms life itself into a dream."[18] James Stephen expressed his own suspicion of what he called "the veil of fiction" in his essay on the Clapham Sect and praised those who sought truth "unadorned by any beauties but such as belong to her celestial nature."[19]

Stephen's essay is peppered with aesthetic judgments, however. He praised the sermons of Clapham priest and poet Thomas Gisborne—who would make an ignominious appearance in Woolf's *Three Guineas* as the author of *The Duties of the Female Sex*[20]—for their "unity of design," their scriptural content, and their uncompromising convictions. This excellence in both form and content produced sermons that were, as Stephen described them, "transparently luminous,"[21] a quality for which Woolf's writing would later be celebrated. Gisborne's sermons were not, however, perfect. What kept them from literary immortality, to Stephen's mind, was their inability to reach a level of profundity to match their authenticity and a quality of imagination to match their taste. Woolf would have encountered in her grandfather's essay not only a history of her ancestors but also a vision of literary greatness built from these kinds of distinctions.

The most striking similarity between grandfather and granddaughter is their shared interest in the way disparate fragments could combine to create new forms. In the section of his essay on the missionary Henry Martyn, known for translating the New Testament into Persian, Stephen wrote that "the chaotic materials" of Martyn's character were "destined to combine . . . into no common forms, whether of beauty and delight, or of deformity and terror."[22] Not only do human beings make their lives out of such fragments, Stephen believed, but this is how God creates as well. Divine power, he wrote, "is a silent invisible influence, obedient to no laws which human wisdom can explore. . . . It works by searching out affinities in the elements of man's moral and social nature; by separating such as are incongruous, and by combining the rest into organic forms, animated by a common life."[23] This passage echoes in Lily Briscoe's reflection on the work of the artist in *To the Lighthouse*. Artists are "lovers whose gift it was to choose out the elements of things and place them together and so, giving them a wholeness not theirs in life, make of some scene, or meeting of people (all now gone and separate), one of those globed compacted things over which thought lingers, and love plays."[24] There is a crucial difference, however, between their accounts of divine and human creativity: in Stephen's vision, God separates out the incongruous and shapes a whole from affinities, whereas in Woolf's, the artist incorporates the incongruous into a new whole, the "globed compacted thing" that inspires both thought and love. For both grandfather and granddaughter, though, this is the heart of creativity, whether divine or human, and the force that moves human history forward: the assembling of "the chaotic materials" of life, the shaping of fragments and disparate elements into new "organic forms."

Woolf understood her Clapham Sect ancestors to be among the "invisible presences who after all play so important a part in every life."[25] When she considered their influence on her, she associated it with feelings of shame, disconnection from her body, and an "ancestral dread" that worked against her "natural love for beauty."[26] Scolding her friend Victoria Ocampo for sending a too-extravagant gift, Woolf apologized for her difficulty in receiving it: "That's what comes of having Scotch clergy in my blood—a detestable race."[27]

Her grandfather, James Stephen, was indeed known for being suspicious of pleasure. "He once smoked a cigar," his son Leslie wrote, "and found it so delicious that he never smoked again."[28] Woolf knew this anecdote—she repeats it in her autobiographical "Sketch of the Past," and she tells a similar story about her own father as a way of describing the resilient strain of puritanism in his life.[29] The Clapham Sect bequeathed to her an inheritance not only of literary accomplishment but also of anxiety about pleasure and the feelings of shame and guilt that arose in its wake.

Woolf's religious inheritance from the Clapham Sect was an ambiguous one. But it also opened the possibility of freedom for creative work in the midst of the constraining Victorian culture within which Woolf grew up. Members of the Clapham Sect, inspired by manuals of spiritual instruction like William Law's *A Serious Call to a Devout and Holy Life* and Henry Venn's *The Complete Duty of Man*, believed passionately that one's entire life—family life, work, all the hours of the day—should be turned toward the service of God. One must, as Law put it, "dedicate every condition of life to His service."[30]

Woolf did not inherit the Christian beliefs undergirding the Clapham Sect's life of devotion to God. She did inherit, however, the conviction that one's life and energies ought to bend in one direction, that one must discover one's work and dedicate oneself to it wholeheartedly, that one's work should reach beyond the boundaries of one's own life to support the good of the world. Woolf's friend John Maynard Keynes thought their generation had benefited from this inheritance. Describing in her diary a conversation with T. S. Eliot about his recently published *After Strange Gods: A Primer of Modern Heresy* in 1934, she remembers Keynes saying to her, "I begin to see that our generation—yours and mine V., owed a great deal to our fathers' religion. . . . We had the best of both worlds. We destroyed Xty & yet had its benefits."[31]

The Clapham Sect's convictions about vocation echo throughout Woolf's life, from her long apprenticeship to writing as a teenager and young adult to her reflections on her devotion to writing toward the end of her life. In 1939, she wrote that, even with another war looming, "I feel that by writing I am doing what is far more necessary than anything else."[32] In the same year, she wrote to her niece, Judith Stephen, that "I'm more and more convinced that it is our duty to catch Hitler in his home haunts and prod him if even with only the end of an old inky pen."[33] Woolf fought the structures of injustice she found built into British society—particularly the barriers to education for women and working people; the oppression of women in families, churches, and universities; and the glorification of war—through activism, teaching, publishing, and lecturing, but most especially through writing, whether she was arguing for the kind of education that would teach young people to hate war in *Three Guineas* or revealing the hidden dimensions of human existence through the inner lives of her characters. She "dedicated every condition" of her life to this work. "The truth is," she wrote in her diary, "that I have an internal, automatic scale of values; which decides what I had better do with my time. . . . Perhaps it's the legacy of puritan grandfathers."[34] Her home, her marriage, her friendships, her travels, her reading, her thinking, her activism, and the way she organized her days all supported her devotion to writing.

Woolf's own religious imagination was shaped, in part, by the children of James Stephen, especially her father, Leslie Stephen, and her aunt, Caroline Emelia Stephen. James Stephen wrote to his wife in 1846, when Leslie was fourteen years old and Caroline twelve, that his "daily and nightly terror is that [the children] should be 'patent Christians'—formalists, praters, cheats—without meaning or even knowing it."[35] He need not have worried. Leslie and Caroline were not destined to become the kind of complacent Christians their Clapham ancestors abhorred. Both sought authenticity and sincerity in regard to religious matters with a fierceness that would lead them to reject their father's evangelical convictions and drive them from the Church of England—Leslie to agnosticism, Caroline to the Society of Friends.

In James Stephen's England, nearly half the population regularly attended church.[36] In the England of his children, rapid urban growth was accompanied by a sharp decline in church attendance.[37] For James Stephen, religion and science were allies in the struggle against "war and superstition," forces of light standing against forces of darkness.[38] For his son, science and religion were no longer on the same side because the insights of the former had unraveled the claims of the latter. James Stephen looked to the Christian faith as the foundation of ethical thought and behavior. Leslie Stephen, as his biographer Noel Annan observed, "would have judged his most notable achievement to have shown that it was possible not to believe in Christianity, yet to live a virtuous life."[39] Through his influential essay collections, *Essays on Freethinking and Plainspeaking* and *An Agnostic's Apology*, the son of James Stephen and Jane Venn—a true child of Clapham—became "one of the great pioneers of Victorian unbelief."[40]

After a delicate childhood marked by interruptions in his schooling, Leslie followed in the footsteps of both his father and his older brother, Fitzjames, and entered Trinity Hall, Cambridge, in 1850.

Both Oxford and Cambridge required membership in the Church of England for admission; nonconformists need not apply. Looking back on those days, Leslie Stephen wrote that the two universities "were simply Anglican seminaries; bulwarks of the establishment which was an essential part of the great conservative fortress; mediaeval in their constitution and altogether behind the age in their teaching."[41] But there were significant differences in ethos between the two universities as well. Cambridge was associated with the evangelicals and, politically, for the most part, with the Whigs, while Oxford, home of John Henry Newman and the Oxford Movement, was the university of high church Anglo-Catholicism and politically aligned with the Tories.[42] An Oxford education at the time focused on the classics, while a Cambridge education was grounded in mathematics,[43] cultivating "a sympathy," as Leslie Stephen put it, "with good hard reasoning."[44]

At Cambridge, the delicate boy became a rowing coach, Alpine climber, and vigorous walker—Leslie Stephen walked at least twenty miles every Sunday for much of his adult life. Stephen would always associate Cambridge with masculinity; his Cambridge years were "the period in which I first called myself a man."[45] Masculinity he associated with vigor, both in body and as a feature of the Cambridge way of thinking. He learned at Cambridge to see "the less romantic side of things," to cultivate the "common sense" by which he could see Newman and his Oxford Movement in "the dry light of reason" and hence be able "to resist the illusions of romantic sentiment."[46] There were no spiritual guides at Cambridge, he proudly remembered, for relying on one would be "enfeebling."[47] At Cambridge, he believed, he had learned to face reality head on, a capacity that would undergird his embrace of agnosticism. He took pride in his association with the university throughout his life and sent his sons (but not his daughters) there to study. Virginia and her sister Vanessa chose their husbands, and many of their friends, from their brother Thoby's Cambridge circle.

The year before Leslie Stephen entered the university, his father was appointed Regius Professor of Modern History at Cambridge and immediately came under fire from a conservative branch of the evangelical movement. The chronicler of the Clapham Sect had published an essay in which he expressed the hope that divine punishment would prove to be less than eternal and the damned eventually released from their torment. "These are dangerous times when an atheist walks about the streets of Cambridge in cap and gown, my friend, in cap and gown!" the Master of Jesus College, George Elwes Corrie, wrote in response to his appointment.[48] Leslie Stephen would himself come to view Christian equivocation on hell as dishonest—although from the perspective of his agnosticism, not from that of Corrie's conservative evangelicalism.

The world of Leslie Stephen's Trinity Hall was much less theologically conservative than Corrie's Jesus College, populated as it was by scholars "who wished to be both rational and Christian."[49] Although this was a position Leslie Stephen would come to critique as illogical, it did make it possible for him, in 1855, to be ordained a deacon in the Church of England, and in 1859, to be ordained a priest. Taking holy orders was required for a tutorship at Cambridge, and he was eager to free his father from having to support him financially. His mother remembers him reading the service from the Book of Common Prayer "in an impressive and beautiful manner."[50]

By 1862, however, Leslie Stephen had decided that it would be wrong for him to continue to lead services in the chapel because he could no longer claim to be a believer. He resigned his Cambridge tutorship, ending the possibility of a university career. There is some debate over Stephen's own understanding of what seemed to some as an abrupt loss of faith. Virginia Woolf reports that her father cast off his faith "with such anguish, Fred Maitland once hinted to me, that he thought of suicide."[51] Noel Annan interprets that anguish as misery over the pain he knew he would cause his deeply religious family more than distress over the actual loss of faith.

Leslie Stephen tells a different story. For him as for many others of his generation, the historical-critical study of the Bible undermined the Christian convictions with which he had been raised. Eventually, he could not bear to hear biblical stories read aloud in services as if they were "as true as the stories of the Lisbon earthquake or the battle of Waterloo." The biblical narratives must be, he reasoned, "true or false, and could not be both at once."[52] He wrote in his *Masoleum Book* that reading Comte convinced him that the story of Noah and the ark, a favorite childhood story he invoked whenever he wrote of his loss of faith, was "a fiction" that could not be read as if it were "a sacred truth."[53] As Eleanor Pargiter would later reflect in *The Years*, the Bible is "what a man said under a fig tree, on a hill. . . . And then another man wrote it down."[54] How could such accounts be trusted? In the light of Comte, Mill's *System of Logic*, and Darwin's account of human origins, the Bible now seemed, to Leslie Stephen, to be a collection of "exploded legends implying a crude and revolting morality."[55] But rather than feeling his foundations crumbling, he felt, instead, a burden lifting. "I was not discovering that my creed was false," he insisted, "but that I had never really believed it."[56]

Whether Leslie Stephen was traumatized or not by the intellectual upheaval that led him to reject Christian belief, he took the matter seriously. Five years after the passing of the Clerical Disabilities Act of 1870, before which it had been impossible for someone ordained as a priest to divest himself of that identity on his own, Leslie Stephen asked the novelist Thomas Hardy to witness his signature on a deed by which he renounced his Holy Orders. This was a symbolic act; he had not functioned as a priest for over a decade. But authenticity and sincerity were bedrock values for Stephen, and he invested the moment with solemnity. Hardy reports that Stephen "thought it as well to cut himself adrift of a calling for which, to say the least, he had always been utterly unfit. The deed was executed with due formality. Our conversation then turned upon theologies decayed and defunct, the origin of things, the constitution of matter, the unreality of time and kindred subjects. He told me that he had 'wasted' much time on systems of religion and metaphysics, and that the new theory of vortex rings had a 'staggering fascination' to him."[57] Hardy's account of their conversation following the signing of the deed reflects nearly everything that severed Leslie Stephen from his family's Christian faith: theologies rendered defunct by unreliable sacred texts, Darwin's theory of human origins, the unreality of "religion and metaphysics," the unending fascination of scientific discovery. These would remain his intellectual preoccupations for the rest of his life and inspire his best writing.

When Leslie Stephen left Cambridge, exchanging, as he put it, "the pulpit for the press,"[58] he began a new career as a journalist and literary critic. With his great capacity for concentration and his appetite for work, he could write three or four articles a week.[59] (Woolf recalls that even the elderly father with whom she grew up "wrote daily and methodically."[60]) One of his early journalistic projects held echoes of the abolitionist commitments of his Clapham Sect ancestors: a severe critique of the *Times* for its biased coverage of the American Civil War. Stephen believed the newspaper's sympathy for the southern aristocracy reflected an upper-class "dread of democracy,"[61] and he made a three-month trip to the United States to study the war firsthand. He arrived in Boston about a week after the fall of Vicksburg to Ulysses S. Grant and his forces. Stephen visited Unitarian and Congregationalist churches, where he found that "though the praying part was bad, the sermons, if less religious, were less palpably rubbish than most English ditto," and he became interested in "American theology."[62] He also met the leading abolitionist William Lloyd Garrison (who had known William Wilberforce and Leslie Stephen's uncle, George Stephen), attended Harvard's commencement, and spent time with Cambridge luminaries like James Russell Lowell and Oliver Wendell Holmes. From Boston, he traveled to New York, Albany, Utica, Trenton Falls, Niagara, Buffalo, Chicago, St. Paul, St. Louis, Cincinnati, Philadelphia, and Washington, D.C., where he met briefly with President Lincoln. He also spent a few days with General Meade and his troops.

After a few weeks in the United States, Stephen wrote to his mother that the North would undoubtedly win and that the end of the war would bring emancipation. Slavery sickened him—"I could have joined John Brown with satisfaction," he wrote in a letter a few years after the Civil War ended[63]—and he especially despised the arguments of some Southern clergy that slavery was a "means of bringing home the blessings of Christianity to the black race."[64] For Stephen, the American conflict was wholly about slavery, and the *Times*'s attempt to make it about the failure of the democratic project disgusted him. He concluded that "everything that the *Times* says is either a lie, a blunder, or a mystification."[65] Two years after he returned home, he published "The *Times* on the American War: A Historical Study," in which he accused the paper of "a public crime." The newspaper, which should have educated the British public on the causes of the American conflict, instead misled them and, in so doing, alienated "the freest nation of the old world from the great nation in the new."[66] Leslie Stephen did not write with the brilliant and biting irony with which his daughter composed political works like *A Room of One's Own* and *Three Guineas*. But his daughter's writing does reflect the same passion for the importance of getting the facts straight in matters of social justice. The footnotes of *Three Guineas* are a tribute to this commitment. Like her father, Woolf believed in patiently amassing her evidence—"I have collected enough powder," she wrote of her research for *Three Guineas*, "to blow up St Pauls."[67] The pamphleteering and sermonizing of the Clapham Sect echo in the confident public voices of Virginia Woolf and her father.

One of the most important things that happened to Leslie Stephen during this first visit to the United States was the lifelong friendship he began with the poet James Russell Lowell. "He fell in love with me," Stephen later wrote of their first encounters.[68] When Virginia Stephen was born, James Russell Lowell became her godfather (or, as Leslie Stephen preferred to describe it, stood "in quasi-sponsorial relation" to her).[69] Lowell was troubled by Stephen's agnosticism—especially by his conviction that holding onto Christian faith was intellectually dishonest once one had taken on board the scientific and historical-critical insights that undermined it. No creed can explain the universe, Lowell conceded to his friend. "But I continue to shut my eyes resolutely in certain speculative directions, and am willing to find solace in certain intimations that seem to me from a region higher than my reason." There are some chapters of the Old Testament, Lowell insisted, that I "wouldn't drop" no matter how vigorously science disproved them.[70] This is the kind of thinking that Leslie Stephen would ordinarily excoriate as a deliberate denial of reality. But this disagreement did not diminish the love between them. At the end of Lowell's life, Stephen made a last trip to Massachusetts to be with him, because he was one of the few people Lowell wanted to see before he died.

Like his writing on the U.S. Civil War, Leslie Stephen's literary criticism reflected his evangelical background. Woolf's friend Desmond MacCarthy argued that Stephen's evangelical upbringing made him "the least aesthetic of noteworthy critics," more concerned with "human nature and morals than about art."[71] The Clapham Sect mistrusted artifice, and Stephen ignored, in his criticism, the ways in which authors work with language and imagery to solve narrative problems and achieve certain effects. What Stephen valued in literature was "sincerity," the quality that made possible the communion between reader and author that he cherished. "The true object of the study of a man's writings is, according to my definition," he told students at St. Andrews, "to make a personal friend of the author."[72]

Stephen's approach to literature did not make for original literary criticism and accounted for what one critic has called "his frequent failure to distinguish between an author and his work."[73] Virginia Woolf, who also cherished communion with authors, had a more specific critique of her father's literary criticism: she objected to his use of codes of Victorian morality to judge authors. Those whose lives demonstrated a devotion to work, common sense, and clear thought her father considered good; those whose lives or books did not meet the norms of Victorian morality he did not.[74] When Woolf read her father, she wrote, "I find not a subtle mind; not an imaginative mind; not a suggestive mind." But she did continue to read his literary criticism all her life, seeking in his essays on novels and poetry "something to fill out; to correct; to stiffen my fluid vision." She always found what she was looking for, even though "he is not a writer for whom I have a natural taste."[75]

Stephen turned to literature not only to commune with authors he admired but also for ethical reflection. Matthew Arnold had suggested that poetry would eventually replace religion because, having attached itself to facts that had failed in the face of modern science, religion could no longer do the work of interpreting, consoling, or sustaining. One might expect Stephen to agree with Arnold on this (as they agreed on the moral criticism of literature), but Stephen saw Arnold's assertion as rooted in sloppy thinking. If poetry is, as Arnold had also claimed, "a criticism of life,"[76] then how could poetry replace religion? Religion, for Leslie Stephen, was an object of critique, not a form of it.[77]

What interested Stephen was not finding a substitute for religion but articulating an ethics that did not depend on religion. And for this, Stephen explored the resources not only of poetry but of the novel as well, at a time when novels were still largely regarded as frivolous reading. To the extent that novels showed "the concrete person in action" rather than getting caught up in "abstract analyses of character" (as he judged even the novels of the great George Eliot were sometimes prone to do),[78] we live through the characters' moral dilemmas as well as their quiet moments, and our moral perspective is enlarged. Leslie Stephen admired the novel's ability to show us both eventful moments of decision and catastrophe as well as the less eventful but equally crucial moments of ordinary life. By treating the novel with the same seriousness that earlier critics treated poetry, Leslie Stephen helped open the way for his daughter to seek a new form for prose fiction, one that would "have something of the exaltation of poetry, but much of the ordinariness of prose."[79]

As a writer, Leslie Stephen's most influential and lasting accomplishment was not his literary criticism. Some have argued that his most lasting achievement was the *Dictionary of National Biography*, for which he served as editor until the overwhelming amount of work the project demanded nearly ruined his health.[80] Woolf notes that others believed *The History of English Thought in the Eighteenth Century* to be his masterpiece, whereas his *Science of Ethics* was "the book which interested him most."[81] Noel Annan argues that Stephen "would have judged his most notable achievement to have shown that it was possible not to believe in Christianity, yet to live a virtuous life."[82] MacCarthy agrees. *Essays in Freethinking and Plainspeaking* and *An Agnostic's Apology*, he wrote, are "the most important part of his life's work" because of the influence they had "upon men's minds."[83]

Stephen's essays on religion and agnosticism still echo in the work of today's "new atheists." The contemporary literary critic James Wood has noted that "the child of evangelicalism . . . is always evangelical" because it is "the only kind of belief that makes sense."[84] In a sentence that could have been written by Leslie Stephen, Wood, like Stephen a child of evangelicalism, asserts that Christianity "is true or it is not true."[85] Like Wood, for whom reinterpretations of "orthodox Christian faith" are pointless at best, "repulsive" at worst, Stephen attacked evangelical Christianity while at the same time lifting it up as the only "genuine theology."[86] If Christianity is not a set of indelible propositions, both ask, then what is it? "I found it easier to admit that the dogmas simply meant what the dogmatists supposed them to mean and to reject them 'in a lump,'" Stephen admitted.[87] Stephen wanted to hold Christianity in place, unchanged and unchanging, while he argued with it. Christians should not change either; those who professed to be Christian while not believing in hell were especially offensive to him. "Hell must be an integral part of the ideal world so long as the radical convictions of Christianity retain their genuine vitality," Stephen wrote. "Simply to suppress it is to substitute a vapid optimism which will never satisfy men nourished upon the Christian version of the unmistakable facts of the universe. Eternal damnation is as much a necessity of the imagination as a logical deduction from the fundamental principles of the creed."[88] Stephen's own father had once dared to hope, in print, that the suffering of the damned would not be eternal and had come under fire from the conservative evangelicals at Cambridge. His son would condemn even such tentative attempts at reinterpretation from the other direction.

Even if Leslie Stephen's embrace of agnosticism did exclude the possibility of reinterpreting the theology with which he had been raised, it would be impossible to overstate the sense of freedom—in the sense of "a burden lifting"—that it offered him and many others. His first biographer and fellow Trinity Hall graduate, Frederic Maitland, remembers him as "one of our liberators."[89] For Stephen, as for many Victorians confronted with new knowledge about the world and the Bible, it was an intellectual and emotional relief to let go of the need to defend God in the face of evil and to reconcile sacred texts with scientific knowledge about the age of the planet and the evolution of diverse forms of life. It freed their minds for other work. Leslie Stephen turned his toward ethics. He believed it was possible to live a moral life without the support of religion and belief in God, and he dedicated his intellectual energy to making the argument. This conviction permeated not only his writings on religion and agnosticism but his literary criticism as well. His essays on George Eliot, for example, argue that the religion around the "lofty moral ideal" upheld in her work is not its foundation. Eliot portrays parsons, he argued, whose goodness does not derive from their creeds, and the "very imperfect and stammering version of truths" articulated by her religious characters are "capable of being very completely dissevered from their dogmatic teaching."[90]

The burden eased by his embrace of agnosticism was not only intellectual. Agnosticism also released Stephen from the religious "mockeries" by which those who grieve are "tortured." The ministrations he received after the deaths of his wives and his step-daughter, Stella, echo in his condemnation of such mockeries. But it is not just the clumsy attempts at comfort by well-meaning Christian friends and relatives that offended Leslie Stephen; even worse was the dogma itself, expressed in the liturgy. "Is there a more cutting piece of satire in the language than the reference in our funeral service to the 'sure and certain hope of a blessed resurrection'?" he asks. Such "dreams" do not offer any real or lasting comfort; "happiness must be won by adapting our lives to the realities."[91]

Images and concerns that appear frequently in Leslie Stephen's writing on religion and agnosticism appear also in the work of his daughter. They share a conviction that full knowledge of the world lies beyond human reach, and so agnosticism is the only rational response to being alive. They both invoke, repeatedly, the world's "vastness." Leslie Stephen invokes "the vast order of which we form an insignificant portion," "the vast scheme of the universe," "vast and enormously complex processes."[92] His sense of vastness echoes in his daughter's statement of her philosophy: "*Hamlet* or a Beethoven quartet is the truth about this vast mass that we call the world."[93] They also share a sense of the dangers lurking in this vastness, the random "blows" and "shocks" that can upend a life and in the face of which Christianity's consolations seem so thin.[94] They are both attentive to the difficulties of truly knowing another person. "Each of us is an absolute unit, cut off by an impassable abyss from a direct knowledge of other consciousness," Stephen wrote.[95] Woolf's work, too, is marked by the presence of the unknowable more of others, but she is also interested in the ways in which the barriers between people can be occasionally crossed.

Father and daughter were both wholly committed to "reality." For Stephen, this meant coming to grips with a universe ungoverned by justice or an omnipotent God. For Woolf, this meant seeking new literary forms capable of giving a fuller account of human experience, including its hidden, interior dimensions. For Stephen, the universe's amoral vastness foreclosed on the possibility of theology. For Woolf, who was not arguing with Christian theologians in the way her father was, reality, with all of its blows and shocks, opened new experimental spaces for reflection for which she often employed religious language: a blow might be "a revelation of some order . . . a token of some real thing behind appearances."[96]

Although she shared his agnosticism, Woolf found the mystery that agnosticism acknowledged more susceptible to exploration, especially literary exploration, than her father, with his attention to "facts," did. In *To the Lighthouse*, when Cam and James look at their father standing in the boat as they arrive at the island, James sees him as the confident atheist, standing "straight and tall, for all the world, James thought, as if he were saying, 'There is no God.'" Cam sees him in a different way. For her, it is "as if he were leaping into space."[97] Woolf transformed the agnosticism she inherited from her father into something less dogmatic, more like a free space into which one might leap than a definite, unchanging stand.

Leslie Stephen cast his distinction between reality and dreams, fact and fiction, reason and sentiment in gendered terms. He considered those who put their faith in reason to be "masculine," whereas those who put their faith in dreams he deemed "effeminate." These distinctions did not always map onto actual men and women. Stephen believed that men should be feminine—that is, "have quick and delicate feelings"—as well as masculine, and that the best women integrated their feminine and masculine dimensions. George Eliot's "wide and calm intelligence," he wrote, reflected her "masculine quality." Male poets like Coventry Patmore and George Herbert he judged "effeminate"—Patmore because he "let[s] his feelings get the better of his intellect and produce[s] a cowardly view of life and the world," Herbert because "he seems to me always to be skulking behind the Thirty-Nine Articles instead of looking facts in the face."[98] Woolf hears her father in his essays "always cracking up sense and manliness; and crying down sentiment and vagueness,"[99] and, indeed, what Leslie Stephen understood by "manliness" was the cornerstone of his agnostic ethics: "One virtue lies at the base of all the others: call it force, energy, vitality, or manliness, or whatever you please."[100] Without a religious grounding, the moral life had to be rooted in self-control through the sheer force of will. As Charles Taylor has noted, Leslie Stephen, before losing his faith, embraced a "muscular Christianity"; his daughter remembers him as a "muscular agnostic."[101] In the move from evangelical Christianity to agnosticism, Leslie Stephen retained a commitment "to form and steel the will," a commitment he associated with masculinity.[102]

The evangelical emphasis on family piety reinforced Victorian expectations of gender roles and the duties that accompanied them, and when members of the Clapham Sect wrote about "the duties of the female sex," as priest and poet Thomas Gisborne did, the results were "appallingly repressive and breathtakingly patronizing."[103] Woolf's Victorian agnostic parents' understanding of gender roles was equally restrictive. The lingering Clapham influence ran in two directions, however. In one, feminine roles were forever fixed in place by women's essential nature. In the other, the Clapham Sect's emphasis on vocation nudged open a space for women's creative work.

Like Katharine Hilbery in *Night and Day*, Woolf and her sister were expected to be present downstairs each afternoon to serve tea and make conversation with whatever guests appeared. But Katharine Hilbery, unlike the Stephen daughters, also had to spend her mornings helping her mother prepare a biography of her father, a famous poet, a project that stood as much chance of successful completion as Mr. Casaubon's doomed "Key to All Mythologies."[104] Woolf describes Katharine's entire day as given over to tasks that had nothing to do with Katharine's real passion: mathematics.

Virginia and Vanessa Stephen's mornings were given over to reading, writing, and painting. "From ten to one Victorian society did not exert any special pressure upon us," Woolf wrote in her memoir. "For three hours we lived in the world which we still inhabit."[105] Many entries in Woolf's early journals track Nessa's disciplined devotion to painting—"Nessa went to her studio . . . Nessa went to her drawing. . . . Nessa went to her _____ drawing"—and Woolf's steady diet of books.[106] By the afternoon, Victorian society began to impinge on them, and by evening, it was operating at full strength, enforced by their stepbrother George Duckworth, who insisted on taking them to society events they despised. But in the mornings, both Virginia and Vanessa honed the practices of their vocations, the work from which their lives would take their shape.

Unlike Katharine Hilbery, Virginia and Vanessa lacked a mother during most of their teenage and young adult years to yoke them to her projects. Had Julia Stephen lived longer, would their mornings have been given over to accompanying their mother as she made her nursing rounds and assisting her with her correspondence? Woolf certainly understood the constraining power her parents wielded. On what would have been her father's ninety-sixth birthday, Woolf wrote in her diary that, had he lived until he was ninety-six, his "life would have entirely ended mine. What would have happened? No writing, no books;—inconceivable."[107] Leslie Stephen was "the most imminent obstacle, the most oppressive stone laid upon our vitality and its struggle to live."[108] Obsessed with his health, Julia Stephen "was too willing," Woolf wrote, "to sacrifice us to him," leaving the children, after her death, to deal with "the legacy of his dependence."[109]

In a talk to a group of professional women in 1931, which later became her essay "Professions for Women," Woolf famously spoke of killing the "Angel in the House"—the fictitious embodiment of Victorian ideals of womanhood her mother had upheld: "[The Angel in the House] was intensely sympathetic. She was immensely charming. She was utterly unselfish. She excelled in the difficult arts of family life."[110] And she whispered in the ear of the writer that it was necessary to be pleasing to men: "Be sympathetic; be tender; flatter," she urged. "Never let anyone guess that you have a mind of your own."[111] In order to write, Woolf told the assembled professional women, the woman writer must first kill the Angel in the House: "If I had not killed her, she would have killed me. She would have plucked the heart out of my writing."[112] There was much Woolf had to resist in her parents in order to become a groundbreaking thinker and writer. When Woolf was seven years old, Julia Stephen signed "An Appeal Against Female Suffrage," which argued against giving women the vote on the grounds that it would weaken the influence of "the special moral qualities of women."[113] (Fifteen years after her mother's death, Virginia Stephen worked for women's suffrage, a fact she continued to recall with pride until the end of her life.)[114] Julia Stephen's Victorian understanding of women's essential nature and the tasks to which it was suited was shared by Woolf's father.

But Julia Stephen could not be reduced to the angel in the house. As Lily Briscoe muses about Mrs. Ramsay in *To the Lighthouse*, "Fifty pairs of eyes were not enough to get round that one woman with."[115] Julia Stephen was not only the angel in the house; she was also one of the writers in the house. Woolf remembers her mother writing at a table with silver candlesticks and a brass inkpot. She left behind nine unpublished children's stories, a book on nursing called *Notes from Sick Rooms*, the entry on her aunt, the photographer Julia Margaret Cameron, for the *Dictionary of National Biography*, and three unpublished essays, including one on women and agnosticism.

Julia Stephen wrote her essay on women and agnosticism in response to a published essay by Bertha Lathbury in the journal *Nineteenth Century*. Lathbury had argued that, without faith in some kind of religious reward, women would have no incentive to do the self-sacrificial work that family life, nursing, and teaching demand of them, nor would they be able to help the working classes to accept their lot in life. Women who claim to be agnostics, she wrote, are simply acting on their love and reverence for the agnostic men in their lives, even though, she goes on to assert, such men prefer women to "cling with womanly inconsistency to all that is refining and soothing in the old creeds."[116] Agnosticism, she insisted, is not a position at which a woman would arrive on her own.

Julia Stephen dismisses Bertha Lathbury's assertion that agnostic men would prefer their wives and daughters to remain Christian believers with the dry humor by which her daughter's own writing is marked: "Who can fathom the depth of a man's heart?" Julia Stephen asks. "We certainly cannot."[117]

It is Bertha Lathbury's insistence that women could not become agnostics on their own and that agnosticism would undermine their ability to do the work for which women are meant that draws out Julia Stephen's most passionate arguments. Although married to one of Victorian England's foremost agnostic thinkers, Julia Stephen had come to agnosticism on her own, following the death of her beloved first husband, Herbert Duckworth. She had been drawn to Leslie Stephen by his essays on agnosticism, which confirmed her own conviction that living a moral life did not require that one believe in God. She read

Leslie Stephen's essays, as her daughter later put it, "with a desire to establish her own sad faith."[118]

When she writes about women and agnosticism, though, Julia Stephen does not sound sad. Woolf described her mother's work of nursing the poor and dying as a reversal of "those natural instincts which were so strong in her of happiness and joy," pressing "the bitterest fruit only to her lips."[119] But Julia did not write of this work as a penance but as a vocation.

> We, having chosen the work of nursing, give to it the best that we have—our lives. We are not thinking that we shall gain a glorious immortality, that we shall be crowned as saints because we have helped our fellow creatures, but they are our work. We are bound to these sufferers by the tie of sisterhood and while life lasts we will help, soothe, and, if we can, love them. Pity has no creed, suffering no limits. And shall we, who are not helpers but sufferers, refuse to be helped in our turn by those who differ from us in doctrine but who are one in heart?[120]

To soothe suffering is a deeply human calling, according to Julia Stephen, for we are all bound together by our shared vulnerability to illness and pain. Agnostics, in fact, make better nurses than Christians, she argued, because, acknowledging that there is much they cannot explain about life and death, agnostics have a broad, inclusive range of sympathy and no desire to evangelize.

Julia and Leslie Stephen shared a conviction that the moral life need not have a religious foundation. Leslie's belief was nurtured by philosophy, Julia's by nursing. Together, they embodied an agnostic version of their inherited notions of vocation and duty that was both intellectually and ethically challenging. Their ways of living and thinking gave their children something to embrace and to resist as they grew into their own vocations.

In her essay on agnosticism and women, Julia Stephen argued that women and men had the same capacity for moral courage but different work to do. Her sense of essential differences between women and men, and the distinction between women's and men's work that such differences evoked, restricted Woolf's and her sister's opportunities, especially in the realm of education. Leslie Stephen did not provide his daughters with a formal university education, as he did his sons—a fact that Woolf resented all her life. But he and Julia did not exempt their daughters from the human duty to contribute to the world through meaningful work either. When Virginia was still a child, Leslie was already imagining that she would become an historian and turning her reading in that direction.[121] Vanessa was given drawing lessons and eventually sent to study art at the Slade and the Royal Academy. Although her father "had no special love for painting," Woolf remembered that "he assured [Vanessa] that so long as she took her work seriously he would give her all the help he could."[122] Most mornings, the two girls were side by side, Vanessa painting or drawing, Virginia reading or writing. From an early age, the Stephen sisters brought to reading, writing, and painting the seriousness and discipline that their mother brought to nursing and their father to study and writing.

Leslie Stephen himself embodied the tension between freedom and constraint that marked their Clapham inheritance. On the one hand, his expectation of "a certain standard of behavior, even of ceremony, in family life" restricted his children's freedom. On the other, as Woolf noted, he insisted on "the right to think one's own thoughts and to follow one's own pursuits."[123] During "that dreadful summer" after Julia Stephen's death, when their father imposed his enormous grief on his children, groaning at the dinner table, worrying out loud, and obsessively, about whether he had communicated clearly enough to his wife how much he had loved her, there were still moments when he could offer a glimpse of a life worth living: "On a walk perhaps he would suddenly brush aside all our curiously conventional relationships, and show us for a minute an inspiriting vision of free life, bathed in an impersonal light. There were numbers of things to be learnt, books to be read, and success and happiness were to be attained there without disloyalty. Indeed it seemed possible at these moments, to continue the old life but in a more significant way, using as he told us, our sorrow to quicken the feeling that remained."[124] These moments passed, and gloom would close over the grieving family once more: "We were made to act parts that we did not feel," Woolf wrote of life in the Stephen household after Julia's death, "to fumble for words that we did not know."[125] But that occasional glimpse of freedom within life's possibilities was vivid enough for Woolf to remember, and be grateful for, decades later. The moments of being her characters experience in her novels owe something to Woolf's memory of those moments when a sense of freedom and possibility broke through her father's oppressive mourning. They were "matches struck unexpectedly in the dark," small revelations that lit the way forward.[126]

Woolf's biographer, Hermione Lee, has observed that Woolf "made her female inheritance count for just as much as her father's influence," and certainly Woolf's father was not the only child of James Stephen who left his mark on Woolf's intellectual and religious imagination.[127] The influence of his younger sister, Caroline Emelia Stephen, the Quaker theologian and self-described "rational mystic," was also profound.

Leslie and Caroline Stephen shared the same evangelical childhood, marked by the Clapham Sect's commitment to family devotional practices. Caroline recalled, in a tribute to her father, the short meditations he would offer on the gospel reading during the family's morning prayers.[128] Leslie's own practice of reading aloud to his children in the evenings retained the form, if not the content, of those family devotions. But although Leslie and Caroline grew up in the same household, they remembered their father differently. Leslie's account of James Stephen's life excluded any exploration of his religious convictions and interior experience; he focused instead on his father's accomplishments as a public man. Caroline intended her own collection of their father's letters and her reminiscences of him to correct what she considered to be Leslie's partial view. Being her father's child, she once wrote, "was like having been brought up in a Cathedral."[129]

In the portrait of her father's religious life that emerges in her edited collection of his letters annotated by her own remembrances, Caroline Stephen did not portray James Stephen as a dogmatic thinker. Rather, she traced her own expansive understanding of faith back to her father's practice of it. Although he approached the Bible with the reverence of an evangelical Christian, she wrote, "it was yet put before us not as infallible, but as inexhaustible—as supplying not so much proof, as edification." It was because of this generous-spirited understanding of scripture, she believed, that the insights of the historical-critical study of the Bible produced in her "no violent disturbance of faith"[130]—a distinct difference from her brother's experience, for whom historical challenges to the literal truth of the story of Noah and the flood pulled the whole rug of faith out from under him. Caroline remembered her father as a truth-seeker, one who, had he lived to read it, would have had his "religious opinions" changed by Darwin's *Origin of Species*, "as have those of all honest thinkers in the last fifty years."[131]

Like Leslie, Caroline experienced the intellectual upheavals that marked the Victorian age and by which, as Caroline wrote, "we have been so severely shaken and sifted."[132] The historical-critical study of the Bible had "laid bare," as she and her brother had discovered, "an unsuspected degree of uncertainty as to the exact words uttered by Jesus of Nazareth"[133] and exposed biblical infallibility as an intellectually untenable position. For Leslie and many others, the scientific insights of Darwin seemed better suited to describe reality than the theological dogmas and doctrines of Christianity and its biblical accounts of creation.

If, for Leslie, it was the loss of confidence in the historical truth of the Bible that led him to renounce his ordination and his academic post, for Caroline, it was the worship mandated by the Church of England's *Book of Common Prayer* that led her out of the church. She found the language of the liturgy, while beautiful, too sure of itself, too systematic. Rather than drawing her into devotion, its confident tone set the other side of the argument going in her mind: "What I felt I wanted in a place of worship was a refuge, or at least the opening of a doorway towards the refuge, from doubts and controversies—not a fresh encounter with them. Yet it seems to me impossible that any one harassed by the conflicting views of truth with which just now the air is thick, should be able to forget controversy while listening to such language as that of the Book of Common Prayer."[134] The theological language of the Church of England's worship had become fraught for her, a burden. The silent worship of the Quakers offered relief.

While on a visit to Leslie and his family at the seaside in 1872, Caroline attended the Quaker Meeting in Falmouth, sat with the Friends in silence, and felt a new world open to her. "I had found a place," she wrote, "where I might, without the faintest suspicion of insincerity, join with others in simply seeking His presence. To sit down in silence could at the least pledge me to nothing; it might open to me (as it did that morning) the very gate of heaven."[135] In a letter to a friend, she described the experience like this: "It is as if my painted roof had been smashed and, instead of the darkness I had dreaded, I had found the stars shining."[136] For a woman who had likened her childhood in her father's house to growing up in a cathedral, this was liberation.

Caroline Stephen tried to pass down something of that freedom to her beloved niece, Leslie's youngest daughter, to whom she left a legacy of £2,500 at her death. Woolf, who, like her aunt, described her childhood as held in a "Cathedral space,"honored the theological and political dimension of her aunt's gift when she referred to it in *A Room of One's Own*.[137] Arguing that a measure of financial independence was required for women to write, Woolf's fictional narrator notes that "my aunt's legacy unveiled the sky to me, and substituted for the large and imposing figure of a gentleman, which Milton recommended for my perpetual adoration, a view of the open sky."[138] For both aunt and niece, breaking through the cathedral space dominated by their fathers and the patriarchal God their fathers worshipped or rejected opened the possibility of a free and open space beyond Christianity or agnosticism.

Caroline Stephen became a Quaker during a period of evangelical Christian influence within the Society of Friends in Britain. Although the Quaker movement had begun "as a mighty protest of soul against the habit of turning religion into the adoption of theological doctrines,"[139] it was not immune to the evangelical revival that swept through Britain in the eighteenth and nineteenth centuries. From Methodism to the evangelical revival movements within the Church of England, including the Clapham Sect, British evangelicalism left its mark on the Society of Friends. In the eighteenth century, itinerant Quaker preachers like Mary Dudley brought a taste of revival preaching to meetings and introduced an emphasis on the saving work of Jesus Christ into a religious society that, in its origins, was distinctly anti-creedal and even theology-averse. Dudley and other Quaker preachers attempted to integrate the mystical dimension of Quaker belief and practice with an evangelical emphasis on salvation through the atoning sacrifice of Christ.[140] As evangelical doctrines gained a foothold among the Quakers, a "growing sensitiveness to unsoundness" in matters of doctrine began to manifest itself.[141] It was accompanied by a growing suspicion of the convictions of the original Quakers: the emphasis on the authority of each individual's experience of the Inner Light; the resistance to paid ministers and to sacraments; the refusal to elevate biblical authority over the authority of religious experience.

The Society of Friends in nineteenth-century Britain was strained by controversies related to the tension between the old Quaker ideals and the newer evangelical emphases. The American Quaker Elias Hicks horrified evangelically inclined Friends with what they considered to be his heretical overemphasis on the authority of the Inner Light and stimulated an evangelical backlash. Hicks elevated the authority of the Inner Light over all external authorities, including the Bible, understood Jesus to be a model of perfect obedience to God rather than a savior, rejected the notion of original sin, and considered the doctrine of the atonement to be a "vulgar error."[142] The schism in the American Society of Friends between the Hicksites and the Orthodox influenced Quaker debates in England, although the British Quakers did not split as the Americans had. As British Friends sought to articulate their position vis-à-vis Hicks, several manifestations of Quaker evangelicalism emerged: those who saw the authority of scripture as balanced by the authority of the Inner Light, those who believed scriptural authority to be greater than the authority of inward religious experience, and, at the furthest extreme, those who believed the "unscriptural notion of the light within"[143] to be opposed to the gospel of Christ, a position taken by Isaac Crewdson in his *Beacon to the Society of Friends*. What came to be known as the Beaconite position rejected the authority of individual experiences of God so cherished by the original Quakers. Other evangelical Quakers found the position of Crewdson and his followers too extreme, and the Beaconites eventually left the Society of Friends for the Church of England and the Plymouth Brethren.[144]

Joseph John Gurney, one of the most important figures in the nineteenth-century evangelical revival within Quakerism, was deeply influenced by intimate friendships with leaders of the Clapham Sect, especially Henry Venn, the grandson of the author of the Clapham spiritual manual, *The Complete Duty of Man*, and William Wilberforce, Clapham's leader in antislavery activism. Gurney considered his friendship with Wilberforce "one of the happiest circumstances of my life."[145]

With such close friends in the evangelical movement exerting so powerful an influence on him, it is a wonder that Gurney did not simply join the Church of England. But the Quaker commitment to "plainness of speech, behavior and apparel" remained deeply meaningful to him, as did the silent worship in which Friends sought the guidance of the Holy Spirit. Itinerant Quaker preachers—Ann Jones in particular—also had a profound effect on him, as did his sister, Elizabeth Fry, whose ministry was focused on prison reform (and who married into a family that would produce Roger Fry, artist and beloved friend of Virginia Woolf, as well as his sister, Margery, who followed in Elizabeth's footsteps as a prison reformer). So, despite some misgivings about the Quaker position on the sacraments and what he believed to be too little emphasis on the saving work of Christ, Gurney committed himself to the Society of Friends.

Gurney's impact on the Society of Friends in nineteenth-century Britain was enormous. He replaced the Quaker emphasis on the inner experience of the presence of God with "an elaborated plan of salvation" grounded in scripture rather than in the individual experience of the Inner Light.[146] For him, the Inner Light was a means to understand scripture better, not an authority on par with it. Gurney, along with other evangelical Friends, pulled nineteenth-century British Quakers toward a theological position focused on salvation and the doctrine of the atonement, a radical change from Quaker beginnings.

Caroline Stephen pulled the Society of Friends in the other direction, back toward its original convictions and practices. Her eloquent defense of the Inner Light and other distinctive Quaker convictions made her conversion to the Society of Friends "one of the most important events in the history of English Quakerism during [this] period," according to Rufus Jones.[147] As British Quakers struggled to integrate the influence both of the evangelical revival and the intellectual upheavals of the day while at the same time retaining a distinctive identity, Caroline Stephen made a crucial contribution with her eloquent and intellectually alive accounts of central Quaker commitments and practices, especially *Quaker Strongholds* (1890) and *Light Arising: Thoughts on the Central Radiance* (1908), both of which Woolf owned.[148] Rufus Jones has called her "the foremost interpreter in the Society in England of Friends's way of worship and of the type of religion which they were endeavoring to maintain and express."[149] Caroline's great-grandfather, Henry Venn, had written the spiritual manual of the Clapham Sect with his *Complete Duty of Man*. With *Quaker Strongholds* and *Light Arising*, Caroline Stephen articulated a Quaker spirituality that pushed back against the pressure that her family's evangelical Christianity exerted on her Quaker faith.

Caroline Stephen was well-suited to articulate the relevance of Quakerism for her time. She had experienced firsthand both the world of evangelical Christianity and the world of religious skepticism, and she understood the attractions of both. She acknowledged the appeal that the vigor of the evangelical revival could have for Quakers who had watched their numbers dwindle. But she also acknowledged the many ways truth, goodness, and beauty could be sought within Christianity and without. She had read modern criticism of the Bible—she writes in a letter of finding Adolph von Harnack's *What Is Christianity?* a "strong and beautiful" book[150]—and the theories of Darwin. She found these intellectual developments unsettling but also thrilling and was not afraid to think about her faith in the light they provided. Like her father, she believed science and religion to be allies, not enemies. She wrote to her friend Harriet Litchfield, Darwin's eldest daughter, that while reading Harriet's father's scientific work did not lead her into the "region of devotion," neither did it "weaken or injure the spirit of rational devotion itself."[151] One need not choose between intuition and reason, she insisted; both were human capacities, both gifts of God.[152]

A sense of "rational devotion" permeates Caroline Stephen's work. Even though evangelical Christianity had drawn so many people to it in her day, she knew that it also drove away others who felt offended by "the glibness, the exasperating completeness, the unconscious blasphemy, of many 'orthodox' vindications of Providence."[153] Although they all occupied different religious locations, Caroline Stephen shared with her father, her brother, and her niece a revulsion toward too-easy religious answers to the profound questions of life. James Stephen despised the complacency of Christians who simply went through the motions. Leslie Stephen disdained what he considered to be the Christian refusal of reality and the embrace of dreams. Woolf mistrusted Christianity's consolations. In between her father's evangelicalism and the agnosticism of her brother and her niece, Caroline Stephen stood in the Quaker stillness, offering a religious practice "unshackled by creeds and formularies," a practice that she believed could accommodate the most rigorous seeking of truth.[154] An invitation to free thinkers like her brother Leslie runs throughout her work. Silent worship, she argued, "throws open the door wide to those who are passing through all degrees of doubt and agnosticism."[155] Even Voltaire, she noted, appreciated the Quaker position.[156]

Reading Caroline Stephen, it is impossible not to be struck by the resonances and similarities between her language, imagery, and ideas and those of Virginia Woolf. As Jane Marcus has observed, Caroline Stephen's "rational mysticism" shares much in common with the way Woolf described her experience of what she called "moments of being." Caroline Stephen described "rational mysticism" as "agnosticism with mystery at the heart of it," a position marked both by her father's devout religious faith and the intellectual upheaval that made it impossible for her and her brother to remain in the Church of England.[157] In her writing and in her life, Woolf also seems to express an "agnosticism with mystery at the heart of it." Although deeply critical of the institutional religious forms of her grandfather's faith, she also mistrusted her father's muscular agnosticism as a gendered, limited view of the world.[158] The space she occupied as an artist and as a human being seems closer to her aunt's fluid, undogmatic view of religion than to the more settled, convinced positions of her agnostic father and Christian grandfather. Caroline Stephen "unveiled the sky" for her niece in more ways than one.

Woolf poked fun at her aunt in her letters, referring to her as "Nun" or "the Quaker," complaining of her nonstop talk, finding "her whole system of toleration and resignation . . . so wooly."[159] She also wrote a comic life of her aunt, which, unfortunately, has not survived.[160] But her aunt's home, "The Porch," was a refuge for her. Woolf spent many Sundays there and went there to live for a few months to recover from an illness that had spiraled into hallucinations, severe headaches, and a suicide attempt following her father's death. She wrote to her friend Violet Dickinson that "this is an ideal retreat for me,"[161] and "I have had no headaches since I came here—so I think the Quaker must be doing good."[162] She and her aunt had long conversations—Woolf reports a Sunday conversation of nine hours in her letters—in which they discussed her aunt's religious experiences. Woolf found Caroline Stephen sometimes maddening and at other times "a very wise and witty old lady."[163] "With all her faults," Woolf wrote, "she is about as tough an old heathen as they make; we shant develop such thews and sinews not if we live 80 years."[164] Woolf was obviously proud of the esteem in which her aunt was held by young Quakers at Cambridge: "she is a kind of modern prophetess."[165] Aunt and niece attended Quaker meeting together, where Woolf experienced firsthand the silent worship that changed Caroline Stephen's life.[166] She thought once of writing about going to Quaker meeting for the *Guardian*, the church weekly in which she got her start as a reviewer, but she was busy helping Frederic Maitland with his life of Leslie Stephen and never produced the essay.[167] Her aunt's way of receiving and responding to the world, though, appeared in her writing in other ways.

Jane Marcus and Quentin Bell famously feuded over whether or not Caroline Emelia Stephen was a literary influence on Woolf.[168] Marcus, whose essay "The Niece of a Nun" was the first extended treatment of Woolf's relationship with her aunt and her aunt's influence on her, argued that she was. Bell, pointing to Woolf's descriptions in her letters of being bored by her aunt's company, argued that she was not. Bell is right that Virginia often ridiculed Caroline Stephen as a comic figure—an elephant trumpeting on the stairs, a quacking Quaker—whose pieties her niece disdained. But Marcus captures something important when she points to echoes of Caroline Stephen's "rational mysticism," her "agnosticism with mystery at the heart of it," in Woolf's own work. That Caroline Stephen was not "Virginia's literary stay maker," as Bell feels compelled to assert, seems obvious.[169] But that she was a particularly influential part of the religion around Virginia Woolf, providing language, ideas, and imagery that Woolf engaged as an artist and used to describe elusive dimensions of human experience also seems clear.

In her autobiographical essay "A Sketch of the Past," Woolf articulated most clearly the relationship between the way she experienced the world and her vocation as a writer. Most of life, she wrote, is made up of "non-being"—moments that flow by without our fully noticing, without marking us in any way. Such moments, Woolf wrote, are "embedded in a kind of nondescript cotton wool"—a phrase that echoes George Eliot's harsher observation in *Middlemarch* that "the quickest of us walk about well wadded with stupidity."[170]

But within the flow of nonbeing erupt "exceptional moments" when we are wrenched fully awake, fully conscious by "a sudden violent shock," a "revelation" of "some order" behind the cotton wool, "a token of some real thing behind appearances." Woolf's ability to experience such moments, to receive such shocks, she believed, is what made her a writer. Moments of being are shattering; the practice of writing allowed her to piece the resulting fragments into a new whole. "Perhaps this is the strongest pleasure known to me," she wrote. "It is the rapture I get when in writing I seem to be discovering what belongs to what; making a scene come right; making a character come together."[171]

Virginia Woolf's idea of the "moment of being" that rises up out of ordinary life like a violent revelation derives from her own experience. But in those long conversations with Caroline Stephen about her aunt's religious experiences, and in her aunt's writing, she would have found something akin to what she struggled to find language to describe. In *Light Arising*, Caroline Stephen writes that some people experience the Inner Light as a dim glimmer, others as glory, and others as "flashes of revelation, which have changed for them the whole aspect of life as the blaze of lightning reveals the midnight landscape."[172] For Caroline Stephen, the ability to apprehend such flashes of revelation belongs to mystics and poets. She understood it to be a religious capacity, for it responds to the way God communicates: like a lighthouse, intermittently.[173] Indeed, for her, faith was defined more by this human capacity for receiving the shock of revelation than by intellectual assent to a set of religious propositions. Faith, she wrote, is "that faculty, come from whence it may, by which we behold the Invisible; the insight which penetrating through all misleading appearances grasps the innermost unchanging truth underlying them."[174]

Virginia Woolf did not clothe her experience in the language of religious conviction as her aunt did, although she did draw on the language of religious experience to describe it: rapture, ecstasy, revelation. Caroline Stephen believed that what Woolf calls "moments of being" could be sought in the silent worship of the Quakers. Woolf does not report seeking such experiences; she writes of them as coming from outside of her, suddenly: "they seemed dominant, myself passive," especially in childhood. For Woolf, moments of being were incomplete without writing; through writing, she gave them shape, wholeness. She found a way to place the severed parts together.[175] George Eliot had warned in *Middlemarch* that such direct experience of reality is dangerous for human beings. "If we had a keen vision and feeling of all ordinary human life . . . we should die of that roar which lies on the other side of silence,"[176] she wrote. Through the practice of writing, Woolf survived her encounter with the "real thing behind appearances"and transformed it into art.[177]

Woolf summed up her account of the relationship between her experience of moments of being and her work as a writer with a statement composed in the rhythmic language of a creed.

> From this I reach what I might call a philosophy; at any rate it is a constant idea of mine; that behind the cotton wool is hidden a pattern; that we—I mean all human beings—are connected with this; that the whole world is a work of art; that we are parts of the work of art. *Hamlet* or a Beethoven quartet is the truth about this vast mass that we call the world. But there is no Shakespeare, there is no Beethoven; certainly and emphatically there is no God; we are the words; we are the music; we are the thing itself. And I see this when I have a shock.[178]

This often-quoted passage from Woolf's autobiography has been used to argue for everything from her mysticism to her atheism. I quote it here to remark on the similarity between Woolf's philosophy and her aunt's. Caroline Stephen did not want to hide, as some of her religious contemporaries did, from the new knowledge produced by the historical-critical study of the Bible, the new advances in scientific understanding of human origins, and the philosophical speculation it engendered. But she believed that each person should "construct out of our own actual experience some sort of creed . . . a real framework" with which to think about new ideas. Caroline Stephen constructed such a framework in her writings, and Woolf did too, in "A Sketch of the Past."

Even more interesting, however, is the similarity between Woolf's image of human beings as the words, the music, the thing itself, and her aunt's reflection on human beings in relation to the divine. In a letter to a friend about a year before her death, Caroline Stephen wrote, "I don't think we can perhaps ever tell where the divine begins and the human ends; indeed I don't think it is like that, as who should say one province was human and another divine? To me it seems as if the human were but a note *in* the divine harmony, a syllable *in* the divine poem."[179] Both Stephen women had a sense of reality as lying just beyond our ordinary existence. Both women imagined the pattern hidden behind the cotton wool of nonbeing as a work of art. And both imagined human beings as part of that work of art—a note in the divine harmony, a syllable in the poem. Woolf made sure to insist that there was no God; the work of art that we are a part of is what is real. Caroline Stephen wrote confidently of that work of art as divine in origin, yet she refused to speculate on where the human ended and the divine began. Her "agnosticism with mystery at the heart of it" tended toward the theistic, Woolf's toward the atheistic. But both expressed a vision of reality that is remarkably similar in form.

There are important differences between Caroline Stephen and Virginia Woolf as well. Like Woolf's mother, Caroline Stephen passed along an ambiguous inheritance in relation to gender. Julia believed both that women and men shared the same capacity for moral courage but were fitted for different kinds of work because of the differences between their essential natures. Caroline Stephen both treasured the ministry of women within the Society of Friends but also, like Julia Stephen, opposed women's suffrage until the end of her life. Formed by her many years as "the daughter at home," Caroline Stephen carried ambivalent feelings about the role of women in society. In her first book, *The Service of the Poor* (1871), she was clearly drawn to the women's communities she studied—Florence Nightingale's Kaiserwerth, the Beguinage at Ghent, the Sisters of Charity in Paris—but argued against such communities because the free labor of the "daughter at home" was crucial to the survival of the patriarchal Victorian family.[180] Once she became a Quaker, however, new possibilities of human community became visible to her: the Quaker meeting in which women and men met on equal footing; the home of a woman living alone and making her own choices about the "channels into which [her] energies should flow, and for which they should be reserved."[181]

Although they are both concerned with interiority and mystical life, Woolf and her aunt diverge in their descriptions of it. For Caroline Stephen, interiority is lit by the Inner Light. "The mystical sense I value," she wrote, "owes nothing to the darkness."[182] Woolf's sense of the mystical was shaped in part by experiences of depression and despair—"I expect they've done instead of religion," she wrote to E. M. Forster in 1922.[183] And so her sense of the mystical, unlike her aunt's, embraces darkness as well as light. In *To the Lighthouse*, when Mrs. Ramsay imagines a form for her inner life, it is a "wedge-shaped core of darkness."[184] Furthermore, in her desire to keep her mysticism "rational," Caroline Stephen eschewed attention to rapture and ecstasy. The Inner Light "consists not in rapture, ecstasy, sensation, but in clear insight into the deepest kind of truth."[185] By contrast, Woolf's earliest and most formative memories are marked by ecstasy and rapture, a rapture she continues to find in her work as a writer: "The rapture I get when in writing I seem to be discovering what belongs to what; making a scene come right; making a character come together."[186] These differences stem from their differences in religious practice. Caroline Stephen's central religious practice was to wait in silence with others for illumination. Virginia Woolf's was the piecing together of fragments to discover "what belongs to what," to discover and create new wholes.

Through relationships with members of her family, Virginia Woolf came into contact with significant currents of religious thought and practice in the world around her. The currents flowed through her as well, leaving behind traces of her parents' agnosticism, her aunt's mysticism, her ancestors' commitment to social change, and their emphasis on vocation. These early influences were crucial to the shaping of the religious dimensions of her own literary project. But they were by no means the only ones. As her world gets larger in adulthood, she will encounter religion in many other forms through reading, travel, art, friendship, and marriage.

2

FRESH CHAPELS

The theological questions that animated the intellectual life of her parents' generation continued to stimulate discussion in Woolf's own. Having been raised without religious faith, Virginia Stephen and her siblings were free from the struggle with religious doubt experienced by their parents and the intellectual labors that doubt engendered for them. But religious argument and debate—a Stephen "family habit"[1]—remained part of their highly conversational lives. Virginia wrote in her diary about a vacation with her siblings in Norfolk in August 1906 during which they tramped the countryside together, "thinking, arguing, & expounding," often about religion. As they explored the fens, meadows, and roads of the area one Sunday, they encountered churchgoers—"10 orthodox Christians, 6 Methodists, & 2 ½ Anabaptists." Two and a half? "Children count only as halves," Virginia explained, "because when they grow up they may think for themselves, & swell the number of the hostile sect, or, presumably, build a fresh chapel for themselves." Leslie Stephen had died two years before, and the Stephen children were just beginning to imagine their own fresh chapels, their distinctive forms of marriage, friendship, and artmaking.

On the morning Virginia recorded in her diary, the Stephen siblings spent their time wondering and arguing about why people continued to go to church now that the Black Death no longer threatened and "the sheep are gone, & Americans live in the Halls of the landowners." Although she was puzzled by the living piety they encountered, when she sat down with her diary that evening, she used religious language to express the creative drive that led her to write an account of the day. "Dont I feel," she wrote, "the steady beat of the great Creator as I write; & doesn't the Church there record its pulse this evening, & for six hundred years of evenings such as these?"[2] The fresh chapels Virginia Woolf created through her writing would reflect both of these elements: a deep mistrust of traditional religious institutions combined with a sense of something hidden, yet alive, in the universe. Her encounters with this reality, as she suggests here and reiterates in her memoirs at the end of her life, made her a writer. Although not connected through traditional belief or piety to the churches she comes upon during her walks, she is connected as an artist, recording the "pulse" of the "great Creator" just as "the great solid chapels" of England's sacred landscape do.

Throughout her childhood and young adulthood, religion reaches Virginia Stephen through friends and relatives, occasional churchgoing, reading, art, and travel. The Stephen children's friends ranged from the grandchildren of Charles Darwin to the children and grandchildren of parish rectors and deans of cathedrals to children who would themselves grow up to be rectors and deans. In her early journals, Virginia experimented with the religious language around her to describe her daily life. Nessa "preaches"; "pilgrimages" are made; a road is "christened"; a good book and the time to read it are a "blessing." Bits of liturgy, hymns, and scripture appear here and there, repurposed—"A ship moves in mysterious ways," she wrote, echoing William Cowper's famous hymn,[3] as she watched the ships move in and out of the bay during a vacation in Cornwall.[4] The Stephen children engage each other and others in theological arguments. They go to church occasionally, to hear the banns of marriage read for their half-sister Stella's wedding, for example, or to hear Evensong in cathedral towns during their holidays. And occasionally religious people surprise them by turning out to be other than they expect. On vacation in

Warboys in 1899, Virginia wrote of dining with a local curate, notable "because I have never sat down to a meal with a curate in my life." The seventeen-year-old Virginia continued: "The fact that a Black Coated gentleman could be a Human Being & not a Hypocrite . . . was quite strange to me."[5] Woolf studied ministers closely throughout her life, reading their diaries, their essays, their letters to the editors of various newspapers, and measuring them against both the satirical treatment they received "at the hands of all wielders of Pens" and her own ideas of how much more they might do with their pulpits and their place in the culture.[6] The ministers who appear in her novels, from Mr. Bax in *The Voyage Out* to Mr. Streatfield in *Between the Acts*, are never simply stock characters with one job to do but capable of both the silliness that merited satirical treatment and the occasional startling insight.

A significant shaping influence on Virginia Woolf's understanding of religion was her cousin Dorothea Stephen, the youngest daughter of her father's brother, Fitzjames Stephen. Eleven years older than Virginia, Dorothea badgered the Stephen children throughout their childhood and into their adulthood about their lack of Christian faith. Dorothea is a vivid character in Woolf's early diaries and letters and continues to appear—a negative touchstone of sorts—in Woolf's letters and diaries well into the 1930s. Dorothea became, over time, a ridiculous figure to Woolf and a token of the kind of religiosity, bent on the conversion of others, that Woolf despised.

Like his brother Leslie, Fitzjames Stephen, Dorothea's father, had lost his faith in adulthood. He and his wife, however, continued to bring their children to church and to have family prayers at home, read by Lady Stephen. Associating Christianity with cultural superiority, Fitzjames asserted that "the best part of the human race" names God as Father.[7] The Stephens continued to impart Victorian Christian ideas about gender, family, and nation to their children. Doctrinally, though, they wanted their children to make up their minds for themselves, so they immersed them in Christian practice while explaining to them that "a great part of what they heard in church and read in the Bible, was not true, and that much of the teaching founded upon it by clergymen and others was most immoral and dangerous."[8] Despite such warnings, however, the churchgoing took root in Dorothea. She became an evangelical Christian eager to convert her cousins and, eventually, a religious teacher in India. Like other members of the Stephen family, she put her ideas into print. In 1918 she published a study of the Rigveda, the Upanishads, and the Bhagavadgita, which concluded that early Indian thought had failed to grasp the importance of personal character.[9] Late in her life, she wrote that she saw herself as part of a "connected argument of the generations" of Stephens about religion.[10]

In Virginia Stephen's diaries, we see Virginia and Dorothea spending long days together. They take walks and go shopping. Virginia typed out her cousin's handwritten poems so that Dorothea could submit them for publication. Throughout it all, Virginia reported, Dorothea talked "loudly and vehemently." Virginia records in her diary that "Nessa and D discussed 'religion & the gospels,' while D was undressing"—their ongoing theological argument, apparently, rarely paused.[11] At seventeen, Virginia found her cousin "overpowering."[12] But by the time she was nineteen, Virginia had begun poking fun at her. Teasing her with jokes about the afterlife, Virginia got the rise out of her that she hoped for: "She glows like a sunset over Mont Blanc . . . and says 'Shut up!'"[13]

In 1903, Virginia wrote to Violet Dickinson, herself a Christian, about an argument Thoby was having with Dorothea about Christianity. "She is trying," Virginia wrote, "to prove that certain sections of her soul are alive and afloat while ours are 'atrophied.'"[14] Thoby and Dorothea continued their argument by letter. Virginia reported jousting with Dorothea herself: "We have quarreled happily!" she wrote to her cousin Emma Vaughan that same year.[15]

By 1905, however, Dorothea's religious intrusions started to sound less like spirited argument and more like frantic attempts to keep Virginia close as Virginia and Vanessa began their new life in Bloomsbury following their father's death: "I find a letter from Dorothea Stephen—that cumbersome, square footed cousin—to say, as one might say it was hot weather—that 'Christianity rests on a fact—the Resurrection. Believe this or be damned. Goodbye.' Why these sudden pieces of news? They are startling in the middle of a dinner party of undergraduates."[16] Dorothea's Victorian morality, in both its evangelical and secular forms, is precisely what Virginia and Vanessa and the Cambridge undergraduates their brother Thoby introduced into their lives were dismantling, dinner party by dinner party. No longer involved in each other's daily lives, their interactions took on a sharper edge, more desperate on Dorothea's side, more cool and cutting on Virginia's.

In 1921, on a visit home from India, Dorothea intruded again, this time to scold Vanessa for her family arrangements. Vanessa remained married to Clive Bell but lived with the painter Duncan Grant, with whom she had a daughter. Grant's lover, David Garnett, sometimes lived with them. Dorothea, unsurprisingly, was scandalized. Virginia rose to Vanessa's defense with this letter to her cousin:

> My dear Dorothea . . .
>
> Your view that one cannot ask a friend who has put aside the recognized conventions about marriage to one's house because of outsiders and servants seems to me incomprehensible. You, for example, accept a religion which I and my servants, who are both agnostics, think wrong and indeed pernicious. Am I therefore to forbid you to come here for my servants sake? Yet I am sure you agree with me that religious beliefs are of far greater importance than social conventions. I am quite willing to suppose that all you said to Vanessa was dictated by kindness and good will, though I do not think it struck her quite in the same way. Anyhow my point is different—it is simply that I could not let you come here without saying first that I entirely sympathise with Vanessa's views and conduct—since, for your own reasons, you have drawn attention to them. If after this you like to come with Katharine, by all means do; and I will risk not only my own morals but my cook's.[17]

Dorothea did come, and Woolf wrote an over-the-top account of the visit—she "so oppressed me with her moral depravity—her sheer repulsiveness and obtuseness and stodge—that I was practically fainting"—for Vanessa to enjoy.[18]

It is in relation to Dorothea, and other relatives like her, who often used the occasion of a death in the family to expound their religious views to the Stephen children, that Woolf developed many of her ideas about religion in general and Christianity in particular. It was hypocrisy that made Christianity "wrong and pernicious," its easy elision with Victorian morality. Woolf despised the colonizing project of British missionaries and found Dorothea's life in India ridiculous: "She lives in a village; can't talk a word of the language, which is Candarese; learns Sanskrit with a pundit, and intends to expound the fallacies of the Buddha."[19] Having been on the receiving end of Dorothea's religious correction all her life, Woolf saw her repeating that same aggressive behavior in India—keeping herself aloof from those around her by refusing to learn their language while having plenty to say about their religious errors.

The abhorrence Woolf felt for Dorothea's proselytizing—"She persists, prods; brutally tramples"—appears in her novels.[20] "Nothing . . . can be more arrogant, though nothing is commoner," she writes in *Orlando*, "than to assume that of Gods there is only one, and of religions none but the speaker's."[21] The revulsion Septimus Warren Smith and Clarissa Dalloway feel for the doctors who are capable of "forcing your soul" reflects Woolf's hatred of attempts at conversion.[22] Ten years after the conflict with Dorothea over Vanessa's family life, Woolf continued to invoke her as an example of the unpardonable sin of interfering with the beliefs of others. In a letter to her friend Ethel Smyth in 1931, she wrote that "what I can't abide is the man who wishes to convert other men's minds; that tampering with beliefs seems to me impertinent, insolent, corrupt beyond measure. I never pass through Hyde Park without cursing separately every God inventor there. This is partly because, unbaptized as we were, our religious friends, some cousins in particular, the daughters of Fitzjames, rasped and agonized us as children by perpetual attempts at conversion. . . . And even now, when no one tries, I still draw in and shiver at the suspicion—he's got a finger in my mind."[23] Her response to proselytizing—"to draw in and shiver" at the intrusion into her mind—echoes her response, as a small child, to her half-brother Gerald Duckworth's invasive assault on her body. "I stiffened and wriggled as his hand approached my private parts," she wrote, "resenting, disliking it."[24] The mind is also a private part for Woolf. To touch it without permission is "corrupt beyond measure."

Dorothea's intrusive proselytizing was not the only kind of engagement with religion available to Virginia Stephen, however.

She pursued her own interest in religion in childhood and young adulthood through her reading, her writing, her friendships, and her travels.

Leslie Stephen, recognizing Virginia's literary gifts early on, directed her reading toward history. At fifteen, she read her grandfather Sir James Stephen's *Essays in Ecclesiastical Biography*, including his essay on the Clapham Sect. In the aftermath of her stepsister Stella's unexpected death, she read at least nine volumes of James Anthony Froude's twelve-volume *History of England*. Froude's history was famously undergirded by his fiercely anti-Catholic views. Indeed, it had been the review of Froude in *Macmillan's Magazine* by Charles Kingsley, the Regius Professor of Modern History at Cambridge, that led John Henry Newman to write his *Apologia Pro Vita Sua*. Kingsley had praised Froude's historical perspective and accused the newly Roman Catholic Newman of deceit. Leslie Stephen may have rejected the Christian faith of his upbringing, but the reading assignments he passed on to his daughter reflected the distinctly Protestant—and anti-Catholic—perspective of his evangelical forebears.

Left to her own devices, Virginia's reading in her teenage and young adult years reflected a more wide-ranging religious curiosity. On a summer holiday with her family in Warboys in August 1899, she noted in her diary that she had read "the diary of some ancient Bishop written in flowing ancient English" while rocking on the water in a punt.[25] Woolf read ministers' diaries and letters throughout her life as part of her research into the lives of the obscure. "For one likes romantically to feel oneself a deliverer advancing with lights across the waste of years to the rescue of some stranded ghost—a Mrs Pilkington, a Rev. Henry Elman, a Mrs Ann Gilbert—waiting, appealing, forgotten, in the growing gloom," she wrote in 1924.[26] But although she was endlessly interested in the details of these obscure lives, it was not only their lives she excavated and cherished; it was also the sound of their forgotten voices, the rhythm of their sentences, their "flowing ancient English."

Four years later, in 1903, Virginia recorded a more purposeful preparation for vacation reading: "I am laying in books. That is what I mean by getting ready."[27] Shakespeare and the Bible, Dante and Burke—she loved "munching steadily through all kinds of books."[28] These would be staples for her for a lifetime—especially Shakespeare and the Bible. By the time she wrote *Three Guineas* in 1938, she could boast that those, like herself, who had read the Bible as a whole and had "not been forced from childhood to hear it . . . dismembered weekly" regarded it as "a work of the greatest interest, much beauty, and deep meaning."[29]

Around the same time, Virginia began reading and rereading Walter Pater's *Marius the Epicurean*. Pater's novel, published in 1885, describes the religious journey of a serious young man in the second-century Roman Empire. Through his experiences with traditional Roman domestic devotion, Epicureanism, Stoicism, and Christianity, Marius encounters a range of religious and philosophical possibilities for ordering his life. Woolf's description of what she calls her "passion" for *Marius the Epicurean* appears in a remarkable set piece at the beginning of her autobiographical essay "Old Bloomsbury," in which Woolf juxtaposes her half-brother George Duckworth's Victorian moralizing with his predatory sexual behavior and Pater's account of the religions of the Roman Empire with the imperial use of religion in her own day.

In two paragraphs, Woolf sketches out an evening in 1903. She and George dined with Lady Carnarvon at her home in Bruton Street. As they left with her to go to the theatre, Virginia saw George kiss their hostess in secret "among the pillars in the hall." But the "indecent French play" they attended together so scandalized George and his lover that they left after the first act. In the cab afterward, George criticized Virginia for talking too much, telling her that she "must really learn how to behave."[30]

George then took her to the home of the painter William Holman Hunt to see "The Light of the World," a literal and sentimental rendering of Jesus's words in Revelation 3:20: "Behold I stand at the door and knock." Holman Hunt's painting of Jesus knocking at a closed door had recently returned, Woolf recalled, from a tour of British colonies.[31] The original intention of the organizers had been to use the painting to help mend the divisions left in the wake of the Boer War in South Africa, but the mandate soon broadened to what the *Times* called "a laudable way of promoting imperial unity through a common sentiment in art, a common culture."[32] From this celebration of religion and art pressed into imperial service, Virginia returned home, got into bed, and "sat reading a page or two of *Marius the Epicurean* for which I had then a passion." Then, as in Holman Hunt's famous painting, there was a knock at her door: "There would be a tap at the door; the light would be turned out and George would fling himself on my bed, cuddling and kissing and otherwise embracing me in order, as he told Dr. Savage later, to comfort me for the fatal illness of my father—who was dying three or four storeys lower down of cancer."[33] In this brief sketch, Woolf evokes the sexual and religious hypocrisy she despised, with George attempting to impose standards for proper behavior while, in secret, forcing himself on his unprotected half-sister. With the juxtaposition of Holman Hunt's "The Light of the World," which traveled the British colonies as an emissary for the empire, and the story of Marius, a religious seeker who dies at the hands of the Roman Empire because they believe him to be a Christian, she also critiqued the kind of religious hypocrisy she saw in her cousin Dorothea's colonial adventures. *Marius the Epicurean* represented for her a more authentic religious searching than Hunt's compromised painting or Dorothea's insistent proselytizing.

Pater has been called "the first modern" and Marius the "first modern character in fiction."[34] The novel's collage-like quality, its emphasis on character and state of mind, and its subversion of the traditional movements of plot helped clear the space within which modernist literary projects would unfold. Critics often point to Marius's epiphany in the hills around Rome as a precursor to Joyce's epiphanies and Woolf's "moments of being." Harold Bloom credits Pater with secularizing the epiphany, "a displacement in which so many were to be his heirs."[35]

Bloom's emphasis on secularization, however, risks obscuring the novel's sustained attention to religion. In an age preoccupied with the truth or falsity of what Arnold called the "facts" of Christianity, Pater's novel explored religion differently: as an orientation toward life that had the potential to illuminate the sacred within ordinary experience and to shape human lives in deliberate, distinctive ways. Pater was interested in the resemblances among religions, their shared hermeneutical character, and he portrayed early Christianity not so much as a break with the pagan past but as a culmination of much of what the pagan past had offered.[36] Marius, for example, is encouraged to look more deeply into Christianity by his Epicureanism, which urged him to investigate anything that attracted him.[37] Pater believed that "trac[ing] the influence of religion upon human character is one of the legitimate functions of the novel."[38] But what he meant by "religion" was not an unchanging set of dogmatic assertions, a collection of religious "facts." For Pater, religion—or better, religions—changed as the world changed.

The novel opens by drawing the reader's attention to the "new religions [that] had arisen with bewildering complexity around the dying old one,"marking religions not as fixed and eternal, but as changing phenomena in a context of historical flux.[39] Pater's Marius explores the religious and philosophical options around him, weighing their ideas and practices and measuring them against each other. Although Marius was mistaken for a dedicated adherent of Christianity at his death, Pater portrayed him not as one who crossed the threshold of faith but as one who stood near, questioning, critiquing, admiring, and experimenting with its ideas and practices in his own life. As one critic has put it, he died "in the porch of the Church, hopeful without certainty to the end."[40] Pater portrays this not as a secular posture, but as a deeply religious one.

When Virginia Stephen, at age 21, sat up late reading and rereading Pater's novel, what would she have found? The motherless young woman whose father was dying of cancer on a floor below might have felt a kinship with the orphaned Marius, who both mourned the loss of his father and, when he thought of him, felt "a not unpleasant sense of liberty."[41] Like Virginia Stephen, Marius's young life was punctuated by losses—his father, his mother, his dear friend Flavian—and his imagination shaped by grief.

She might also have recognized Marius as a fellow passionate reader for whom words worked on all the senses. Just as she read Pater's book with "a passion," Marius read Apuleius's "golden book" with a similar passion, finding in the story of Cupid and Psyche the shape of his own aspirations. Reading Apuleius with his friend Flavian, Marius experienced "a revelation in colour and form" which gave his poetic aspirations "a direction emphatically sensuous."[42] Virginia Stephen, reading Pater, found a "writer who from words made blue and gold and green . . . all things that the hand delighted to touch and the nostrils to smell, while the mind traced subtle winding paths and surprised recondite secrets." Pater, she wrote when she reread him in 1920, "makes the nerve of the eye vibrate."[43] Through reading, Marius sharpened his attention to the revelatory dimensions of everyday life, dimensions that Virginia Woolf would explore in her novels.

She would also have discovered a useful model of literary portraiture in Pater's novel, one that she would bring to life in her own novels, especially *Jacob's Room* and *Orlando*. Critics have sometimes faulted Pater for the frozen, static quality of his "imaginary portraits."[44] And certainly Pater held his imaginary portrait of a religiously seeking young man still enough for an apprentice writer like Virginia Stephen to study. With Marius in the center of his canvas, Pater focused less on plot and more on opening the young man's inner life for the reader as well as filling in the world around him, from Marius's ancestral home to the Rome of Marcus Aurelius to the Campagna.

Pater's novel epitomized many of the literary concerns that Woolf would come to share. Perry Meisel has identified some of the most important of these. Pater and Woolf, he notes, share an "appetite for sensation and a careful attention to the patterns it weaves in the mind; a Keatsian fascination with death, decay and dissolution . . . a modernist emphasis on the loneliness and isolation of the individual and a concomitant desire for companionship and the knowledge of others; a prevailing atmosphere of loss and an elegiac mood suffusing the narrator's imagination . . . [and] the vision of a universe in constant flux, with an attendant . . . strategy for seizing and arresting the particularly intense and revelatory node of experience known as the privileged moment."[45] There are also important differences between Pater's project and Woolf's. Pater believed that perfection was both possible and desirable in art. For him, a work of art that is "closed, finished, perfect"[46] possesses a religious power: "A perfect poem like *Lycidas*, a perfect fiction like *Esmond*, the perfect handling of a theory like Newman's *Idea of a University*, has . . . something of the uses of a religious 'retreat.'"[47] Woolf was not looking for a retreat. She wanted to create art that was closer to "life & the world, in action."[48] And while Marius experiences the "something more" in the universe as a friendly hand on his shoulder, the experiences Woolf describes are of something more dangerous—a violent shock or blow, a fin on the horizon. But in *Marius the Epicurean*, Pater would have given Virginia Stephen the opportunity to study how one writer shaped a literary form for the exploration of these preoccupations and how he sustained that exploration over the course of a novel. In her 1905 diary, we see Woolf studying Pater's writings with care, trying "to see how the trick's done."[49]

Many of Pater's contemporaries had been transformed and even undone by *Marius the Epicurean*. Oscar Wilde referred to it as his "golden book," a nod to the role Apuleius's *The Golden Ass* plays in Marius's formation as a lover of beauty. The poet Yeats found in *Marius* "the only great prose in modern English." But, as is typical even in the comments of Pater's greatest admirers, Yeats worried about Pater's seductive influence. He wondered "if *Marius*, or the attitude of mind of which it was the noblest expression, had not caused the disaster of my friends. It taught us to walk upon a rope, tightly stretched through serene air, and we were left to keep our feet upon a swaying rope in a storm."[50] Pater was often portrayed as a seducer of the young who drew them into a decadent love of beauty unmoored from any doctrinal foundation. He was considered by many a "pagan" influence, liable to undermine the faith of what were assumed to be his young, besotted followers.[51]

The fear of Pater-as-seducer had begun with the first edition of his *Studies in the History of the Renaissance*, a book Virginia Stephen read in January 1905.[52] Both Christians and agnostics had objected to its conclusion when it was first published in 1878, with its emphasis on the flux both within us and around us, "that strange, perpetual weaving and unweaving of ourselves" out of which "a single sharp impression" occasionally arises. These are the moments worth living for, Pater argued. "Not the fruit of experience, but experience itself, is the end," the thing itself. "To burn always with this hard, gemlike flame, to maintain this ecstasy, is," he insisted, "success in life." Not to seek out the brilliance in all the moments we are given would be "to sleep before evening." Life is short, and "our one chance lies in expanding that interval, in getting as many pulsations as possible into the given time. . . . Of this wisdom, the poetic passion, the desire of beauty, the love of art for art's sake, has most; for art comes to you professing frankly to give nothing but the highest quality to your moments as they pass, and simply for those moments' sake."[53] It was this sentiment most of all—"the love of art for art's sake"—that scandalized many of the book's first readers, Christians and agnostics alike. His criticism was demeaned as "aestheticized," "secular," "decadent." In the minds of many, Pater argued for a radical separation of art from morality, emphasizing sensation at the expense of ethics. Two years after Pater published *The Renaissance*, Leslie Stephen published an essay in *Cornhill Magazine* called "Art and Morality." Although he does not mention Pater by name, he asserts forcefully that "all art and poetry should be moral and even didactic." Art should "purify and sustain the mind" and "make society so far healthier and happier."[54] Artists who do not share these goals, Woolf's father wrote, "corrupt the social atmosphere."[55] It is not true to say, though, that Pater did not have ethical aspirations for his art. He did not join Leslie Stephen in calling for art to make whole societies "healthier and happier," but he did believe that art transforms the one who experiences it and "accomplishes," as Hilary Fraser has put it, "an important ethical result in enlarging and orientating the soul."[56]

Such an uproar greeted Pater's conclusion to *The Renaissance* that he removed it from the second edition of the book, a concession to fears that it might mislead his readers. He brought the conclusion back, revised, in the third edition, with a note that readers should look to *Marius the Epicurean* for a fuller discussion of the ideas contained in it. But readers have been undecided about how *Marius* relates to *The Renaissance*. For some, the novel was the fulfillment of what they saw as the decadent, aestheticized approach of Pater's art criticism. For others, *Marius* seemed to be a modification, even a correction, of "the more extreme positions" of *The Renaissance* that moved beyond what Iain Fletcher has called Pater's "self-regarding ethic that sought the meaning of life in the intensity of highly charged moments of experience."[57]

Nevertheless, *Marius* attracted a great deal of the same kind of criticism *The Renaissance* attracted, and Pater was accused of doing for religion in the novel what his criticism had done for art. Many Christian readers of *Marius the Epicurean* objected to what they saw as Pater's dangerous reduction of Christianity to ritual and beauty and sensation. Mrs. Humphrey Ward, the author of *Robert Elsmere*, a novel about a doubting Christian clergyman, criticized *Marius* for what she called its "evasive" ending. As much as any evangelical, the theologically liberal Mrs. Humphrey Ward wanted Marius to make a decision, yay or nay, about Christianity. Pater had left his protagonist on the threshold—as Woolf will later leave her "seedy nondescript man" on the steps of St. Paul's. Marius is a Christian in the eyes of the empire who made him a martyr, but an undecided seeker in his own. It was not only evangelicals who insisted on a decision from Pater about Christian faith; doubters and agnostics did as well.

The fiercest religious critique of *Marius* would arrive decades after Virginia Stephen first encountered Pater's novel. In his 1930 essay "Arnold and Pater," T.S. Eliot argued that Marius was born from "the repudiation of revealed religion by men of culture and intellectual leadership."[58] Eliot found religion reduced to feeling in *Marius* and compared Pater's sensuous love of ritual and liturgy unfavorably with the muscular passion for Christianity's "dogmatic essentials" of Newman, Pusey, and the Tractarians. Witheringly, he described Pater's novel as a "hodge-podge" of donnish learning, Italian tourism, and "a prolonged flirtation with the liturgy" without concern for dogma. He accused Pater of knowing "almost nothing" about "the essence of Christian faith"; he asserted that *Marius* had had no influence on any "first-rate" minds and blamed Pater for the morally "untidy lives" of some unnamed people. Like many of the moral critiques of Pater's approach to religion and art, Eliot's bears the sneering tone of the thinly veiled accusations of homosexuality often directed at both Pater and his followers.

Virginia Stephen, indifferent to the theology and moralism of Pater's critics, read Pater's book, not in the context of Christian attempts to protect the "essence" of Christianity from Pater's decadent attachment to the sensual, but in the context of her own life and artistic aspirations—and her own interest in religion. *Marius* offered a way to think about religion and explore the ways it moved through human history and human lives that was markedly different from what she had encountered in her family. Pater did not portray religion as a set of propositions that could be promulgated, as Dorothea did through her proselytizing, or dismantled, as Leslie Stephen did through his passionately argued agnosticism. Pater's novel illustrated multiple ways of being religious. Standing in sharp relief to the Protestantism of both her cousin and her father, the Roman religion of Marius's childhood was "something to be done, rather than something to be thought, or believed, or loved."[59]

Pater portrayed religion and its rituals as products of human creativity that could have both ill and salutary effects in the world. Like many of his contemporaries who had read Renan's *Histoire des Origines du Christianisme* and other accounts of early Christianity, Pater believed there had been a moment when "the gracious spirit of the primitive church" gave way to a post-Constantinian "opposition between the soul and the body, the world and the spirit" that undermined the early form of Christianity Marius encountered in Cecilia's house-church. Pater also pointed to a damaging tendency to deny the body in the Stoicism of Marcus Aurelius. Pater shows Marius being attracted to religion in its many forms and also revolted by it, especially by the animal sacrifices he witnesses in Marcus Aurelius's Rome. Pater's novel demonstrated that one could observe the jostling of religions for position in one's culture with profound interest but also "as an indifferent outsider might, not too deeply concerned in the question which, if any of them, was to be the survivor."[60]

Religion, in Pater's novel, could be shaped by attention to "the sacredness of time, of life and its events, and the circumstances of family fellowship"[61] and reveal the spiritual significance of ordinary objects and experiences. It could be understood as a "formal, habitual recognition" of the demands of conscience.[62] It could be wholly dedicated to relieving pain, as in the medical rituals and practices of the temples of Aesculapius. It could be focused on the soul-making engagement with the practices of particular philosophical schools, as in Marcus Aurelius's Stoicism. It could reveal new forms of beauty through its rituals, as did Cecilia's Christian house-church. When Christianity appears on the scene at the end of the novel, it is one religion among many, both distinct from and continuous with the religions that came before it. In both form and content, Pater's novel leans more toward religious hope than religious belief.[63] Pater demonstrated that one could speak about religion, religious ideas, even the idea of God, with an epistemological humility; throughout his novel, Pater used words and phrases like "it was as if," "dared one hope," and "hypothesis" when he spoke about religions and their beliefs.

Virginia Stephen would have found in Pater's novel a portrait of religion that resonated with her own ideas. Pater once told a friend at Oxford that he wrote *Marius* "to show the necessity of religion." Woolf remembers writing "a long picturesque essay upon the Christian religion" called "Religio Laici" when she was fifteen or sixteen, "proving that man has need of a God; but the God was described in process of change."[64] Their shared convictions about the work that religion can do in human life and the flux within which everything, including the idea of God, moves and changes shaped both the content and form of their work. Marius's childhood love of ritual would have likely appealed to Virginia. The rituals of reading and writing while Nessa painted, listening to her father read aloud in the evenings, and taking daily walks in London grounded her existence and stood in opposition to the chaos introduced into her life by sickness, death, and sexual abuse. When Pater wrote about Marius's childhood love of ritual taking a new literary shape, "a kind of sacred service to the mother-tongue," Virginia might have heard her own aspirations expressed.[65] Marius arrives in Rome "under poetic vocation, to receive . . . the very impress of life itself" and to find "golden words" with which to describe it.[66] Sixteen years after her passionate reading and rereading of Pater's novel, Woolf would use similar language to describe the work of the novelist: to make oneself available to "life itself" and "to convey this incessantly varying spirit" in language.[67] Just as Marius hoped to discover what was "behind this vain show of things,"[68] Virginia Stephen wanted, as she wrote in her diary during a trip to Italy in 1908, to "discover real things beneath the show."[69]

Pater represented religious searching as something wholly unlike Dorothea's confident proselytizing. Where Dorothea was doctrinal, Marius was attuned to the sacredness of "the elementary conditions of life"; where Dorothea was confident and certain in her religious convictions, Marius was searching and undecided about his; where Dorothea talked nonstop, Marius was contemplative and quiet; where Dorothea judged the Stephen children severely for their lack of faith, Marius rooted his moral judgments in a deep sympathy for the suffering of animals, a sympathy "which had in it something of the religious veneration for life as such." Dorothea embodied what Woolf considered the worst of a Victorian sensibility. Marius, growing up in the graceful Italian countryside, seemed, in Pater's romantic vision, inoculated against vulgarity.[70]

Marius also provided a contrast to Leslie Stephen's confident agnosticism. Marius remains a questioner in regard to religious and spiritual matters throughout his life, a seeker who finds himself both attracted to, and also critical of, the religious options he encounters, from the domestic worship of his youth to the Stoicism of Marcus Aurelius to the Christianity he discovers in Cecilia's house-church. He is less interested in winning theological debates and more interested in the beauty, hermeneutics, and lived moral choices inspired by particular religions. When Marius, for example, encounters indifference to cruelty in Marcus Aurelius, he rejects the Stoicism that allows such cruelty to flourish unchecked, just as Orlando, in Woolf's novel of the same name, breaks off an engagement to a fiancé who beats a dog.[71] Marius finds Christianity beautiful because of its commitment to sacrifice on behalf of others. His attempt to emulate that commitment leads to his death.

Of all the family members who helped shape Woolf's understanding of religion, it is probably Caroline Emelia Stephen, her Quaker aunt, who has the most in common with Marius. Woolf would likely have found Marius's philosophical and literary engagements with religion to be more rigorous and so more attractive than her aunt's "general benignity, which does seem to me so woolly."[72] But her aunt's "agnosticism with mystery at the heart of it" is not unlike Marius's religious stance, which cast a questioning and skeptical eye on the religious ideas he encountered but also remained curious about and open to what might lie "behind this vain show of things."[73] For Caroline Stephen, intermittent "flashes of revelation" were more important than dogma, religious experience more revelatory than systematic assertions. Woolf's expression of a similar idea as "moments of being" was prepared for, literarily, by Marius's epiphany in the Roman Campagna.

Marius's epiphany occurs on one of his solitary excursions into the hills around Rome. "As if by favor of an invisible power," Marius feels as awake and alive as he has ever felt, in "possession of his own best and happiest self."[74] His epiphany grows upon him slowly, "as if the spirit of life in nature were but withholding any too precipitate revelation of itself, in its slow, wise, maturing work."[75] He does not experience the violent shock of Virginia Woolf's "moments of being" nor does he experience the illumination of any "mysterious light" like the Quaker Caroline Stephen. But in contemplating the interplay between his relationships and his love of solitude, he comes to see that, even when he is alone, it was "as if there were not one only, but two wayfarers, side by side." In the quiet of the countryside, Marius moves "from that mere fantasy of a self not himself . . . to those divinations of a living and companionable spirit at work in all things. . . . Through one reflection upon another, he passed from such instinctive divinations, to the thoughts which give them logical consistency, formulating at last, as the necessary exponent of our own and the world's life, that reasonable Ideal to which the Old Testament gives the name of *Creator*, which for the philosophers of Greece is the *Eternal Reason*, and in the New Testament the *Father of Men*—even as one builds up from act and word and expression of the friend actually visible at one's side, an ideal of the spirit within him."[76] Intellectually, the ideal that Marius apprehends remains an "hypothesis." But, for a moment, he becomes convinced of the presence of an other with "boundless power of memory" to whom he might entrust his own memories and experiences. Marius's epiphany is both mystical and ethical; his sense of a companion evoked for him "the faculty of conscience." He never has exactly the same experience again, Pater writes, yet the rest of his life is enriched by it. Marius's epiphany refocuses his purpose and his vocation: it is "a gathering together of every trace or token of [that Ideal], which his actual experience might present."[77]

Traces of Marius's epiphany appear in Virginia Stephen's writing in the first decade of the twentieth century, the years in which she was most attached to Pater's novel. Her 1906 account of the Blo' Norton holiday, in which she writes about the "steady beat of the Great Creator" pulsing beneath her own creativity, is one example. As she comes into her own as a writer, Marius's ideal creator is most visible in the act of creation itself. For Marius, this presence sustains his breath and sight and intellect, "rounding, supporting his imperfect thoughts."[78] For the young writer who will become Virginia Woolf, it is the creative pulse itself that connects her across time and space with others who have participated in it.

During that same holiday, Virginia Stephen wrote a long story about a medieval historian, Rosamond Merridew, who discovers a diary kept in the fifteenth century by a teenager named Joan Martyn. Joan's diary soon takes over the story and establishes many of the preoccupations that Woolf will explore for the rest of her life: the role of women as the preservers of culture and civilization in the face of violence and war, the relationship between past and present, the lives of the obscure. It also offers a portrait of a young woman for whom religion is woven throughout her daily life—who goes to mass, tends the graves of her ancestors, and says her prayers. Each year, Joan makes a midsummer pilgrimage to the shrine of Our Lady at Walsingham, where Mary, the mother of Jesus, had appeared to a local noblewoman in the eleventh century and taken her to Nazareth to show her the house where she had raised her son. It is on this pilgrimage to a site made holy by layered accounts of the experiences of women that Joan has her own epiphany.

Like Marius in the Campagna, Joan's epiphany on her pilgrimage is both mystical and ethical. It has two significant moments. First, as she joins hands with other pilgrims—many of whom she has been taught to "rule; and tread underfoot" so that they do not "tear us to pieces with their fangs"—she longs to know them: "My eyes sought their faces curiously, and I thought desperately for a moment that it was terrible that flesh and [fens?] should divide us. They would have strange, merry stories to tell."[79] Virginia Stephen, like Chaucer before her and Victor and Edith Turner after her, saw how the kinds of encounters pilgrimage makes possible had the potential to erode social hierarchy, if only for a time.

As the pilgrims move together toward the shrine of Our Lady, bleached white from the sun, Joan's mind becomes so filled with the image that "no other thought had room there. For one moment I submitted myself to her as I have never submitted to man or woman, and bruised my lips on the rough stone of her garment. White light and heat steamed on my bare head; and when the ecstasy passed the country beneath flew out like a sudden banner unfurled."[80] Virginia portrays Joan's Marian devotion as the distilled essence of Joan's admiration for her mother, who, with the men away fighting, manages the land, runs and protects the household, and rules the community around her with wisdom and power. "It is a great thing to be the daughter of such a woman," Joan writes in her diary, "and to hope that one day the same power may be mine."[81] Just as Woolf saw her own mother as a kind of divinity at the center of the "Cathedral space" of Woolf's childhood, Joan's mother and the Lady of Walsingham both compel her devotion. Her mother teaches her about the significance of women's strength. If England survives its wars to thrive as a country, her mother tells her, it will be thanks to the women who cultivated their homes and land and protected their households from the chaos all around.

Joan admires her mother's vision, but she wants to do more: to write, to tell stories, to create. Just as her mind was filled with the image at the shrine, her mind fills after the pilgrimage with the images of the knights and ladies whose stories she would like to tell. The story ends with Joan visiting the graves of her ancestors with her father. Like Marius, who stood at the graves of his ancestors and wished he could do something for them, Joan "would fain do some small act that would give them pleasure . . . something secret, and unthought of—a kiss or a stroke, such as you give a living person."[82]

Perhaps it was Virginia Stephen's passion for *Marius the Epicurean* that opened the space for her to explore a religious character in fiction not as someone who confused dreams with reality, as her father believed religious people did, but rather someone for whom religion was an organic part of life. Louise DeSalvo has argued that Virginia Stephen's adolescent journals and essays provided a place for her to resist her father's influence and develop her own ideas and commitments. "Religio Laici," the essay in which Virginia Woolf remembers arguing "that man has need of a God; but the God was described in process of change," was, DeSalvo suggests, one such act of resistance.[83] "The Journal of Mistress Joan Martyn" also bears the marks of that resistance. A lengthy story built around a sympathetic Roman Catholic character, an epiphanic description of Marian devotion, and the recognition of women's power to preserve culture and civilization contradicted Leslie

Stephen's patriarchal stance, his Protestant prejudices, and his agnostic pieties and verities. Leslie Stephen's approach to religion—based on the dismantling of unchanging religious "facts"—is nowhere in evidence in "The Journal of Mistress Joan Martyn." But Pater's approach—focused on religious practice and religious hope as integral parts of life—very much is.

Woolf would encounter other approaches to religion that, like Pater's, emphasized practice over belief. One such approach that would be crucial to the shaping of her fiction was that of the scholar of ancient religions and cultures Jane Ellen Harrison. The first woman in England to have a full-time academic career, Harrison was a scholar of ancient Greece and a fellow of Newnham College.[84] One of her students remembered Harrison's lectures revealing "a pattern in the chaos; the soil became transparent and one found oneself looking straight down to the roots."[85] Harrison's attempt to discover the origins of religion and art appealed to Woolf's interest in prehistory, a preoccupation that left its mark on her fiction.

Woolf may have met Harrison as early as 1904. While living with her aunt in the weeks following her father's death, Virginia wrote to Violet Dickinson that Florence Maitland was going to introduce her to Jane Harrison "and all the other learned Ladies" at Newnham.[86] Years later, Woolf and Harrison became friends. Woolf admired her erudition, her knowledge of languages, and "her superb high thinking agnostic ways."[87] Leonard and Virginia's Hogarth Press would publish Harrison's memoir, *Reminiscences of a Student's Life* (1925), and *The Life of the Archpriest Avvakum by Himself* (1924), translated by Harrison and Hope Mirrlees, Harrison's partner and former student. The Hogarth Press had also published Mirrlees's poem *Paris* in 1920, a work that Julia Briggs has argued influenced T. S. Eliot's *The Waste Land* and Woolf's novel *Jacob's Room*.[88] Woolf pronounced *Paris* "very obscure, indecent and brilliant" in a letter to the head of the Women's Co-operative Guild, Margaret Llewelyn Davies, in 1919 and admiringly noted that Mirrlees "knows Greek and Russian better than I do French" and "is Jane Harrison's favourite pupil."[89] Woolf would visit Harrison and Mirrlees in Paris in 1923, where they moved after Cambridge reaffirmed its refusal to grant university degrees to women.[90]

That Christmas, Harrison sent Woolf a copy of the second edition of her 1913 volume *Ancient Art and Ritual* as a gift. Notes on this volume in Woolf's reading notebooks indicate that she was particularly interested in Harrison's description and analysis of ancient spring festivals.[91]

Like Woolf and her Bloomsbury friends, Harrison kept her eye on Woolf's generation's religious proclivities and gossiped with her about recent conversions. In a hilarious letter to her friend Jacques Raverat, husband of Charles Darwin's granddaughter, Gwen, Woolf reported a conversation with Harrison in Paris in which Harrison had bemoaned the "miserable defection" of poet and daughter of Frederic and Florence Maitland, Fredegond Shove, to Roman Catholicism and praised Woolf and Vanessa Bell and "perhaps Lytton Strachey" with standing firm in the face of this religious revival. "'There are thousands of Darwins' I said, to cheer her up," Woolf wrote. To which Harrison replied: "'The Darwins are the blackest traitors of them all! With that name!'" Harrison then went on to say, Woolf reported, that Gwen Raverat, her mind weakened by her marriage to a Frenchman, "'goes to Church (if not mass, still Church) every Sunday of her life.'" Learning from Jacques that this was not, in fact, true, Woolf wrote, "I at once sent word to dear old Jane, who replied, a little inconsistently, 'Thank God.'"[92]

Although Harrison was, in many ways, an old-school agnostic in the mold of Leslie Stephen, she was much more interested in theology, and in the ways in which the study of ancient religions could illuminate what she called "the religion of to-day," than Woolf's father was. "Those of us who are free-thinkers used to think of [theology] rationalistically as a bundle of dead errors, or at least as a subject dead and dry," she wrote in 1921. "But conceive of it in this new light and theology becomes a subject of passionate and absorbing interest, it is the science of the images of human desire, impulse, aspiration."[93] The "new light" to which she refers in this passage is modern psychology, which had, she believed, illuminated how religion can offer "incalculable solace and relief" to frail, insecure human beings. Harrison was constantly revising and expanding her work in the light of new scholarship in several fields, from anthropology to archeology to philosophy to the psychological theories of Freud and Jung, which helped shape her 1921 *Epilegomena to the Study of Greek Religion*—"Jane's pamphlet," as Woolf called it in her diary.[94]

Through her study of Harrison's work, Woolf encountered Harrison's theory of religion and her ideas about how the practice of ancient religion could help us think about "religious questions of to-day."[95] For Harrison, religion was grounded in the human desire to create and preserve life—grounded, as Woolf would say, in "life itself." Harrison argued that religion arises from ritual; it is something people do. A "living and vigorous religion" did not require a theology, she wrote. For religion to be religion, no deity was necessary, nor were priests; indeed, she wrote, the idea of a god can hinder religion's own purposes. Ritual gave rise to gods and myths, not the other way around. Harrison argued that the gods emerged from rituals that were repeated annually, the ritual figures gradually coming to take on lives separate from the lives of the humans who first conjured them.

Harrison believed that, while magic could be individual, religion was always, from its origins to the present, social. The Victorian emphasis on individualism had obscured this fact, she knew. But "scientific examination of religious phenomena among primitive peoples" had shown, she argued, that "religion is a social factor and can only be properly studied in relation to social structure."[96] Religion supports the life of the community through its mimetic rituals and strengthens the solidarity between its members through its commemorative ones. The desire for such solidarity, according to Harrison, sends people both to church and to the theater.[97] Ritual provides a bridge between life and art, life and myth, life and the gods.

Harrison insisted that religion "grows and shifts with human growth,"[98] a conviction Woolf would repeat when she wrote in 1924 that "when human relations change there is at the same time a change in religion, conduct, politics and literature."[99] Harrison understood that the way in which "the religion of to-day" enacted the religious impulse to create and preserve life was to focus on what she called "the betterment of life." She believed "the religion of to-day" to be, at its best, an ascetic, self-sacrificial way of life rather than a cosmology or a theology. Leslie Stephen had offered his daughter a view of life that included Clapham's ethics without the dogma. Jane Harrison offered something similar, but with more space for religion—one that, like Woolf's father's view of ethics, did not require a deity, but which was crucial to apprehending "life itself."

Although encountering new understandings of religion through reading was crucial to the influence of religion on her work, Woolf's travels at home and abroad were also important. "The Journal of Mistress Joan Martyn" reflects not only her interest in religion but her lifelong love of English landscapes. In later travels, Woolf would come to believe Marius's Roman Campagna to be the most beautiful countryside in the world. But in her travels in her home country as a young woman, the English countryside was her Campagna, her sacred landscape. Her Clapham ancestors had regarded nature as "a mirror of the divine goodness,"[100] a sense that echoes in Leslie Stephen's passion for mountain climbing and walking and in his daughter's love of the countryside. "A day spent happily in the open air," she wrote in the diary she kept during a 1903 visit to Salisbury, "counts, I am sure 'whatever Gods there be' as worship; the air is a Temple in which one is purged of one's sins."[101] Her walks became "pilgrimages" on which she experienced "little visions," "sights which surprise the solitary walker & linger in the mind."[102] Twenty years later, she would write a long passage in *Mrs. Dalloway* about the visions of a solitary traveler that drew both on these memories and on Jane Harrison's research into goddess religions.[103]

Virginia Stephen visited many churches and cathedrals on her travels in England. Sometimes the cathedrals seemed to her to interrupt the natural beauty of the countryside. Salisbury Cathedral, for example, "is like a great forest oak; nothing can grow healthily beneath its shade . . . A bare hilltop would have pleased me better than all the Closes & Cathedrals in England."[104] She liked the cathedral in Wells, though. "If Christianity is ever tolerable," she wrote, "it is tolerable in these old sanctuaries; partly because age has robbed it of its power."[105] Stonehenge, "naked to the sun," seemed to her the holiest site of all, an "altar made of earth, on which the whole world might do sacrifice."[106] Like Marius in the Roman Campagna, it is in the countryside where she often senses "something more" abroad in the world. "But coming home in the evening through great open spaces of field it was born in upon the mind that something was alive enough," she wrote in her diary in 1906. "Call it what you will. For the whole air was rich with energy, & brilliant with colour."[107] Virginia Woolf would seek to express that living "something" in everything she wrote.

Her travels abroad brought her into even more diverse religious environments. Having studied Greek language and literature for years, first with Walter Pater's sister, Clara, and then with Janet Case, Virginia Stephen embarked in 1906 on a trip to Greece and Turkey with her three siblings and their friend Violet Dickinson. In Athens, she wrote, "every step is on sacred ground." Greece engaged her creative powers—in Olympia, she noted that whereas guide books and archaeologists could organize one's approach to the statues, "the final work must be done by each fresh mind that sees them."[108] Just as Joan Martyn felt white light and heat on her head as she venerated the image of Our Lady of Walsingham, the sunlight at the Parthenon was so intense that it was difficult for Virginia and her siblings to gaze at it, and they experienced "a numb feeling as though our minds had been struck inarticulate by something too great for them to grasp."[109] Out of this visit to Greece, she wrote a story—"A Dialogue upon Mount Pentelicus"—in which she experimented with Marius's epiphanic sense of an unseen presence in the universe. But while the presence Marius felt was a personal one—"some other companion, an unfailing companion, ever at his side throughout"—Virginia Stephen's characters together encounter a more impersonal force that "survives trees and even plants them," an "original hearth"[110] that lit the flame in the eyes of a monk they meet.

In Constantinople, Virginia Stephen was first struck by the "uncomfortable" sense that life was being successfully and beautifully lived in this city "with no thought or need of certain great countries yonder to the west."[111] London and Paris did not provide the pattern for life here, nor did Christianity serve as the model for religion or for art. She witnessed with interest the ways in which Santa Sophia had been transformed from a Christian to a Muslim space by the erasure of images "till it has no virtue or vice left in it." At first, she found this "not very sympathetic to the stranger," but as the days passed, she began to admire more deeply the mosques she entered.[112] She began to see Muslim worship as continuous with "real life," part of the ordinary round of daily activities. She liked the way friends would greet each other in the mosques, the way voices at prayer sounded like voices in the market, the way children ran in and out, the way the practice of devotion was a natural part of daily life. Although the absence of religious images at first seemed to her to render the space of the mosque "secular," after a few days, she came to appreciate the religious power of devotion performed in "the light of day," undimmed by stained glass.[113]

In her final diary entries in Constantinople, she returned to the otherness of the place: "No Christian, or even European, can hope to understand the Turkish point of view."[114] Decades later she would describe Orlando throwing "aside his shoes and join[ing] the worshippers in the Mosques."[115] But Woolf understood, watching the worshippers in Santa Sophia from the gallery above, that this was something she was being allowed to watch, but not to join. "So we watched," she wrote, "a scene which we shall never understand; & heard the true gospels expounded in an unknown tongue."[116] She exhorted herself, in her diary, to remember what she had seen and heard in the mosques.

In Siena two years later, the differences between the Roman Catholic worship of Italy and the Anglican worship of England would fascinate her: "A strange worship compared with ours!" she wrote after observing a feast of the Virgin in the Siena Duomo. She was interested in the way the priests seemed to be doing one thing while each person in the crowd seemed to be doing something else: "The people looked, wandered about, sank on their knees, & rose again; their faith seemed warm & private, not to be regulated by any common need."[117] The worship of the Church of England seemed to her more regimented, and considerably less warm, than what she saw happening in either the mosques of Constantinople or the churches of Italy. She would later invest one of her religious characters, Doris Kilman in *Mrs. Dalloway*, with a spirituality so personal and intense that it troubles her fellow worshippers in Westminster Abbey.

For Vanessa and Virginia Stephen, Italy meant art, and it was in response to the religious art she saw there that Virginia pondered her own artistic aspirations. In her diary, she described the power of art to subvert the authority of viewers who believed they understood it. As her experience in the gallery of Santa Sophia had taught her, gazing on something, even from above, does not give us power over it: "We seem to think each verdict we pass [on the art we see] has power to change it. . . . When we look at it in another way though, it is more humiliating; for it is the unchanging thing, & shows us up as shadows against it. It bids us reveal ourselves."[118] Virginia Stephen's experience with visual art would shape her own art as well as her understanding of the practice of reading, during which, as she would later write, we are ourselves read.

In 1908 she visited the Collegio del Cambio in Perugia, frescoed by Perugino, the teacher of Raphael. In the richly decorated rooms, Perugino's elegant figures mingle beneath God and the angels, seemingly oblivious to the divine beings hovering overhead. The figures are grouped, she writes in her journal, according to Perugino's own idea of beauty, the way certain combinations of lines and colors "compose one idea in his mind."[119] To her, Perugino's idea of beauty "has nothing to do with anything to be put into words." His paintings were governed, she thought, by "certain & invisible forms."

Virginia Stephen stood before the frescoes and pondered her own vocation as an artist, weighing the differences between the beauty sought by Perugino and the beauty she sought to express. His beautiful figures seemed "sealed" and "infinitely silent; as though beauty had swum up to the top, and stayed there."[120] Woolf loved beauty but was wary of it, too. In *To the Lighthouse*, Lily Briscoe thinks of beauty as a "penalty" that freezes life, smooths out "the little agitations; the flush, the pallor, some queer distortion, some light or shadow."[121]

Contemplating Perugino's frescoes, Virginia Stephen understood that she wanted both: beauty and the little agitations. Or better, beauty made from the little agitations. She thought this through in her diary.

> As for writing—I want to express beauty too—but beauty (symmetry?) of life & the world, in action. Conflict?—is that it? . . .
>
> I attain a different kind of beauty, achieve a symmetry by means of infinite discords, showing all the traces of the minds passage through the world; & achieve in the end, some kind of whole made of shivering fragments; to me this seems the natural process; the flight of the mind. Do they really reach the same thing?[122]

In *To the Lighthouse*, Lily Briscoe expressed Woolf's conviction, a conviction she held from a young age, that making new wholes is the heart of the artistic vocation. Artists seek to create from incongruous combinations "a globed, compacted thing over which thought lingers and love plays." But unlike Perugino's beautifully rounded figures, the whole Woolf sought to create would not be present in any single figure but in the way each figure related to every other, and out of the fragments each character contributed. Perugino's groupings interested her because of the questions they raised—questions that were artistic and religious at once. What were the invisible forms according to which he grouped his figures? What was the idea that led him to place them in this, rather than that, relation to each other? What sort of beauty did he seek? She would continue to ponder these questions in her writing, and in her study of other forms of art, for the rest of her life.

Such questions also preoccupied her sister, the painter Vanessa Bell.[123] As devoted to her art as Virginia was to hers, Vanessa became an important contributor to the Postimpressionist movement in Great Britain. The questions Virginia Stephen put to herself while standing before Perugino's frescoes in the Collegio del Cambio were questions that Vanessa put to herself every time she picked up her brush: how can I bring forms in a work of art into relation with each other? How can I achieve the kind of beauty I am after?

In a painting she completed around 1912, *Studland Beach*, Vanessa (by then Vanessa Bell, having married Clive Bell in 1907) worked on these questions. In the painting, there are two groups of figures—two figures in hats in the bottom left-hand corner, sitting at the foot of a dune, and on the right-hand side, a figure standing on the threshold of a tent at the edge of the ocean, with four smaller figures at her feet. All the figures in the painting have their backs to us; we cannot see their faces. The two groups are related by what appears to be the gaze of the two hatted figures upon the standing figure and the children and by the great planes of color that slash across the canvas: one white, one blue.

The line between white and blue, sand and sea is broken only by the tent at the edge of the water. It recalls the bathing tents on Studland Beach where swimmers would change their clothes. In a 1909 photo, Virginia Stephen and Clive Bell sit in front of two such bathing tents, with their pointed tops, like the one in Vanessa's painting. On Vanessa's canvas, though, the bathing hut is transformed: it has been moved from the dunes to the very edge of the water, and inside it is shining white, whiter than the sand, a threshold to some luminous, unknown place. The figure standing on that threshold, dressed in a long blue garment with her hair hanging down her back, radiates stillness and solemnity, a sense of waiting, a sense of ritual.

Like her sister, Vanessa often thought about her own art in relation to works of religious art. Both Frances Spalding and Lisa Tickner have noted the influence of the early Renaissance artist Piero della Francesca on Bell's painting—especially his *Madonna della Misericordia* (1462), the central panel of a polyptych he created for a religious confraternity in San Sepolcro, and the *Madonna del Parto* (ca. 1460), a painting of the pregnant Madonna he made for a church in Monterchi.[124] Piero's geometric approach to painting pointed toward the abstract forms that would interest Vanessa throughout her career. She loved Piero's work, and as Frances Spalding has noted, she "catches an echo of his statuesque simplicity and contemplative mood in certain of her post-impressionist pictures."[125] Certainly this is true of *Studland Beach*.

The Bloomsbury artists all admired Piero for his geometric precision as well as the stillness and gravity of his figures, the dignity of their posture, their expressive hands. For Roger Fry, he was "an almost pure artist."[126] Like Piero, Bell used color to explore the relations between forms and groups of forms in *Studland Beach* and relied on a similar combination of blue, white, red, and black. The echoes of his paintings in Bell's own are unmistakable, not only in color and form and the relations between forms but also in her painting's religious power.

In Piero's *Madonna della Misericordia*, the Madonna stands still and straight, holding open her cloak, which is blue on the outside and white on the inside, to reveal eight adult figures, men and women, kneeling at her feet. One female figure is dressed in blue, with long golden hair down her back, like the standing figure in Bell's painting. One figure is dressed in the black hooded garb of the confraternity that commissioned the painting. The Madonna towers over them; if they stood, they would come up only to her waist. She is the mother of mercy, monumental, sheltering her children beneath her mantle.

In the *Madonna del Parto*, the Madonna is again larger and taller than the other figures in the painting—in this case, two angels, who are about two-thirds her height. The angels hold back the flaps of a tent that is red on the outside and white on the inside to reveal the Madonna, standing with her hand on her hip, leaning slightly under the weight of her pregnancy. The Madonna's dress is blue with a slit open in the front to reveal white beneath. Like the bathing tent in Bell's painting, the inside of Piero's tent, cloak, and dress are all white. They are tabernacles, sheltering the Madonna, who is herself a tabernacle, a sacred space. The monumental presence of the Madonna, her gravity and stillness, all find modern expression in Vanessa Bell's painting.

In *Studland Beach*, the figure standing before the tent wears a blue dress, her hair falling down her back. Like the Madonna della Misericordia, she stands still and straight. Unlike Piero's Madonna, she seems as if she might be on the verge of moving across the threshold, a sense of potential movement that contributes to the painting's ritual quality. Four figures cluster at her feet—not small adults, or angels, but actual children in ordinary proportion to the standing figure. As in the *Madonna della Misericordia*, one is wearing hooded garb, but in this case, the garb is shining white, like the tent at the edge of the water or the inside of the Madonna's various coverings—cloak, tent, dress—in Piero's paintings. The figures in *Studland Beach* are not kneeling; they seem, rather, to be playing in the sand, and they appear connected to the woman standing just outside the tent. Unlike Piero's pregnant Madonna, though, the woman is not standing beneath the tent; unlike his Madonna of mercy, she has her back turned to those who have gathered around her. Both the standing figure and the figures of the children around her seem much more exposed than Piero's figures. But the children seem nevertheless to be sheltering in her presence, the way Piero's Madonna is sheltered by her white-lined clothing, the way her body shelters the baby in her womb.

Lisa Tickner has convincingly argued that *Studland Beach* is Vanessa Bell's *To the Lighthouse*, enlivened by the "psychic charge" that comes from the connection between the standing figure in the painting and Julia Stephen, Vanessa and Virginia's mother.[127] Julia Stephen was both a monumental presence in the lives of her daughters—dwelling "in the very centre of that great Cathedral space which was childhood"[128]—and a frequently absent one, dividing herself among the needs of her husband, her seven children, and those to whom she provided nursing care. As Woolf wrote of Mrs. Ramsay in *To the Lighthouse*, "It was her instinct to go . . . turning her infallibly to the human race, making her nest in its heart."[129] Tickner argues that Bell links motherhood to "ambivalence and loss" in *Studland Beach* and that this accounts for the sense of melancholy that Tickner finds pervading the painting. Julia's death when Vanessa was fifteen and Virginia thirteen made of her a permanently absent presence with whom her daughters would struggle and whom they would memorialize in their art. "Fifty pairs of eyes were not enough to get round that one woman with," Lily Briscoe thinks as she struggles to finish her painting of Mrs. Ramsay. In *Studland Beach*, Vanessa focuses several pairs of eyes—her own, ours, and the watchers in the painting itself—on a figure invested with the absent, yet powerful, presence of her mother.

Bell did not believe, however, that paintings required narrative background to arouse emotion. In a letter to Leonard Woolf in 1913, around the time she would have been finishing *Studland Beach*, Bell wrote that forms did not need to be associated with objects in life to communicate their power: "I often look at a picture—for instance I did at the Picasso trees by the side of a lake—without seeing in the least what the things are. . . . I got quite a strong emotion from the forms and colours, but it wasn't changed when weeks afterwards it was pointed out to me by chance that the blue was a lake."[130] *Studland Beach* also does not depend on the story of Julia Stephen to communicate its power, and the questions it poses are not limited to the biographical. With their backs to us, toward what are the figures in the painting turned? Does the luminous white inside the tent open onto some greater spaciousness, or does it constrict space and block the view? Are the emotions the painting evokes generated solely from line and color and the relations between the forms, as Vanessa Bell wanted to argue? Or do they emerge from the history of forms that echo the explicitly religious images of Piero della Francesca, or Giotto, or Bellini? The painting has undeniable psychological power, ritual power, religious power. How does it reach us?

Tickner argues that the power of Vanessa Bell's *Studland Beach* communicates through what her husband, the Bloomsbury art critic Clive Bell, called "significant form." In his 1914 book *Art*, he argued that significant form is inherently religious because it communicates a sense of the ultimate reality beyond form. Significant form is the thing that all great works of art have in common, he argued—"Sta Sophia and the windows at Chartres, Mexican sculpture, a Persian bowl, Chinese carpets, Giotto's frescoes at Padua, and the masterpieces of Poussin, Piero della Francesca, and Cézanne."[131] Clive Bell understood significant form to be made up of particular combinations of lines and colors, forms and the relationship between forms that stimulate transcendent, even ecstatic, "aesthetic emotions." Some of these forms—like Giotto's frescoes at Padua—are associated with narrative content, and some—like the design on a bowl or a carpet—are not. For both Clive and Vanessa Bell, aesthetic emotions are not dependent on narrative content but on form itself. The "first commandment" of art, Clive argued, is "thou shalt create form."[132]

Of all his Bloomsbury colleagues, Clive Bell wrote the most explicitly about art as a religion. Art was not, for him, "the expression of any particular religion" but, like other religions, "a manifestation of the religious sense" itself. Art was not only *a* religion, it was also the *best* religion—the most "adaptable and catholic," the only religion of "unlimited forms and frequent revolutions." Without dogma or priests, art was uncompromising. Others religions, Clive asserted, capitulate to mammon. "Artists," on the other hand, "have been more willing to go lean."[133]

For Clive Bell, religion, including the religion of art, is marked by exalted experiences of both creation and contemplation. "Religion, as I understand it, is an expression of the individual's sense of the emotional significance of the universe; I should not be surprised to find that art was an expression of the same thing."[134] Viewing religion as essentially mystical, Clive had no interest in joining Leslie Stephen's battle over contested religious "facts." He agreed with Stephen that dogma could not satisfy the deepest religious longings of human beings. But in his comparisons of religious and scientific approaches to the world, Bell found the religious "more open-minded" than the scientific, their assumptions "less arrogant." As an example of "scientific bigotry," he offered the reductive view of a "man of science" who claimed that Matisse's pictures could be explained by a diagnosis of astigmatism.

"Few things of importance can be proved," Clive asserted; "important things have to be felt and expressed."[135] He believed art had the potential to serve as a fresh chapel for "an age grown too acute for dogmatic religion."[136] The "religious spirit" of the age could be seen and experienced in the art of Cézanne, whose work, Clive believed, might be the beginning of a new and fertile artistic "slope," just as the Byzantine art of the sixth century had been the beginning of a Christian slope within which the art of Giotto and Piero were apogees. Clive believed that people could find the "new religion" they were looking for in the contemplation of the significant form of Cézanne and others. He regarded such contemplation as analogous to prayer and worship. Some people go to look at paintings for the same reasons that others go to church: to "find that emotional confidence, that assurance of absolute good, which makes of life a momentous and harmonious whole."[137] Indeed, for "those who can feel the significance of form, art can never be less than a religion."[138]

Both Vanessa and Virginia linked their art more closely with life than Clive's transcendent theory does. For example, in her 1913 letter to Leonard Woolf, Vanessa noted that she disagreed with Clive that "one gets the same emotion from flat patterns that one does from pictures." Although she did not believe aesthetic emotions depended on narrative content, she did believe, as Frances Spalding has noted, that forms must have a "sensuous relationship with the everyday world" to arouse the emotions of the viewer.[139] Virginia, even at her most abstract, always had her eye on history. Neither Virginia nor Vanessa seemed to regard art as a religion in the rather literal way that Clive did. They found in explicitly religious art clues about the kind of art they wanted to create, and they produced art with tremendous religious power. But they did not move from there to a general theory about art as religion.

Even so, in *To the Lighthouse*, the novel in which Woolf explored the art of painting most explicitly, it is possible to hear echoes of Clive's book. His description of "the thrill that answers the reception of sheer rightness of form" comes to life during Mrs. Ramsay's dinner party when Lily Briscoe feels "as if she had found a treasure" every time she remembers her painting and ponders how she might solve its formal dilemmas. Lily's reflection, at the end of the novel, that "one wanted . . . to feel simply that's a chair, that's a table, and yet at the same time, It's a miracle, it's an ecstasy," is nearly a direct quotation from Clive's description of the impact of religion on a particular life: "His life became a miracle and an ecstasy."[140]

In *To the Lighthouse*, Woolf engaged both Clive's theory of significant form and Vanessa's experiments with it in *Studland Beach*. When Lily ponders her painting in the novel, it is often formal dilemmas that preoccupy her. "It was a question, she remembered, how to connect this mass on the right hand with that on the left,"[141] Lily thinks as if she were painting *Studland Beach* itself. But Lily is most concerned with how to capture "the quivering thing, the living thing,"[142] how to reveal forms that are hidden and invisible, like Mrs. Ramsay's own understanding of her interior life as a "wedge-shaped core of darkness." When Lily can finally see what her painting needs in order to be complete—a line down the center—she reaches for language that echoes both the Christian scriptures and Clive Bell's understanding of art as religion: "It was done; it was finished . . . I have had my vision."[143]

If *Studland Beach* draws its power from Vanessa's memories of Julia Stephen, so, of course, does Woolf's novel. When Vanessa first read it, she wrote to her sister that her portrait of their mother in Mrs. Ramsay "is more like her to me than anything I could ever have conceived of as possible. It is almost painful," she continued, "to have her so raised from the dead." She acknowledged Virginia's aesthetic accomplishment in the strongest language she had ever used about her sister's work, exclaiming that, after finishing the novel, her own "pride was humbled and I was eating dust at your feet. . . . So you see as far as portrait painting goes you seem to me to be a supreme artist and it is so shattering to find oneself face to face with those two again that I can hardly consider anything else."[144] But Vanessa also recognized *To the Lighthouse* as a work of art whose power did not rely on being a memorial of their parents: "So your vision of [our mother] stands as a whole by itself and not only as reminding one of facts." She described herself as moved not only "personally" because she knew the protagonists but also "impersonally" because, reading the novel, "I am excited and thrilled and taken into another world as one only is by a great work of art."[145] In 1905, the philosopher George Santayana wrote that the power of religion lay in the "vistas it opens and the mysteries it propounds"; they offer, according to Santayana, "another world to live in."[146] Woolf's ability not only to create such a world in language but to open hidden vistas of interiority within it helps account for the religious power of her work.

What Vanessa acknowledges in her letter is that her sister's novel is like a painting, with a significant form of its own. Woolf considered the form of *To the Lighthouse* as deeply as Lily considered the form of her painting. She wanted a form that could express multiple journeys—Lily's artistic journey, the journey to the lighthouse, the journey of humanity through the First World War. She sought to cultivate a form that could hold the intimate particularities of family life, the interior lives of women, the terror of history, the passage of time, and the sound of the sea. The kingdom of art, Clive Bell wrote, "is not of this world."[147] Woolf's art was very much of this world, even as it opened hidden spaces within it. The "other world" to which Vanessa felt transported by reading *To the Lighthouse* was not a Platonic world of forms but a world now past, conjured from a mix of form and narrative, the abstract and the particular, the impersonal and the deeply personal.

Clive Bell's formalist theories and Vanessa's and Virginia's experiments with form took shape within a vibrant, changing artistic milieu. In 1910, Roger Fry, with the help of the Bells, organized "Manet and the Post-Impressionists" at the Grafton Galleries, exhibiting the art of Gauguin, Van Gogh, Cézanne, and others. Fry had the same Platonic aspirations as a painter and art critic that Woolf had as a novelist: "To penetrate beneath appearance to reality."[148] Woolf remembers Fry's excitement, his desire that everyone who looked at the pictures "share his sense of revelation."[149] Some did, but the public "was thrown," as Woolf put it, "into paroxysms of rage and laughter. . . . The pictures were a joke, and a joke at their expense."[150] An art critic for *The Times* called the exhibition "the rejection of all that civilisation has done."[151] Some of the critique ridiculed the evangelistic fervor with which Roger Fry and Clive Bell embraced the new art. Professor Henry Tonks, Vanessa Bell's former teacher at the Slade, created a caricature of Fry, mouth open and hair flying, testifying to "the religion of Cézannah."[152] Others were less amused; the writer Wilfrid Blunt, for example, wrote that the paintings were "the works of idleness and impotent stupidity, a pornographic show."[153] Undeterred (Desmond MacCarthy recalls that Fry "did not give a single damn"[154]) by what he called an "outbreak of militant Philistinism," Fry arranged the "Second Post-Impressionist Exhibition," for which Leonard Woolf served as secretary, two years later. The offending French artists were exhibited again, this time alongside the work of young British Postimpressionist artists like Duncan Grant and Vanessa Bell, as well as Russian painters.[155]

Not all critics were appalled by Roger Fry's exhibits. Christina Walsh, in the Labour paper, the *Daily Herald*, drew a line from the Postimpressionist project to revolutionary political movements: "The Post-Impressionists are in the company of the Great Rebels of the World. In politics the only movements worth considering are Woman Suffrage and Socialism. They are both Post-Impressionist in their desire to scrap old decaying forms and find for themselves a new working ideal."[156] Virginia Woolf was looking back to the first Postimpressionist exhibit when she famously wrote that "on or about December 1910 human character changed."[157] The year 1910 was also the year Edward VII died and George V took the throne, a shift by which she marked the distance between writers like Arnold Bennett and herself—he was Edwardian, she was Georgian. By 1910, protest movements in England had arisen in support of women's rights, working people's rights, and Irish home rule and in resistance to imperial overreach and economic injustice.[158] For Woolf, 1910 marked a growing instability in the traditional ordering of masters over servants, husbands over wives, parents over children—and this had the potential to change everything. For "when human relations change," Woolf continued, "there is at the same time a change in religion, conduct, politics and literature."[159]

Art led the way in imagining changes in human relations. Fry saw Postimpressionism as expanding the invitation to engage with art beyond the educated classes. It was class anxiety, he believed, that accounted for the accusations of anarchy leveled against

Postimpressionism. The "cultured public" who had received his lectures on the Italian Renaissance so warmly now condemned him because art for them, he realized, was merely a "social asset," providing a "distinctive cachet" that set them apart from those lower down the social ladder. "One could feel fairly sure," Fry wrote, "that one's maid could not rival one" in appreciating a painting by Amico di Sandro "but might by a mere haphazard gift of Providence surpass one" in appreciating a painting by Matisse.[160] The educated classes, Fry realized, were not interested in art that threatened the status quo. In *To the Lighthouse*, Woolf describes another modest experiment with cultural change that those who felt threatened by the Postimpressionist exhibit would no doubt also have found anarchic. Sitting across from "the little atheist" Charles Tansley at Mrs. Ramsay's dinner party, Lily Briscoe reflects that they were participating in an invisible social contract: she should make him feel good about himself at the dinner table, while he was obligated to rescue her if the Tube caught fire. "But how would it be, she thought, if neither of us did either of these things?"[161]

Clive Bell's call for a shift from a religion of dogma to a religion of art was influenced, in part, by the Russian artist Wassily Kandinsky, author of *Concerning the Spiritual in Art* and a painter often credited with creating the first purely abstract painting, "Abstract Watercolor," in 1910, Woolf's auspicious year. (In fact, another painter deeply concerned with the spiritual in art, Swedish artist Hilma af Klint, was creating abstract images years before Kandinsky painted "Abstract Watercolor."[162]) Both his paintings and his ideas about the spiritual in art made an impact on the Bells and on Woolf. Art, Clive argued, is an end in itself and has the potential to reveal "its essential reality, of the God in the everything, of the universal in the particular, of the all-pervading rhythm."[163] Kandinsky sought to reveal that same all-pervading rhythm in his work.

The Russian Orthodox Kandinsky did not regard art as a religion, as Bell did, but he did understand art to be "one of the mightiest elements"[164] of the spiritual life, which he opposed to the unconscious life of materialism and "the despair of unbelief."[165] Kandinsky and Bell agreed on the spiritual power of form. Bell believed significant form pointed to a hidden ultimate reality by arousing ecstatic aesthetic emotions. Kandinksy had a more sacramental understanding: "the outward expression of an inner meaning."[166] The more abstract the form, he argued, the purer the inner meaning and the more purely received.

Kandinsky identified the form of the spiritual life as a triangle with the broadest section at the bottom and the narrowest at the top. "The whole triangle," he wrote, "is moving slowly, almost invisibly forwards and upwards."[167] This shape is important to both *Studland Beach* and *To the Lighthouse*. In *Studland Beach*, there is a triangle at the top of the bathing tent, and the grouping of the three children near the tent and the two watchers in their hats also form triangles. The sand dune and the vast swaths of white and blue that divide the painting are also triangular. In *To the Lighthouse*, Woolf uses a triangular form to describe the thing that Kandinsky cares about most: interior life. Mrs. Ramsay imagines her own interior life as a "wedge-shaped core of darkness." Although it is "invisible to others," Lily Briscoe, the artist, perceives it and paints Mrs. Ramsay reading to her son as "a triangular purple shape." Such an "internal truth," Kandinsky insists, "only art can divine."[168]

Like the Bells, Kandinsky found in the painting of Cézanne the opening of new possibilities for art. Cézanne had reinvigorated the form of the triangle, Kandinsky argued, which had had the life drained out of it by "academic usage." Cézanne's renewal of the triangle could be seen most clearly in his *Large Bathers* (which Kandinsky calls "Bathing Women"), in which the nude bodies of the female bathers participate in the triangular shape of the canopy of trees that rises, cathedral-like, over the pond in which they swim. Rather than simply using the form to balance the figures, he has made the figures obedient to the form itself. In this way, Kandinsky insists, Cézanne's painting is religious in a way that Raphael's *Holy Family*, in which the triangle is used merely to group the figures harmoniously, is not. By pulling the figures themselves into the triangle, making the bodies of some of the bathers seem almost part of the trunks of the trees, their limbs growing "narrower from bottom to top," Cézanne reveals his painting's "mystical motive."[169] The religious power of Cézanne's painting is the same kind of power Vanessa Bell's *Studland Beach* communicates and depends on similar elements: some figures in Cézanne's painting have their backs to us; the canopy of trees creates the kind of numinous space that the bathing tent in *Studland*

Beach also suggests; the blue of the water in Cézanne's painting is the same deep blue that dominates Bell's painting.

Kandinsky and Vanessa Bell both responded powerfully to color. If, for Clive, form is the crucial spiritual component of art, color is that component for Kandinsky. Color creates a "corresponding spiritual vibration" in the viewer; it "can make of the picture a living thing."[170] For artists, Kandinsky insisted, "the study of color and its effects on man" is the foundational spiritual exercise to which the artist must commit in order to fulfill the artistic responsibility of shaping the "spiritual atmosphere" of the age. Kandinsky wrote about the spiritual responsibility of the artist in a much more explicit way than Clive Bell did—indeed, Bell would worry that articulating such responsibility would reduce art to an instrument. Kandinsky, however, wrote fervently about how the artist must direct the power of art "to the improvement and refinement of the human soul—to, in fact, the raising of the spiritual triangle."[171]

Although Clive Bell understood art as a religion, he did not agree with Kandinsky that the power of art should be deployed in a particular direction, even in service of the spiritual atmosphere of the age. Clive believed that beauty and the state of mind induced by aesthetic contemplation were goods in themselves, and so the creation of art increased the amount of intrinsic value present in the world. This faith in the intrinsic goodness of beauty—and truth and love—had been instilled in Clive and his fellow Cambridge students by their beloved professor and mentor, G. E. Moore. The male members of Bloomsbury had all been students at Cambridge, and most of them—although not Clive—had been members of the Cambridge Apostles, a secret society dedicated to intellectual debate. As Leon Edel has put it, the Apostles cultivated "a religion of the mind" and "an enduring sense of fellowship."[172] Moore had himself been an Apostle in his student days, and his influence on Leonard Woolf, John Maynard Keynes, Lytton Strachey, and other close friends of Virginia and Vanessa Stephen was transmitted, in large part, through this group.

Moore's philosophy provided a fresh chapel for the young men around him, both through his philosophy and his personal presence. Leonard Woolf associated being around Moore as a Cambridge undergraduate with "the entrancing excitement of feeling life open out in one and before one."[173] For Leonard, a Jewish student among the descendants of the Clapham Sect and the Quakers, Moore offered a deeply satisfying alternative to the religious voices he and his fellow students had heard in childhood. Moore, he wrote, "answered our questions, not with the religious voice of Jehovah from Mount Sinai or Jesus with his sermon from the Mount, but with the more divine voice of plain common-sense."[174]

Moore has been called "Bloomsbury's Prophet" and his *Principia Ethica* its sacred text.[175] John Maynard Keynes, in a paper read aloud to the Memoir Club in 1938, described Moore's philosophy as the "youthful religion" to which he and his friends ascribed. He breathlessly communicates how thrilling reading Moore's work was for him, Leonard Woolf, Lytton Strachey, Clive Bell, and others: "[Moore's influence] was exciting, exhilarating, the beginning of a renaissance, the opening of a new heaven on a new earth, we were the forerunners of a new dispensation, we were not afraid of anything."[176] Keynes and his friends not only felt freed by Moore from the strictures of the religions in which they had been raised and the need to defend them, they also felt liberated from the demands of utilitarianism. Moore offered Keynes and his friends "a religion without god"[177] in which truth, love, and beauty were intrinsic goods and communion with friends and lovers and the contemplation of art were the practices that brought one into relationship with those goods. Art need not be "moral" in the sense that Leslie Stephen insisted on in "Art and Morality." As an end in itself, art need only be art, capable of producing aesthetic emotions. In "Art, Morals and Religion," Moore described religion as "merely a subdivision of Art." Both art and religion, he argued, produce the same kinds of emotions. The difference between them is that the religious person must believe in the "existence of the objects that he contemplates." For Moore, faith is not a matter of maintaining this kind of belief; it is, rather "what profoundly moves and occupies your minds. And this kind of faith we all have in the objects of Art as much as a religious person in the objects of religion."[178]

Like Walter Pater in the previous century, Moore was criticized for elitism, separating art from morals, and corrupting the young. The economist Beatrice Webb complained that, at Cambridge, there is "a pernicious set presided over by Lowes Dickinson, which makes a sort of ideal of anarchic ways in sexual questions. . . . The intellectual star is the metaphysical George Moore with his *Principia Ethica*—a book they all talk of as 'The Truth'! I never can see anything in it, except a metaphysical justification for doing what you like and what other people disapprove of! So far as I can understand the philosophy it is a denial of the scientific method and of religion—as a rule, that is the net result on the minds of young men—it seems to disintegrate their intellects and their characters."[179] Also like Pater, Moore's work continues to generate a range of contradictory judgments. *Principia Ethica* has been read as a call to radical individual freedom and as deeply, even cosmically, conservative.[180] Admirers of Moore often criticize Clive Bell and Bloomsbury for claiming that Moore's thought undergirded their theories. Even John Maynard Keynes, for whom Moore offered a new religion, argued that Bloomsbury had "accepted Moore's religion, so to speak, and discarded his morals."[181] Most recently, Alisdair MacIntyre has criticized Moore for his role in what MacIntyre considers to be the ongoing erosion of Western civilization, finding in Moore a dangerous emotivism that keeps us from appealing to anything—virtues, duties—outside ourselves.[182] Moore's philosophy detached his followers, including the members of the Bloomsbury group, MacIntyre claims, from "traditional and inherited moral language."[183]

Moore's work, from the beginning, attracted strong responses, especially among those who loved it. For the young men who would become the friends of Virginia and Vanessa Stephen, *Principia Ethica* was a text of liberation. Clive Bell built his formalist aesthetic theory out of it. Lytton Strachey hailed it as the beginning of a new Age of Reason. John Maynard Keynes claimed that its last chapter, on "The Ideal," was "better than Plato because it is quite free from *fancy*."[184]

Leonard Woolf, who adored Moore and called him "the only great man whom I have ever met or known in the world of ordinary, real life," claimed Moore and his *Principia Ethica* as an important influence also on Virginia Woolf's literary style.[185] In his autobiography, he wrote that Virginia was "deeply affected by the astringent influence of Moore and the purification of that divinely cathartic question . . .

'What do you mean by that?' Artistically the purification can, I think, be traced in the clarity, light, absence of humbug in Virginia's literary style."[186] Vanessa Bell's biographer, Frances Spalding, likewise argues that Moore's "insistence on the precise definition of meaning may have indirectly encouraged Vanessa's use of elemental shapes and the extreme openness and honesty of her abstract style."[187] V. S. Pritchett made a similar claim about the effect of Moore's question—What exactly do you mean?—on the development of the art of conversation within Bloomsbury and pointed to Woolf's essay "A Conversation with Walter Sickert," as an example of how Moore's question could be taken up usefully by artists.[188]

Virginia had read *Principia Ethica* in 1908, at the urging of Clive Bell. She read ten pages a night, "climbing Moore like some industrious insect, who is determined to build a nest on the top of a Cathedral spire." She read him from her perspective as a writer: "One sentence, a string of 'desires' makes my head spin with the infinite meaning of words unadorned."[189] When she finished, she wrote to Vanessa of her admiration for him: "He is so humane in spite of his desire to know the truth,"[190] she noted.

Virginia and Vanessa had, of course, grown up with someone who desired to know the truth: their father, whose intellectual endeavors often left him insecure and needy, feelings he often performed within the family, leaning especially hard on Julia, Stella, and, later, Vanessa. G. E. Moore might have seemed to Virginia like a modern, humanized version of her father. Moore had emerged from the same "intellectual aristocracy" as Leslie Stephen. He was raised a Quaker, became an evangelical, then, coming to believe that Christian faith was not rational, rejected his faith. Like Leslie Stephen, Moore loved the novels of Jane Austen and the poetry of Wordsworth, and he read Sir Walter Scott's Waverly novels over and over again. But unlike her father, he did not believe that art required a particular kind of moral content in order to contribute to the good of the world nor that the meaning of an art object was wholly carried by its content. Music had taught Moore that art could be nonrepresentational. He left room for the kinds of formal experiments that both Stephen daughters undertook in their respective arts in a way that their father did not and liberated art from his Victorian moralism.

Years after reading his book, Virginia would cultivate a friendship with Moore. He was an occasional houseguest of hers and Leonard's and would sometimes sing to them in the evenings. Paul Levy has argued that Moore's influence on Leonard and his fellow students was more personal than doctrinal,[191] and Virginia certainly found him "much more human than his followers." He is "solid and direct: and not the least hard to talk to," she wrote to Saxon Sydney-Turner in 1916. "He knows all the wild flowers and butterflies."[192]

Moore's emphasis on the importance of friendship and beauty certainly influenced her. But Virginia Woolf did not take Moore with the hyperbolic seriousness of the men of Bloomsbury, whose lives he had changed. She writes in her diary about a conversation with Lytton Strachey's sister, Ray, and Leonard about "the moral eminence of Moore, comparable to that of Christ or Socrates, so R. & L. hold." Virginia argued that Vanessa, Duncan, Lytton, and Desmond MacCarthy possessed "something different but of equal value."[193] One gathers Ray and Leonard were unmoved. A year later, in 1920, Virginia writes of G. E. Moore again in her diary. "I dont see altogether why he was the dominator & dictator of youth," she writes. "Perhaps Cambridge is too much of a cave."[194]

Virginia Woolf did acknowledge the importance of *Principia Ethica* to her moral formation and that of her friends. In 1939, after a visit from Moore, she wrote to her niece, Judith Stephen, "did you ever read the book that made us all so wise and good: *Principia Ethica*?"[195] Rather than a direct influence on her literary style, though, she seemed most interested in the way *Principia Ethica* could serve as a window on character in her fiction. In an early story written from the perspective of two "daughters at home" who attend a party in Bloomsbury, the sisters engage in conversation with a young woman who has clearly read *Principia Ethica* and absorbed the "divinely cathartic question" that Leonard Woolf seemed so sure had shaped Virginia's prose: "'O do tell me,' broke forth Sylvia, 'exactly what you mean. I want to know. I like to know about people. After all you know, the human soul is the thing.'"[196] Moore's book appears again in Woolf's first novel, *The Voyage Out*. As Helen Ambrose sits reading a book of philosophy, Richard Dalloway takes it from her and begins reading from the first chapter of *Principia*

Ethica: "'Good, then, is indefinable,' he read out. 'How jolly to think that's going on still! . . . That's just the kind of thing we used to talk about when we were boys.'"[197] Woolf did not only use Moore and his book to sketch out the occasional character, however. She was also moved by his profound influence on her husband and her friends. When Keynes read "My Early Beliefs" to the Memoir Club in 1938, Woolf found it "a very packed profound & impressive paper so far as I could follow, about Cambridge youth; their philosophy; its consequences; Moore; what it lacked; what it gave. The beauty and unworldliness of it. I was impressed by M[aynard] & felt a little flittery & stupid."[198]

Moore and his philosophy were part of the Cambridge world she was denied. She could read his systematic, philosophical language with understanding and appreciation, but it was not her chosen language. "The male atmosphere is disconcerting to me," she wrote in her diary in 1919. "I think what an abrupt precipice cleaves asunder the male intelligence, & how they pride themselves upon a point of view which much resembles stupidity."[199] She did not feel that way about Moore's point of view, but she did sometimes struggle to connect with the systematic philosophical language that meant so much to many of the men around her—"a scholasticism which outdid St. Thomas," as Keynes put it.[200] Once, when Moore was her houseguest, he kept her awake taking a cold bath in the middle of the night, and "consequently I was too muddled next morning to follow his explanation of Berkeley."[201]

The "religion" of Moore that Keynes found "a very good one to grow up under" and "is still my religion under the surface" also helped shape the fresh chapel Virginia Woolf was building and the religious thinker her novels show her to be.[202] But Moore and his book were among the shivering fragments from which she constructed her whole, not the whole itself. One of Moore's recent interpreters argues that the common sense so admired by the Bloomsbury men led Moore to believe that "reality does not come in a welter, but consists of discrete, naturally unified objects."[203] Woolf's own common sense led her in another direction—she believed reality came to us chaotically and the work of the artist is to create new wholes from that welter of experience.

Woolf's relationships with family members and friends, her encounters with art and philosophy, the books she read, the places she traveled, the artistic problems she addressed in her writing—her work as a writer, a religious thinker, and a creator of fresh chapels—cannot be traced back to any one of them alone. Woolf helped shape modernism's "culture of experiment" through her commitment to bringing fresh wholes from new combinations.[204] She was drawn, like Kandinksy, to "the immense possibilities of depth and strength to be gained by combination or by discord between the various arts."[205] The years of her childhood and young adulthood, during which she formed some of her closest relationships and worked out the ideas and practices to which she would be most committed, offered her countless shivering fragments whose discords and possible combinations she would explore in her fiction and essays, her diaries and letters for the rest of her life.

3

RELIGIOUS READING

Virginia Woolf understood from an early age that she could tune her interior life by reading. When her half-sister Stella returned ill from her honeymoon in 1897, Virginia wrote in her diary that "my Macaulay . . . is the only calm and un-anxious thing in this most agitating time."[1] Stella had been a crucial presence in Virginia's life after the death of Julia Stephen, and throughout the months of Stella's illness Virginia read to steady herself, finding in books "the greatest help and comfort."[2] When Stella's condition worsened, Virginia "read Mr. [Henry] James to quiet me, and my beloved Macaulay." She read continuously and, as she put it, "religiously."[3] Ten days after Stella's death, we find her "attacking" the twelve volumes of James Anthony Froude's *History of England*—a fifteen-year-old girl hurling herself against a monument of words, seeking relief from her sorrow.

Seven years later, after the death of her father, Virginia would herself become ill. Her doctor, believing that reading and writing agitated her, limited the hours she could devote to them. She complained to her friend Violet Dickinson that Dr. Savage refused to let her return to the home she shared with Vanessa in London. "I long for a room to myself, with books and nothing else," she wrote, "where I can shut myself up, and see no one, and read myself into peace."[4]

Throughout her life, Woolf strengthened her spirit through reading. In 1939, as the war intensified, Woolf wrote in her diary, "Lord this is the worst of all my life's experiences" and looked to "a solid book like Tawney, an exercise of the muscles" for a "cure."[5] In the months before her death, she struggled with depression as German planes on bombing raids flew low over her house, and she and Leonard discussed killing themselves if Germany invaded England. In the weeks before she died, she wrote again in her diary about her attempt to read herself out of the "trough of despair." To read "a good hard rather rocky book," she wrote, "is my prescription"—just as it had been when she was a young girl, reckoning with loss after terrible loss.[6] In one of the two letters she left for Leonard before she drowned herself, she wrote that she was hearing voices again and could not concentrate.[7] "You see I cant even write this properly. I cant read."[8] The practice of reading had nurtured in her the capacities that made life worth living; it was a source of creativity and communion with others. Being unable to read isolated her in her despair.

Reading was the most formative practice of Virginia Woolf's life. So powerfully did she articulate the deep pleasures and complex demands of reading in her essays and reviews that the editor of her essays has asserted that her love of, and belief in, the practice of reading was "almost pathologically impassioned."[9] What Woolf's essays communicate, though, is not pathology but devotion to and faith in a practice by which she navigated her life, a spiritual and ethical practice she believed "has changed the world and continues to change it."[10]

Through reading, Paul J. Griffiths has argued, religious readers cultivate a religious account of the world.[11] And certainly it was from her own practice of reading that Woolf constructed what she would come to call her "philosophy." Reading illuminated for her the connections between disparate ideas, histories, places, and people. At twenty-one, she began to try to put this experience into words: "I read some history: it is suddenly all alive, branching forwards & backwards & connected with every kind of thing that seemed entirely remote before. . . . I think I see for a moment how our minds are all threaded together—how any live mind today is of the very same stuff as Plato's & Euripides. It is only a continuation & development of the same thing. It is this common mind that binds the whole world together."[12] Thirty-six years later, Woolf would still be turning these ideas over and over. The "rapture I get when in writing I seem to be discovering what belongs to what" leads to similar conclusions about reality as her experience of reading.

> From this I reach what I might call a philosophy; at any rate it is a constant idea of mine; that behind the cotton wool is hidden a pattern; that we—I mean all human beings—are connected with this; that the whole world is a work of art; that we are parts of the work of art. *Hamlet* or a Beethoven quartet is the truth about this vast mass that we call the world. But there is no Shakespeare, there is no Beethoven; certainly and emphatically there is no God; we are the words; we are the music; we are the thing itself.[13]

In both instances, Woolf notes the temporary quality of these revelations. When the twenty-one-year-old woman returned to her Greek the next morning, her sense of the common mind had flown. For the woman of fifty-eight, it is only "when I have a shock" that the pattern behind the cotton wool comes, for a moment, into view. The work of art that is the world, the common mind that threads across time and space reveal themselves only in glimpses. Out of those glimpses, Woolf formed her bedrock convictions about reality. Like a religious reader excavating a hidden meaning or seeking an experience of the divine, however fleeting, Woolf read and wrote to "discover real things beneath the show."[14]

Woolf came from a long line of serious readers for whom reading was a religious practice. For members of the Clapham Sect, both individual spiritual reading and family devotional reading were an integral part of daily life and household worship. William Wilberforce "kindled at the very sight of books."[15] On Sundays, families gathered to pray together and to hear scripture read aloud and interpreted; Samuel Wilberforce, hoping to associate the Sabbath with pleasure, wrote a collection of stories for parents to read to their children on Sunday evenings.[16] Even when families with evangelical Christian roots fell away from Christian faith, they retained forms of Sunday family worship. Katharine Trevelyan, for example, described in her autobiography a family ritual known as Sunday Reading, in which texts as diverse as the Song of Songs and the Life of the Buddha were read aloud in the family circle, hymns sung from the Labour Hymn Book, and prayers for humanity composed and recited.[17] Leslie Stephen also continued the Clapham practice of reading aloud to his family. Rather than being part of a domestic liturgy, however, his reading aloud of poetry, history, and fiction was the liturgy itself. Especially poetry. As his biographer Noel Annan put it, "Poetry was his breviary, his matins, terce and compline."[18]

Woolf recalled her father reading aloud *Treasure Island* and the Waverley novels, Carlyle's history of the French revolution, Hawthorne, Shakespeare, and all of Jane Austen. When it came to poetry, though, he recited from memory; the poems of Wordsworth, Tennyson, and Arnold were among his favorites. His mother, Jane Venn, had also known a great deal of poetry by heart. As a teenager, she made a record of her reading in her diary, as her granddaughter would later do, and noted her memorization of Scott's *Marmion* and poems by William Cowper,[19] parts of which would later make an appearance in *To the Lighthouse*. Leslie Stephen shared with his mother and other religious readers delight in the freedom from the written text that allowed him to savor a poem whether the book were to hand or not. Reciting poetry aloud was an ethical act because it cultivated a capacity for listening in his hearers; it was a creative act because, in the recitation of a memorized text, he recreated it.[20] Reading and reciting to his family in the evenings was a practice of spiritual and ethical formation, the fulfillment of a Claphamite responsibility.

The last poem Leslie Stephen ever tried to recite was Milton's "Ode on the Morning of Christ's Nativity," a poem he performed for his family every Christmas. On the night of his last Christmas, Woolf recalled that her father "remembered the words, but was then too weak to speak them."[21] Stephen had written that Milton's "absolute faith in the historical revelation" of Christianity forced the critic "to justify admiration at the cost of condoning palpable absurdities."[22] That Milton's poetic power muscled through the "innumerable trammels" created by those absurdities to create poetry that would survive its time was what Stephen found remarkable in the poet. Many of the poems her father recited for his family remained for Woolf forever linked with him. "I hear in them," she wrote, "not only his voice, but in some sort his teaching and belief."[23]

The roots of Woolf's practice of reading lie even further back, beyond the reading practices of her parents, grandparents, and great-grandparents, in the reading practices cultivated in European monasteries in the Western Middle Ages. Practices like *lectio divina* and the compilation of *florilegia* anticipated a great deal in modern understandings of reading: the recognition of the way "reading *overflows* itself in all directions and at every moment,"[24] the ways in which reading can transform both reader and text, the fluid boundaries between reading and writing, the ways in which texts speak to each other, and the ways in which, as Woolf herself put it, literature "will not suffer itself to be read passively, but takes us and reads us."[25]

Lectio divina is a ruminative form of reading that integrates reading, meditation, and prayer. Its purpose is to make the reader available to an experience of the presence of God.[26] Described by the Carthusian monk Guigo II in the twelfth century as the first rung on a ladder that stretches from earth to heaven, reading was often described as the foundational practice of Christian spirituality. It did not require a material book, for "listening," as Guigo had insisted in a world where a book was a rare and precious thing, "is a kind of reading."[27] Five centuries earlier, Isidore of Seville had helped lay a foundation for Guigo's ladder by asserting that "all progress [in the spiritual life] comes from reading and meditation. He who wishes to be always with God must pray frequently and read."[28]

For medieval people, reading was an activity of the body as well as the mind. Ancient doctors used to prescribe reading as a form of exercise,[29] an idea that Woolf—whose doctors often forbade her to read—would have appreciated. For Woolf, the true reader—as opposed to what she called the "man of learning"—approaches reading more like "brisk exercise in the open air than of sheltered study . . . not a sedentary pursuit at all."[30] She saw her father, and herself, as this kind of reader.

In the monasteries of the Middle Ages, reading was an aid to good works, a path to God, and a portable sacred space. "Thus there will be no need to go to the oratory to begin to pray," wrote the Cistercian monk Arnoul of Bohériss, "but in reading itself, means will be found for prayer and contemplation."[31] A written text was a chapel one could enter any time of the day or night, a pilgrimage trail one could walk without ever leaving one's room. And if the text were memorized, as Leslie Stephen knew, the reader's freedom was even greater, because the text was always accessible, even if books were not.

In the *lectio divina* of medieval Christian monasticism, reading aloud and recitation from memory turned reading into a form of prayer. Reading aloud enabled the reader to taste the words *in ore cordis*, in the mouth of the heart,[32] and to draw more deeply on the ethical dimension of reading in words shared aloud within a community that both read and listened, a community that both read and was read by the books it cherished. Having been formed in the reading circle of her family, Woolf, throughout her life, loved reading aloud and listening to others read. In the weeks after Stella's death, she began reading Dickens's *David Copperfield* aloud to Vanessa as she painted. Later in her life, Woolf and her friends would gather to read plays together and to read their autobiographical essays aloud to one another.

Woolf shared many of her father's beliefs about reading and the relationship between reader and writer. "To read a book in the true sense—to read it, that is, not as the critic but in the spirit of enjoyment—is to lay aside for the moment one's personality, and to become a part of the author,"[33] Leslie Stephen wrote. Woolf also urged readers to seek communion with the author before beginning to analyze and criticize. "Do not dictate to your author," she insisted; "try to become him. Be his fellow-worker and accomplice."[34] Readers who open their minds to what the author is trying to do will find themselves, she argued, in "the presence of a human being unlike any other."[35] Both father and daughter believed that the boundaries between us keep us from having immediate knowledge of each other's "souls" (as Woolf put it) or "consciousness" (as her father put it).[36] But each sought to cross those boundaries and to transcend the limits of their own selves through the practice of reading.

Woolf's notion of self-transcendence through reading appears in a letter to her friend Ethel Smyth, the composer, in 1934, a letter in which she refers to reading, not as a practice, but as a "rapture" and a "state." Smyth was another of Woolf's Christian friends—of the "same persuasion" as T. S. Eliot,[37] as Woolf put it—and Woolf enjoyed arguing with her, as she did with Eliot, about her religion: "How can you belong," she once asked her, "to such a canting creed?"[38] In one of her letters to Smyth, echoing the sentiments of religious readers for whom reading "ends only with death and perhaps not then,"[39] Woolf wrote, "Sometimes I think heaven must be one continuous unexhausted reading. It's a disembodied trance-like intense rapture that used to seize me as a girl, and comes back now and again down here, with a violence that lays me low. Did I say I was flying? How then can I be low? Because, my dear Ethel, the state of reading consists in the complete elimination of the *ego*; and it's the ego that erects itself like another part of the body I dont dare to name."[40] Five years later, Woolf will use the language of rapture and violence to describe the moments of being that punctuated her experience and the practice of writing by which she transformed them into art. In her letter to Ethel Smyth, she described how the practice of reading can itself become a moment of being with the power to induce a rapture so violent and intense that it overcomes the assertion of the self and its desires. In her reference to the male erection and the invoking of her young reading self, there is also perhaps an echo of the relief she found in reading when she was young—not only as an escape from the ego but from the intrusive sexuality of her half-brothers. Kate Flint has drawn out the connection between Woolf's commitment to reading as mutual engagement between reader and writer and her vision of sexual pleasure. "Like sex," Flint writes, "reading should ideally be a reciprocal transaction . . . rather than a process of establishing dominance."[41] For Woolf, both reading and good sex require a willingness to put the shared work of intimacy before the individual ego.

Woolf advocated freedom in reading, a commitment she also shared with her father. "To read what one liked because one liked it, never to pretend to admire what one did not—that was his only lesson in the art of reading," she recalled.[42] In her essay "How Should One Read a Book," she passed along his perspective: "The only advice, indeed, that one person can give another about reading is to take no advice, to follow your own instincts, to use your own reason, to come to your own conclusions."[43] Both believed books were not separate from life but an irreplaceable part of it. Leslie Stephen urged the students of St. Andrews to "read what you really like and not what someone tells you that you ought to like; let your reading be part of your lives."[44] Stephen's unpretentious approach to reading, grounded in pleasure, also encouraged his daughter to let books and life "mix indistinguishably" from childhood forward. When Louis, in *The Waves*, meditates on his life by repeating the poem "O western wind, when wilt thou blow?" and using it as a plumb line into his own existence, we catch a glimpse of religious reading. "I open a little book," says Louis. "I read one poem. One poem is enough." The poem glides like a knife through the banalities of his life, carves out a place for him to look unflinchingly at his loneliness, reveals his multiplicity. "There is always more to be understood," Louis says, "a discord to be listened for; a falsity to be reprimanded."[45] Through a few lines of poetry, repeated like a prayer, Louis listens for discords, resists falsity, and allows his understanding to open a little further.

Woolf believed deeply in the democratizing power of books and reading. Echoing the rhythms of Paul's letter to the Galatians, in which Paul argues that Christ dissolves the distinctions between Jew and Greek, slave and free, male and female, Woolf writes that, in the realm of reading, "simple and learned, man and woman are alike."[46] In *Orlando*, reading weakens any distinction conferred by wealth. Orlando, a wealthy nobleman, "had only to open a book for the whole vast accumulation to turn to mist." When Orlando reads, he becomes "a naked man."[47]

When we read, Woolf insists, we enter free territory. "Literature is no one's private ground," she wrote; "literature is common ground."[48] For Woolf, entering this common ground alters the way we see the world, shifts our perspective, enlarges it.

> [The pleasure of reading] is so curious, so complex, so immensely fertilising to the mind of anyone who enjoys it, and so wide in its effects, that it would not be in the

> least surprising to discover, on the day of judgement when secrets are revealed and the obscure is made plain, that the reason why we have grown from pigs to men and women, and come out from our caves, and dropped our bows and arrows, and sat round the fire and talked and drunk and made merry and given to the poor and helped the sick and made pavements and houses and erected some sort of shelter and society on the waste of the world, is nothing but this: we have loved reading.[49]

For Orlando, the power of reading to transform lives was greater than the power of religion: "A silly song of Shakespeare's has done more for the poor and the wicked," he reflects, "than all the preachers and philanthropists in the world."[50] The deep pleasure of reading could not, for Woolf, be disconnected from its power to shape us and the world in which we live. Even in the terrible days of the Second World War, Woolf urged the members of the Workers' Educational Association in Brighton to borrow books from the public libraries because, in the postwar future for which she hoped, "money is no longer going to do our thinking for us." In order to cross the gulf between war and peace and shape a society no longer based on class, "commoners and outsiders like ourselves" will need to read "omnivorously, simultaneously, poems, plays, novels, histories, biographies, the old and the new."[51]

Woolf's conviction that reading opened democratic common ground that belonged to everyone undergirded her notion of the "common reader," a phrase she borrowed from Samuel Johnson. Woolf first used it in an unpublished essay she was working on in 1922, "Byron and Mr. Briggs," in which she imagined the reading experiences of a Cornhill spectacle maker and his grandchildren. Denied the university education provided to her brothers, Woolf numbered herself among common readers: "I too," Woolf wrote, "am a grandchild of . . . Briggs."[52] In the extant draft of the essay she argued that it was the common reader who kept literature alive. Critics are also important to the life of literature, she acknowledged—but even the most honored critics are "powerless to unseat the judgement of an ignorant boy or girl who has read [*King Lear*] to the end." That young person has had a direct experience of Shakespeare that no critic can supersede. For Woolf, it is the living exchange between readers and writers that keeps literature alive in the world, an exchange that has a decidedly religious quality. Because she believed Britain drew its spiritual life not from "hymn books and ledgers" but from literature,[53] she and her fellow common readers not only kept literature alive but the spiritual life it nourished.

What interested Woolf most about common readers was their desire to create something whole from the fragments of their reading.[54] Books themselves perform a similar generativity: they "are always overflowing their boundaries . . . breeding new species from unexpected matches among themselves."[55] Certain books provide a "resting point for the mind"[56] and renew "the zest of imagination."[57] Reading transforms life, flooding it with excess presence. The practice of reading, Woolf passionately believed, "is the best way of rejuvenating one's own creative power."[58] Like a writer, the reader, especially the "common reader" with whom Woolf identified so strongly and for whom she wrote, creates from the fragments of her reading "a portrait of a man, a sketch of an age, a theory of the art of writing."[59] It is "the desire to create,"[60] she believed, that readers and writers share.

For theorist of religious reading Paul J. Griffiths, it is precisely Woolf's "desire to create" that disqualifies her from being understood as a religious reader. "Writerly creativity," he argues, is a concern only of what he calls "consumerist readers"—readers who read only to write. True religious readers, he argues, do not care about writing at all.[61]

But Woolf stands in a long line of religious readers who created something new from their reading, like the thirteenth-century Carthusian writer Marguerite d'Oingt, who wrote her own text in response to the one God had written on her heart, or the sixteenth-century Carmelite John of the Cross, whose reading of the Song of Songs led him to write not only his own poetry, but commentaries on it.[62] As Duncan Robertson has noted in his book on the practice of *lectio divina*, "in the work of quoting, copying, and paraphrasing, the activity of reading flows into writing in an unbroken continuum" for religious readers.[63] Medieval *florilegia*, which created new texts from the arrangement of bits and pieces of the reader's reading, demonstrate how fluid the distinction between reading and writing can be.

One of the places in which the relationship between reading and creativity is most visible in medieval Christian practices of religious reading is in allegorical readings of scripture that excavate meanings hidden beneath the literal. Ideally, as Duncan Robertson has shown, this is "an exercise in freedom, one that may take the form of a muscular human intervention into the scriptural text."[64] Woolf embraced freedom in reading, but she objected to "muscular human intervention," especially interventions that insisted on particular meanings. After *To the Lighthouse* was published, Roger Fry wrote to ask her what the image of the lighthouse meant. She wrote back emphatically: "I meant *nothing* by The Lighthouse." She explained that she expected her readers to attach a range of emotions to the image. "I can't manage Symbolism except in this vague, generalized way," she told him. "Whether its right or wrong I don't know, but directly I'm told what a thing means, it becomes hateful to me."[65]

Medieval Christian practitioners of *lectio divina* often brought submerged allegorical meanings to the surface. Although Woolf shared with those readers a willingness to allow many meanings to exist simultaneously, she preferred "to allow the sunken meanings to remain sunken, suggested, not stated; lapsing and flowing into each other like reeds on the bed of a river."[66] Although they did not have the same ends in view, Woolf and the medieval allegorists did share similar methods. The best medieval allegorists worked not with a fixed set of possible meanings of the texts they read but allowed themselves to be led in their interpretations by echoes and resonances. Woolf wrote about how words "shuffle" and "change" when they are repeated over and over, when, in reverie, they come into contact with the fragments of one's reading that exist in memory. The phrase "Passing Russell Square" read from the tram might lead to "Passing away saith the world, passing away"; "incarnadine" might open onto "multitudinous seas."[67] The most creative allegorists moved in this intuitive way as well. Like a medieval allegorist, Woolf knew the limits of language—words never quite say what we want them to say and often seem to have a will of their own, revealing more than we intend. But, like an allegorist, she proceeded with the faith that, in listening for reverberations among echoes and fragments, language might be found for "fuller and finer truths."[68]

It would be wrong, though, to associate religious reading only with the excavation of meaning. As Griffiths puts it, for religious readers, there can "be no final act of reading in which everything is uncovered."[69] Religious readers apprehend more than meaning in the texts they read. Anselm of Canterbury (1033–1109) noted in his *Prayers and Meditations* that sacred texts possess a power that communicates to the reader even before the reader comprehends the words.[70] In her commentary on the Song of Songs, Teresa of Avila wrote that the Song stirred her soul, even when she heard it read aloud in Latin, a language she could not understand. Sounding very like Vanessa Bell writing to Leonard Woolf about her response to an abstract painting by Picasso, Teresa continues: "Even when the Latin words were translated for me into the vernacular, I did not understand the text any more."[71] Teresa apprehended the Song of Songs the way we hear music or the sound of the ocean. This is also a kind of religious reading.

Woolf explored the tension between receiving religious language as a kind of music and understanding it according to reason in scenes of churchgoing in her novels. For example, Terence Hewet in *The Voyage Out* is able "to enjoy the beauty of the language" of the Sunday morning service "without hindrance" because he had never tried to make that language "fit any feeling or idea of his."[72] *The Years* contains a scene of explicitly religious reading: that is, the reading of the burial service from the 1928 *Book of Common Prayer* for Rose Pargiter by Rose's children's cousin, James, an Anglican priest. When he reads the opening line of the service, from the gospel of John—"I am the resurrection and the life"—Delia Pargiter responds powerfully to the words. They came at her with a "rush of extraordinary beauty" and "filled her," Woolf writes, "with glory. . . . But then, as Cousin James went on reading, something slipped. The sense was blurred. She could not follow with her reason."[73] The next lines in the gospel, and in the burial service, turn from the stark beauty of "I am the resurrection and the life" to the relationship between belief and life: "He that believeth in me, though he were dead, yet shall he live: and whosoever liveth and believeth in me shall never die." The passage ends with a question posed directly to the listener: "Believest thou this?"[74] Delia does not hear these words as music; she hears them as an argument put forward. Like Woolf's aunt

Caroline Stephen, who found that the language of the *Book of Common Prayer* generated a "fresh encounter" with "doubts and controversies," Delia listens differently to what she understands to be the language of theological argument than she does to language that is more musical than doctrinal. The portions of the burial service that offer her the most comfort are those that describe the rhythms of life and death in nature.

> "And fade away suddenly like the grass, in the morning it is green, and groweth up; but in the evening it is cut down, dried up, and withered." She could feel the beauty of that. Again it was like music; but then Cousin James seemed to hurry, as if he did not altogether believe what he was saying. He seemed to pass from the known to the unknown; from what he believed to what he did not believe; even his voice altered. He looked clean, he looked starched and ironed like his robes. But what did he mean by what he was saying? She gave it up. Either one understood or one did not understand, she thought.[75]

The passage following the Psalm that speaks of the grass growing and withering is a passage from Paul's first letter to the Corinthians, dense with distinctions between natural bodies and spiritual bodies, the glory of the sun and the glory of the moon. Cousin James speeds up his reading in such passages, ones that are difficult to believe or understand. In the middle of the passage, Paul says to his readers: "Some have not the knowledge of God."[76] Delia seems to take these words to heart: "Either one understood or one did not understand." She places herself among those who do not understand and lets her mind wander.

Certain sentences, certain images continue to capture her attention, though, as when the mourners arrive at the grave and Cousin James reads the graveside prayer: "Then it all began again. The splendid gust of music blew through them—'Man that is born of woman': the ceremony had renewed itself; once more they were grouped; united."[77] Delia has a religious experience that is at once communal and private. She feels bound to the others present by the language of the service, and then she looks down into the grave and is "possessed by a sense of something everlasting; of life mixing with death, of death becoming life." But this apprehension of something real and true is ruined for her in the next moment when Cousin James reads: "'We give thee hearty thanks, for that it has pleased thee to deliver this our sister out of the miseries of this sinful world—' What a lie! she cried to herself. What a damnable lie! He had robbed her of the one feeling that was genuine; he had spoilt her one moment of understanding."[78] For Delia, "in the midst of life we are in death" rings true. But the idea of giving God "hearty thanks" for "delivering" her mother from "this sinful world" rings loudly false. The world, with its natural rhythms, its grass that flourishes and then fades, communicates powerfully to Delia. The words of the prayerbook that seem to condemn the world do not. Delia struggles, as many of Woolf's characters do, with reading that is explicitly religious—the reading of scripture, the reading of the liturgy—because they are unsure whether to hear it as music or as a set of propositions that demand a decision: believest thou this? Delia swings between those two options, arrested by the beauty and truth of some of the language, frustrated by the demands of reason in relation to the more propositional parts.

Her sister Eleanor's religious reading is also marked by a tension between beauty and belief. Eleanor, wanting to understand Christianity, reads, as Woolf did, Renan's *Life of Jesus*, which exposes her to historical-critical problems inherent in scripture: "It was what a man said under a fig tree, on a hill, she thought. And then another man wrote it down. But suppose that what that man says is just as false as what this man—she touched the press cuttings with her spoon—says about Digby?"[79] Such historical-critical problems, though, do not keep Eleanor from feeling "a little spark from what someone said all those years ago." That spark came to her "skipping over all those mountains, all those seas." The current that ignited when someone said, centuries ago, that the "kingdom of Heaven is within us" or "God is love" finds Eleanor in the early twentieth century as she sits reading Renan, trying to discover how Christianity began, "what it meant, originally." Her mind wanders, though, and she cannot "fix her mind on Renan" even though she wants to. But the spark that travels from the man under the fig tree on a hill via words on a page reaches her nevertheless.

As these scenes show, one of the ways Virginia Woolf explored the hidden, unseen part of her characters was to study them as they read or as something is read aloud to them. Scenes of reading in Woolf's novels are very often scenes of religious reading, although of a different sort than Cousin James's reading of the burial service or even Eleanor's reading of Renan. When Edward Pargiter reads *Antigone* in Greek in his room at Oxford, the scene has a monastic feel: Edward has divided his day into hours and half-hours and waits until the moment the Oxford bells finish tolling to begin reading. The text itself is laid out under his lamp "in a sharp circle of bright light from the surrounding dimness." He is beset by doubts before he begins, including, in an ugly flash of anti-Semitism, his sense of intellectual competition with "the clever little Jew-boy from Birmingham."[80]

As he reads, everything else falls away. "All sounds were blotted out. He saw nothing but the Greek in front of him." Meaning reveals itself in bits and pieces until it is there before him, "clean and entire." After he raises his eyes from the book, his mind continues to move "without impediments through a world of pure meaning"[81] for a few moments. But the meaning gradually recedes and his room comes back into focus along with the sound of the bells.

When he turns to *Antigone* again, he brings a glass of wine with him. This time, the wine "seemed to press open little dividing doors in his brain."[82] He conjures from his reading an Antigone who looks very like his cousin Kitty, with whom he is in love. Thoughts about Kitty pull him from the book. Reading awakens Edward, focuses his mind, draws him away from himself and quiets his hateful prejudices. But he cannot stay there, where meaning is encountered "clean and entire." Reading's revelations are temporary.

Later in the novel, other characters have their reading interrupted by their own anti-Semitism. North recites Andrew Marvell's "The Garden" aloud to Sara, the only poem he knows by heart. The words sound beautiful to him in the darkness and seem "like actual presences, hard and independent," and they change as they make contact with Sara, listening. North and Sara seem drawn together for a moment, held in space made sacred by Marvell's words. But then the sound of one of Sara's neighbors running a bath intrudes, and they begin a long, hateful conversation about "the Jew" in the bath. "Damn the Jew!" North exclaims.[83] Sara and North had seemed on the verge of a revelation. But as soon as the bath water begins to run, their worst, meanest tendencies emerge. Some readers have seen this passage as a reflection of Woolf's own anti-Semitism; others have argued that Woolf was shining a light on British anti-Semitism so that it could be analyzed and resisted.[84] There is no question that anti-Semitism is part of Woolf's religious inheritance and that being married to a Jewish husband did not dissolve it. Indeed, her letters and diaries show that, whether criticizing or praising Leonard Woolf's family, she never stopped seeing them, as Maren Linett has put it, "as a collection of Jews."[85] But perhaps this passage reflects something more than Woolf's anti-Semitism. Perhaps, as she faced, along with all of Europe, the rise of fascism in 1937, *The Years* became a place for her to ponder the limits of reading, its failures. She had argued in a 1926 essay that reading is a practice that moves human history forward, that it can change us and lead us in new directions.[86] By 1937, perhaps, she was becoming less optimistic about the work reading could do.

Woolf's earlier novels reflected more confidence in the transformative power of reading. Fourteen years earlier, in *Mrs. Dalloway*, Woolf had drawn on monastic images to convey the power of a kind of religious reading. As Jane Marcus has shown, Clarissa Dalloway likely gets her name from the Clarissans, a group of Third Order Franciscan women about whom Woolf would have read both in her grandfather's *Essays in Ecclesiastical Biography* and her aunt's history of religious communities of women, *The Service of the Poor*. The Clarissans were married women who entered into vows of celibacy with their husbands. They were, as Marcus called them, "secret nuns," living a monastic life at home.[87]

Taking its structure from the chiming of Big Ben and St. Margaret's, the novel makes use of the liturgical hours of the monastic Divine Office—indeed, *The Hours* was her working title for the book.[88] The scope of time in the novel is, famously, one day in June after the end of the First World War. But within that day, Woolf stretches time like taffy and, suddenly, the scope of the novel becomes vast. Some sentences, like this one describing the singing of an old woman outside a Tube station, begin in prehistory and finish with the end of all things.

> Through all ages—when the pavement was grass, when it was swamp, through the age of tusk and mammoth, through the age of silent sunrise, the battered woman—for she wore a skirt—with her right hand exposed, her left clutching at her side, stood singing of love—love which has lasted a million years, she sang, love which prevails, and millions of years ago, her lover, who had been dead these centuries, had walked, she crooned, with her in May; but in the course of ages, long as summer days, and flaming, she remembered, with nothing but red asters, he had gone; death's enormous sickle had swept those tremendous hills, and when at last she laid her hoary and immensely aged head on the earth, now become a mere cinder of ice, she implored the Gods to lay by her side a bunch of purple heather, there on her high burial place which the last rays of the last sun caressed; for then the pageant of the universe would be over.[89]

The hours of monastic time also acknowledge time's elasticity and seek, in their rhythms and repetitions, a place to stand within time's flow. As the moments pass, the hours of the Divine Office render them sacred. As a form, the liturgical hours fit the novel perfectly.

Clarissa's day begins with the "freshness and stillness" of Lauds, the dawn office, the hour of resurrection.[90] In the first pages of the novel, nature, London, and Clarissa herself return to life. Attentive to the "waves of that divine vitality"—what the twelfth-century visionary writer Hildegard of Bingen called *viriditas*[91]—Clarissa loves life with "an absurd and faithful passion" and offers her praise to "life; London; this moment of June."

The next hour, Prime, is devoted to the "dedication of and preparation for the day's labors and conflicts."[92] As Clarissa prepares for her party, people in the neighborhood are drawn together for a moment by a "violent explosion," the sound of a car backfiring or its tire exploding. The car, which might be carrying the prime minister through the streets, connects Clarissa for a moment to Septimus Warren Smith, who also sees the car. Having experienced in the war how dangerous those who possess such power can be, Septimus feels fearful: "The world has raised its whip; where will it descend?" The power wielded by the unknown authority figure is "the spirit of religion . . . with her eyes bandaged tight and her lips gaping wide," drawing the crowd together around a mystery, veiled by the drawn blinds at the car's window. Here, again, Woolf stretches time as far as it can go. It is only, she writes, "when London is a grass-grown path and all those hurrying along the pavement this Wednesday morning are but bones with a few wedding rings mixed up in their dust and the gold stoppings of innumerable decayed teeth" that the identity of the person in the car will be revealed.[93]

Clarissa stands with the flowers for the party in her arms wearing "a look of extreme dignity," imagining it is the queen in the car, off to do some good work. She imagines a party that evening at Buckingham Palace and remembers her own party. "She would stand at the top of her stairs" and make her offering. At Prime, she feels her party consecrated by the unknown authority figure in the car, an authority who inspires citizens to follow its power, "if need be, to the cannon's mouth."[94] By the end of the day, she will understand her party to have been consecrated instead by the death of a shell-shocked veteran.

Next come the three "little hours": Terce, Sext, and None. At the midmorning hour of Terce, which recalls the descent of the Holy Spirit at Pentecost, Clarissa remembers the "revelation, the religious feeling" of kissing her friend Sally Seton when they were young.[95] At Sext, the noon office commemorating the crucifixion of Jesus, Septimus Warren Smith faces the forces of hell at his appointment with Sir William Bradshaw, that "obscurely evil" forcer of souls, who prescribes for Septimus the same enervating rest cure that Woolf had endured. At None, the afternoon office that emphasizes perseverance in the last days, Clarissa perseveres in making the offering of her party in the face of criticism from Peter, her friend, and Richard, her husband. The men cannot understand what she is doing. "She could not imagine Peter or Richard taking the trouble to give a party for no reason whatever," she thinks. Her party is "an offering for the sake of offering . . . it was her gift."[96]

Vespers, the first evening hour of the Divine Office, recalls both the evening offering of Psalm 141:2—"Let my prayer be set before thee as incense; and the lifting up of my hands as the evening sacrifice"—and the Passover meal Jesus shared with his disciples the night before his death. Clarissa's vespers begins with the offering of her party. She is herself the sacrifice, standing on the threshold, "drenched in fire"[97] until it becomes clear that the party will succeed, will resolve itself into "something now, not nothing," an event in which it would be "possible to go much deeper." It closes with Clarissa learning of Septimus's death from Lady Bradshaw.[98] Septimus has made his own offering—"I'll give it you!"[99] he cries as he throws himself out of the window.

During the second evening hour of Compline, Clarissa steps away from her party and enters an empty room to receive Septimus's offering and examine her own life in its shadow. She feels his death in her own body: the spikes of the fence, the thudding in his brain, the suffocating blackness. He had preserved the thing "that mattered," she thinks, the thing that she too often "let drop every day in corruption, lies, chatter." She feels her own "awful fear" about life and shame at her desire for success, "Lady Bexborough and the rest of it." She feels her deep love of life itself. She feels, finally, "somehow very like him—the young man who had killed himself."[100]

In the midst of these meditations, as the clock strikes 3:00 a.m., Clarissa looks out the window at the "solemn sky" and notices the old woman who lives across the way staring straight at her, another nun at home, just finishing her night vigil: Matins, the first liturgical hour of the new day. Clarissa gathers herself and returns to the party, transformed, her presence intensified. So powerful has been Clarissa's experience of Septimus's death that Peter can feel it when she returns to the party:

> What is this terror? what is this ecstasy? he thought to himself. What is it that fills me with extraordinary excitement?
>
> It is Clarissa, he said.
>
> For there she was.[101]

Within the structure of monastic time, Woolf consecrates a spirituality of praise and wonder, sexual desire between women, a critique of war and male dominance, attention to solitude in the midst of community and death in the midst of life. Woolf reinforces the structure of monastic time that shapes the novel by attaching monastic language to Clarissa. She is "like a nun withdrawing"; virginity clings to her.[102] As in all of her books, Woolf gives close attention to the hidden "treasure" each person carries within, our "unseen part." Clarissa's unseen part is often described as a "diamond," recalling the diamond castle at the heart of each person that sixteenth-century monastic reformer Teresa of Avila describes in her *Interior Castle*,[103] a text that is both theological anthropology and manual of spiritual instruction. Addressed to the nuns in Teresa's care, *Interior Castle* offers an itinerary into the interior space of the self, the place where God dwells. Woolf would have encountered Teresa of Avila in the prologue to George Eliot's *Middlemarch*, where she is lifted up as an exemplar of the epic life for which Dorothea Brooke longs. She might also have heard about Teresa from her aunt, Caroline Emelia Stephen, and also possibly from her lover, Vita Sackville-West, who would, after Woolf's death, write about Teresa of Avila in *The Eagle and the Dove*.[104]

Woolf uses the image of the diamond to describe the kiss between Clarissa and Sally, an essential dimension of Clarissa's unseen part, her secret self. When Sally kisses her, Clarissa feels "she had been given a present, wrapped up, and told just to keep it, not to look at it—a diamond, something infinitely precious, wrapped up."[105] But this diamond is so radiant with revelation and religious feeling that it burns through its wrapping. Woolf also uses the image of the diamond to describe the self that Clarissa draws together in order to be present to the world: "One centre, one diamond, one woman who sat in her drawing-room and made a meeting-point, a radiancy no doubt in some dull lives, a refuge for the lonely to come to, perhaps."[106]

As she limns the unseen dimensions of Mrs. Dalloway, Woolf refuses to sum her up as one thing or another. Clarissa is middle-aged, but her youth is still very present to her. She is connected to others yet she is also alone. She loves the hum of life in London, and she is attuned to the silence beneath it. "She sliced like a knife through everything," Woolf writes, and "at the same time was outside, looking on."[107]

As Clarissa herself recognizes as she thinks about Septimus Warren Smith's death, "she was never wholly admirable." Mrs. Dalloway "could not think, write, even play the piano. She muddled Armenians and

Turks; loved success; hated discomfort; must be liked; talked oceans of nonsense: and to this day, ask her what the Equator was, and she did not know."[108] She is a snob who does not want to invite lonely Ellie Henderson to her party. But she also "feels the existence of others" and longs to bring them together. She is a mystic who is able to "plunge into the heart of the moment" without hesitation or effort, and her life is punctuated by revelation. Practicing what Peter Walsh calls her "atheist's religion,"[109] she seems far more available to the mystery at the heart of things than the fiercely religious Doris Kilman, whose approach to God was "so rough." But Clarissa is aware enough to know that Doris Kilman's spirituality must struggle to take root amid her insecurity and the daily humiliations of her poverty, whereas Clarissa can depend on her servants for the space and time to cultivate her attention to "life; London; this moment of June." Mrs. Dalloway does not waste her great good fortune. Having come through an illness that has weakened her heart, she attends to each moment as it passes and tries not to miss a thing. Woolf writes that Clarissa "would not say of herself, I am this, I am that."[110] Like a text prayed over and meditated on in *lectio divina*, many things are true of her at once.

Within the structure of monastic time in *Mrs. Dalloway*, Woolf explored religious reading. Early in the novel, soon after Clarissa steps out into the humming green morning to buy flowers for her party, she pauses in front of Hatchards bookshop. During this hour of Lauds, she finds a book "spread open" in the window like a sacred text or a scroll. In its open pages, she reads: "Fear no more the heat o' the sun / Nor the furious winter's rages." Shakespeare's song about the inevitability of death from *Cymbeline* (IV.2) will be Clarissa's text for *lectio divina*. Like a monastic reader, she meditates on it throughout the day, repeating it over and over in her mind until her body begins to pray it on its own.

Unlike a monastic reader, though, for whom sacred texts are easily identifiable, Mrs. Dalloway is confronted with multiple texts "spread open" like Bibles in the window of Hatchards: Jorrocks's *Jaunts and Jollities*, *Soapy Sponge*, Mrs. Asquith's *Memoirs* and *Big Game Shooting in Nigeria*, titles intent on distracting from "the sadness at the back of life" that Woolf admired in the Greeks. Shakespeare's words, on the other hand, give rise to this thought: "This late age of the world's experience had bred in them all, all men and women, a well of tears."[111] In two lines, Shakespeare has brought to the surface of Mrs. Dalloway's mind what her society has tried very hard to repress with books like *Jaunts and Jollities*: the fact of the war, only recently ended, and the losses embodied by the shell-shocked and broken Septimus Warren Smith. Clarissa recognizes these lines from *Cymbeline* as the sacred text in Hatchards's window and repeats them as she walks toward Bond Street.

We next see her repeating Shakespeare's words—"Fear no more the heat o' the sun, Nor the furious winter's rages"—when she returns home and finds that Lady Bruton has invited Clarissa's husband, Richard Dalloway, to lunch without her. The exclusion sounds the note of sexual failure that reverberates within her marriage. Not to have been invited makes her feel the dwindling of her life, the shrinking number of moments that will be available to her. She feels "suddenly shriveled, aged, breastless," unable to absorb "as in the youthful years, the colours, salts, tones of existence" and fill a room with her presence. Rocking and shivering, she repeats Shakespeare's words to steady herself: "'Fear no more,' said Clarissa. Fear no more the heat o' the sun."[112] The reverie this phrase undergirds eventually leads her away from thoughts of age and sexual disappointment to a meditation on the revelatory sexual feelings that she experiences with women and to her memory of Sally Seton's kiss. Such experiences bring her to the threshold of a revelation. They are "an illumination; a match burning in a crocus; an inner meaning almost expressed."[113]

We next hear Shakespeare's words during a contemplative moment in the novel, as Clarissa sits quietly mending her green dress for the party. The rhythm of her needle matches the rhythm of the words, and it is her heart that repeats them, not her conscious mind: "*Fear no more*, says the heart. *Fear no more*, says the heart, committing its burden to some sea, which sighs collectively for all sorrows, and renews, begins, collects, lets fall. And the body alone listens to the passing bee; the wave breaking; the dog barking, far away barking and barking."[114] Donald J. Childs has shown how this scene echoes Matthew Arnold's "the waves draw back and fling / . . . and bring the eternal note of sadness in" from "Dover Beach."[115] But it also echoes Woolf's memories of hearing the waves breaking from her childhood bed at St. Ives and "feeling," as she will write in her memoir, "the purest ecstasy I can conceive."[116] Even as Arnold's sea of faith recedes, the possibility of ecstasy remains. As her heart takes up the practice of *lectio divina*, the words gather up more than Clarissa's anxieties. The heart "sighs collectively for all sorrows," not just Clarissa's own, and prepares her for the ecstatic identification that she will feel with Septimus Warren Smith later in the novel.

The next time Shakespeare's text appears in the novel, it is Septimus's heart that is praying it. Lying on the sofa in his apartment, watching the light and shadow change the colors of the walls and the objects in the room, Septimus hears the same sounds Mrs. Dalloway hears as she mends her dress: the waves, the dogs "barking and barking far away." As if connected to Clarissa by an invisible thread winding through the streets of London, his heart also begins to repeat Shakespeare's words: "Fear no more, says the heart in the body; fear no more."[117] For a few moments, Septimus and his wife, Rezia, enjoy gossiping about the neighbors and making a hat together. It will be the last moment of ordinary happiness they enjoy.

When we encounter Shakespeare's words for the last time in the novel, we are back in Clarissa's house. Although he is a stranger to her, she feels the violation of Septimus's soul by his doctors in her own soul, feels the violence of his death in her own body. Although they are unknown to one another, she honors his death as she stands alone in an empty room while the sounds of her party, her offering, echo through her house. As the clock strikes for the last time, Clarissa watches the solitary woman across the way getting ready to go to bed. When the woman turns out her light, Shakespeare's words come to Mrs. Dalloway one last time: Fear no more the heat of the sun. In that moment, she identifies with Septimus and feels grateful to him: "He made her feel the beauty; made her feel the fun." Like Dionysius, who died and rose again within the community as the god of wine and festival, Septimus illuminates all she has to live for.

Septimus and Clarissa are connected through their shared *lectio*, just as monks who pray the psalms each day pray with all those who have ever prayed them. With that thread pulled taut between them, Clarissa can "assemble" herself, return to the party, wholly alive, wholly herself.

Septimus will never suffer, or fear, again. Clarissa, choosing to go on living, inevitably will. The practice of *lectio divina* opens to her what is unknowable—the life of another—just as it did for the monks for whom it was the first rung on a ladder to God. But it also has its limits. Her mystical encounter cannot save Septimus. When, earlier in the novel, Peter Walsh had seen Septimus and Rezia in the park and believed them to be arguing, he wished Clarissa were there to speak to them. That missed opportunity creates a terrible absence in the novel, one that echoes down to the last word of the last page.

In *To the Lighthouse*, published two years after *Mrs. Dalloway*, another woman makes an offering to life through gathering people together and helping them move beyond their separate selves toward being a community that makes "their common cause against that fluidity out there."[118] With her dinner party, Mrs. Ramsay brings her guests together in a moment of being in which "anything might happen," and they sit together in "the still space that lies about the heart of things, where one could move or rest."[119]

Scenes of reading circulate around the account of Mrs. Ramsay's dinner party, from Mrs. Ramsay reading the fairy tale "The Fisherman and His Wife" to her young son in the opening of the novel, to Mr. Ramsay's sudden recitations of poetry that startle his guests, to Mr. Carmichael lying awake reading Virgil in the darkness that deepens into the years of the First World War. One particular scene at the end of the dinner party describes a form of religious reading.

After the dinner party, when the children have gone to their rooms and the guests have scattered, Mr. and Mrs. Ramsay sit together and read. Mr. Ramsay reads a novel by Sir Walter Scott while Mrs. Ramsay reads poetry: Charles Isaac Elton's "Luriana, Lurilee," William Browne's "Sirens' Song," and Shakespeare's "Sonnet 98." As Mrs. Ramsay knows, Mr. Ramsay has chosen Scott because Charles Tansley, a young acolyte of Mr. Ramsay's, had said at dinner that nobody reads Scott any more. Tansley's comment had pricked Mr. Ramsay's own anxieties about whether or not his own books would continue to be read after his death and so he has picked up his beloved Scott to comfort himself with a few passages. Reading Scott fills him with vigor and delight. Mr. Ramsay fortifies himself with Scott's story; it smooths off the rough edges of his anxieties and frustrations. He acts the part of one of the characters, "tossing the pages over." Scott's novel makes him "feel so vigorous, so relieved of something that he felt roused and triumphant and could not choke back his tears." For a moment Mr. Ramsay transcends himself: he forgets his worries, his anxieties, and even himself in the wake of the pleasure reading Scott gives him. But he soon returns to himself, sorting out in his mind what is "fiddlesticks" and what is "first-rate" in the novel and feeling "that he had been arguing with somebody, and had got the better of him."[120]

The dinner party has drained Mrs. Ramsay of energy. "The whole of the effort of merging and flowing and creating," Woolf writes, "rested on her."[121] She joins her husband in a room to read because she wants "something more."[122] As Mr. Ramsay tosses over the pages of his book, Mrs. Ramsay grows still "like a tree which has been tossing and quivering and now, when the breeze falls, settles, leaf by leaf, into quiet."[123] She closes her eyes and lets a line from "Luriana, Lurilee," which her husband and Mr. Carmichael had recited toward the end of dinner, rise into her mind, the words lighting up in color and washing around inside her like water. She picks up a book to read a few lines with a sense that she is climbing, "shoving her way up under petals that curved over her."[124] Just as a book can serve as an oratory for a religious reader, nature often functions as sacred space in Woolf's novels. Here, Mrs. Ramsay enters the natural world through the pages of a book, to which she responds like an insect in a field of flowers or an animal in the branches of a tree. Woolf herself read poetry in this way. She wrote longingly in her diary in 1921, when her doctors limited her work and exercise, of wishing for a good long walk, followed by "some bout of poetry after dinner, half read, half lived, as if the flesh were dissolved and through it the flowers burst red and white."[125]

Sounding again like Vanessa Bell responding to Picasso's abstract forms, Woolf writes that Mrs. Ramsay "did not know at first what the words meant at all." She is led into the poem by its colors. She climbs it like a tree, "swinging herself, zigzagging this way and that, from one line to another as from one branch to another" until finally, as Woolf writes, "there it was, suddenly entire; she held it in her hands, beautiful and reasonable, clear and complete, the essence sucked out of life and held rounded here—the sonnet."[126] Mrs. Ramsay has not read her way to a summation of existence or an answer to every question, but she has experienced a "moment of being," a glimpse of the real beneath appearances. Mrs. Ramsay's ability to apprehend the essence of life in a sonnet is the same ability that allows her to see in a collection of people more than their individual selves, to see who they might become when they are drawn together in community.

Woolf once wrote that the best time to read poetry is "when we are almost able to write it."[127] Mrs. Ramsay has realized her vision for her dinner party—she has created her masterpiece—and now she is so ready for poetry that she inhabits it like an animal in a tree. Reading and writing move fluidly in both directions for Woolf, one leading to the other and back again, both creative acts.

In 1931, Woolf explored the political dimensions of the relationship between reading and writing in an introduction she wrote for a book edited by her friend Margaret Llewelyn Davies and published by the Hogarth Press. Characterized by Kate Flint as one of Woolf's "most sustained and impassioned pieces of radical writing," Woolf describes the effect Davies's volume has had on her.[128] Called *Life as We Have Known It*, Davies's book collected the writing of members of the Women's Co-operative Guild, for which she served as general secretary for two decades. These accounts offered portraits of women who worked, raised families, and participated in radical social movements for the rights of workers and women. In her introduction, Woolf seems particularly struck by the power of reading in the lives of women who barely had a moment to read: they read as they cooked and while they ate; they read in the night when they might have been sleeping instead. "Naturally," Woolf wrote, "such reading led to argument" and to debates on factory floors.[129] For these women, reading was not just a stolen pleasure; reading helped them see more clearly the unjust systems in which they were enmeshed and wrought transformations inside of them that made a difference not only in their own lives, but in the lives of others and in the communities in which they lived and worked.

For the women in Davies's book, reading led not only to debates on the factory floor but to writing, a "work of labour and difficulty . . .

done in kitchens, at odds and ends of leisure, in the midst of distractions and obstacles."[130] Woolf lifts up some of the writers whose pieces in the volume most powerfully affected her: the felt-hat worker who lovingly described the life of the moors, a worker's precise and graceful observations of the matchbox factory where she worked, the woman who recalled the stranger who invited her and other children coming home from a long day of working in the fields to eat their supper inside her house rather than under a hedge. But the account that arrests Woolf the most, the one she wants her readers to be sure not to miss, is a portion of a letter that an office worker for the Women's Co-operative Guild, Harriet A. Kidd, described by Davies as a woman who "never spared herself in battling for the rights of women and labour," wrote to Davies before taking up the job Davies had offered her. "The writing of this letter is one of, nay, it *is*, the hardest task I have ever been called on to perform during the whole of my life," Harriet Kidd wrote, before describing, with tremendous dignity, how, as a seventeen-year-old girl, she had been lured to her employer's home and raped by him. "At eighteen," Miss Kidd wrote, fearing she would be condemned and rejected, "I was a mother."[131]

Woolf listens, and asks her readers to listen, as Harriet Kidd's voice emerges from silence and obscurity. For Woolf, Harriet Kidd's letter "explains much and reveals much" about a woman Davies describes as so angry about the exploitation of workers that she "was not an easy person to live or work with."[132] Having read her letter, Woolf can imagine more clearly the hidden dimensions of Harriet Kidd's life: "Such then was the burden that rested on that somber figure as she sat typing your letters, such were the memories she brooded as she guarded your door with her grim and indomitable fidelity."[133] By retelling Harriet Kidd's story, a woman Woolf knew and yet did not know, Woolf focuses her readers' attention not only on the hidden sorrows those around us carry but also the ways in which writing can erode the boundaries that keep us from knowing one another and caring about what has happened to each other. Harriet Kidd, Davies reported, "had been a great reader and writer, often after work at the mill spending the whole night reading in bed."[134] In Miss Kidd's life, in the lives of the other women who contributed to Davies's volume, and in Woolf's own life, reading and writing flowed into one another and undergirded political engagement.

Reading and writing were, for Woolf, political and mystical at once, practices with the power to reshape the interior life of the reader and writer as well as the life of the world around them, practices that could dissolve, for a moment, the boundaries between ourselves and others, between ourselves and the world. If Woolf cultivated a modern form of *lectio divina* in which readers and writers cooperate in the creation of the text and through which the "common mind" that threads through time and space is illuminated, it cannot be separated from a kind of *scriptio divina*, the discovery, exploration, and clarification, through writing, of the hidden connections that are the scaffolding of the real.[135]

This mystical understanding of the practice of writing can be found in the medieval European mystical writing that echoes in Woolf's work, especially in the writing of women. Because their authority to write at all was in question, women frequently grounded their authorial claims in accounts of mystical experience and often gave extended accounts of how and why they wrote. One such writer, Marguerite d'Oingt (d. 1310) explicitly linked her experience of writing to the practice of *lectio divina*. Reading her account of the development of her vocation as a writer next to Woolf's helps illuminate the mystical dimension of writing for Woolf (and the literary dimension of writing for Marguerite).[136]

Like Guigo II, Marguerite was a member of the Carthusian order whose spiritual life took shape around the practices of reading, prayer, and the copying of manuscripts. In her *Page of Meditations*, she describes her ascent of Guigo's ladder of monks, beginning with hearing a scriptural text read aloud in the liturgy, meditating on it by using other parts of the Bible to interpret it, and through these meditations being drawn to prayer. Her prayer culminates, as Guigo's ladder of monks does, with contemplation, an experience of God's presence. Guigo's highest rung is not the end for Marguerite, however. Experiencing God as an author who writes on her heart, she finds herself stuck at the top of the ladder, overwhelmed by God's writing. "I was so full of these thoughts," she writes, "that I lost my appetite and my sleep. And I thought that I would either die or languish if I did not remove these thoughts from my heart."[137] Marguerite's solution to this dilemma is to write, which both heals her and gives her a new text for *lectio divina*, one she would be able to meditate on "little by little." She writes what comes "into my innermost self in order" as her pen moves across the page and "assemble[s] everything" that will increase her love for God.[138]

In "A Sketch of the Past," Woolf describes being similarly wounded—not by God writing on her heart, but by the "sudden shocks" of existence that came to her in childhood with "sledge-hammer force" and in adulthood as "a revelation of some order . . . a token of some real thing behind appearances." Like Marguerite d'Oingt, she survives these experiences through writing: "I make it real by putting it into words. It is only by putting it into words that I make it whole; this wholeness means that it has lost its power to hurt me; it gives me, perhaps because by doing so I take away the pain, a great delight to put the severed parts together. Perhaps this is the strongest pleasure known to me. It is the rapture I get when in writing I seem to be discovering what belongs to what; making a scene come right; making a character come together."[139] This mystical understanding of writing as a way to experience reality carries with it, for Woolf, a political demand as well. Because of her bedrock sense that "there is a pattern hid behind the cotton wool" of daily life, and because, through writing, she apprehends that pattern and makes it real, she feels she must write. She considers the fact that other work might seem more useful "if war comes." But her conviction is strong: "I feel that by writing I am doing what is far more necessary than anything else."[140]

In her novels, many of Woolf's characters have some practice that illuminates the hidden connections between things and gives them a glimpse of the real beneath appearances. Rachel Vinrace has music, Katharine Hilbery has mathematics, Lily Briscoe has painting, Mrs. Dalloway and Mrs. Ramsay their parties. Edward Pargiter, whose knowledge is otherwise sealed up inside him, his nephew North complains, has translation.[141] Orlando, like Woolf, has reading and writing, and moves between them, picking up Sir Thomas Browne and reading for an hour, putting the book down to write poetry, turning back to the "divine melody" of Sir Thomas Browne's prose again.[142]

In *The Waves*, Woolf leaves her readers some directions about cultivating just such a practice. Julia Briggs has noted that Woolf put instructions for reading this demanding novel into the text itself.[143]

> Certainly, one cannot read this poem without effort. The page is often corrupt and mud-stained, and torn and stuck together with faded leaves, with scraps of verbena or geranium. To read this poem one must have myriad eyes. . . . One must put aside antipathies and jealousies and not interrupt. One must have patience and infinite care and let the light sound, whether of spiders' delicate feet on a leaf or the chuckle of water in some irrelevant drain-pipe, unfold too. Nothing is to be rejected in fear or horror. . . . One must be sceptical, but throw caution to the winds and when the door opens accept absolutely. Also sometimes weep; also cut away ruthlessly with a slice of the blade soot, bark, hard accretions of all sorts. And so (while they talk) let down one's net deeper and deeper and gently draw in and bring to the surface what he said and she said and make poetry.[144]

Woolf commends here a practice of reading that requires patience, attention, and effort, a way of reading with "myriad eyes" that sees the fragments from which the text is made and resists reducing it to one meaning. Woolf urges us to let the world in as we read, to question, and also to accept. She encourages us to peel away the accretions that stand between us and "the thing itself." We are to go deeper, and then even deeper. And like the common reader to whom she addressed herself, we are to make something new out of what we bring to the surface.

Briggs notes that these instructions not only teach us how to read *The Waves* but also describe how Woolf wrote it. But although the form of *The Waves* was unique, Woolf followed these instructions, to some extent, in everything she wrote. Woolf takes care to help us hear the "chuckling and burbling noise in the gutters"[145] in her novels; she works to see all the way around her characters as if she had "fifty pairs of eyes."[146] Like the fishermen Jesus instructs, in the gospel of Luke, to "launch out into the deep, and let down your nets," she sends her nets deeper and deeper, into the hidden places in her characters, bringing to the surface things that may seem incongruous, but out of which she makes poetry.[147] Her reading and her writing are both skeptical and open, ruthless and generous. As they do for religious readers of many times and places, reading and writing flow into and out of one another, illuminating what is hidden and finding ways to breach the boundaries of the real.

4

"STILL DENSER DEPTHS OF DARKNESS"

VIRGINIA WOOLF AND GOD

In the Stephen household, the phrase "There is no God" served as shorthand for the family's intellectual commitments. Woolf's older brother, Thoby, inscribed it in a book he gave to her as a gift when they were in their mid-twenties.[1] She used the phrase at the end of *To the Lighthouse* to describe James Ramsay's view of his father, who "rose and stood in the bow of the boat, very straight and tall, for all the world, James thought, as if he were saying, 'There is no God.'"[2] And when Woolf wrote her credo toward the end of her life, she intensified what Hermione Lee has called the "family message": "certainly and emphatically," she wrote, "there is no God."[3]

Despite, or perhaps because of, the pervasiveness of the family message, the idea of God preoccupied Woolf during her childhood. "I dreamt one night that I was God," she wrote at thirteen in the *Hyde Park Gate News*, a newspaper produced for their family by Virginia and her siblings.[4]

> The whole world was at my disposal and the whole of mankind. With one stroke of my hand, worlds would shiver and

> break, and with another worlds would spring from the air. I was a man alone playing with Time. People were my toys and the world was my playground. People scheming below, trying to dissect life and death and knowing nothing. There was no Heaven and no Hell. Heaven is held out as a kind of sugar-plum after medicine, Hell as a scourge if you rebel. I created several worlds in order to see which one was best. In one people were only born once in a hundred years, and they only died once in a hundred years, and their births and deaths were felt all over the world. The people lived as one great familly [*sic*]. But were they real? And what was I? Why did I exist? Who made me? and who was my maker? Was everything a dream, but who were the dreamers? So I wondered in my dream, and the only solution I could find was by waking, and finding my self a person.[5]

Both Virginia Stephen's precociousness and her father's influence are on display here. The God of this account is marked by what Leslie Stephen viewed as the immoral capriciousness of the God of the Bible and the manipulative use of the idea of heaven and hell by the church. Years later, in *To the Lighthouse*, the God of Virginia Stephen's dream, for whom the world was a playground, would reappear in Nancy Ramsay's own playful capriciousness as she blocked the sun over a tide pool with her hand, bringing "darkness and desolation, like God himself."[6]

The God of Virginia's dream, however, seems more interested in experimentation and self-reflection than Leslie Stephen's fickle deity. Her God asks the same questions that characters in her novels will later pose: What am I? Why do I exist? It is also clear that, months before the steady toll of family deaths would begin with the death of her mother, Virginia was already pondering death and grief. As the God of her dream, she asked: What kind of world would do justice to the gravity of birth and death and minimize the pain of loss? Her God "created several worlds in order to see which one is best." What if births and deaths happened only once in a hundred years? Would that allow the world's people to live "as one great familly" within which each birth and death would be keenly felt? With this bit of theological speculation, Virginia was perhaps searching for ways to withstand the overwhelming feelings she would later describe welling up in Nancy Ramsay as she played God on the beach. Nancy found herself immobilized "by the intensity of the feelings which reduced her own body, her own life, and the lives of all the people in the world, for ever, to nothingness."[7]

While Woolf left Nancy Ramsay brooding silently over the world of the tidepool, Virginia Stephen kept asking questions. What is real? Human beings? A divine creator? Why would there be a God, and where would that God have come from? Is the world only a dream? If so, who are the dreamers? Her father often made a distinction between dreams and reality as a way of distinguishing agnostics, who recognized and accepted the truth about the world, from religious people who obscured reality with dreams. Leslie Stephen's essay "Dreams and Realities" had been published in his collection, *An Agnostic's Apology*, two years before his daughter published an account of her dream in the family newspaper. Echoing her father, Woolf often invoked "dreams and realities" in her essays and used the phrase as the working title of her second novel, which was eventually called *Night and Day*. In the account of her dream in the *Hyde Park Gate News*, she played with, and resisted, her father's distinction—in this instance, by imagining that reality might itself be a dream. But the solution she offered to her list of questions—to wake up and see herself as a human being—must have pleased him.

A few years later, as we have already seen, Woolf began writing the "long picturesque essay upon the Christian religion" she called "Religio Laici." Writing in the style of the Elizabethan prose writers she adored, she argued that "man has need of a God"—a bold stance against the family creed. Her God was not the same as the unchanging deity of her Clapham ancestors; the God of "Religio Laici," she recalled in her diary, was a God "in process of change."[8] Virginia Stephen's idea of God bears a striking resemblance to the ideas of the philosopher Alfred North Whitehead, on whose work process theology—with its understanding of God as affected by what happens in the world—would be built.[9] Virginia Stephen expressed her idea of a God who changes almost thirty years before Whitehead began exploring the theological implications of his view of reality in his 1925 Lowell Lectures at Harvard. During the time she was writing about a God "in process of change," Whitehead, a fellow of Trinity College and a Cambridge Apostle, was working on his foundational studies in mathematics.

Like other Cambridge Apostles and fellows of Trinity, Whitehead and his work were known by the Bloomsbury Group, but Bloomsbury did not revere him as it did G. E. Moore. As Leonard Woolf remarked in a letter to Whitehead's biographer, Victor Lowe, he and his friends respected the work Whitehead had done with Bertrand Russell in *Principia Mathematica*, but they felt that "he went much too 'religious' in his later books."[10] And there was no love lost between Virginia Woolf and Whitehead's wife, Evelyn, who had been scandalized by Virginia's and Vanessa's Gauguin-inspired dresses at the Post-Impressionist Ball in 1910.[11] Woolf gave her the Puritan-inflected moniker "the Widow Whitehead" in her letters and named the invalid Evelyn Whitbread in *Mrs. Dalloway* after her. Woolf does not record any thoughts about Whitehead in her diaries or letters, and none of his books are mentioned in her reading notebooks. She did not socialize with him as she did with G. E. Moore and Bertrand Russell, whose books she did read. But some of his ideas about reality resonated with hers. The understanding of God that evolved from those ideas, so different from the God Leslie Stephen had rejected, was part of the religion around her as well.[12]

Ideas, arguments, and conversations about God wound through Woolf's childhood. Long conversations with her aunt Caroline Stephen, contentious debates with her cousin Dorothea, lively discussions with her siblings, and the pervasive influence of her parents' agnosticism all left their mark on Woolf's ideas about God, as did the books she read and reread, like Sir Thomas Browne's *Religio medici* and Walter Pater's *Marius the Epicurean*. In her early twenties, despite not being a "believer" in the traditional sense, she appealed to the idea of God in her letters and diaries. In a letter to her Christian friend Violet Dickinson in 1903, she wrote that "the only reason I have to believe in God is that some life grows in one and outgrows most things," once again connecting the idea of God with her experience of growth and flux and change.[13] God sometimes appears in her early journals as the creative force undergirding her own creativity. Her diary entry from 1906, made at the end of a day of tramping through the West Suffolk countryside with Vanessa, Thoby, and Adrian, described how she felt "the steady beat of the great Creator" as she wrote and imagined the practice of writing as grounded in a pervasive divine creativity, a steady beat she sensed as her pen scratched across the page.[14]

By the time Virginia Stephen becomes Virginia Woolf, she no longer writes of God as a "great Creator" or a "God in the process of change" whose creative power she draws on as she writes. As Barbara K. Olson has noted, Woolf would become "increasingly uncomfortable with using theological analogies for either authorship or narration."[15] She attaches the word God more often to a heavy-handed dispenser of suffering or an impediment to freedom. She comes to see her beloved Sir Thomas Browne, whose ecstatic attention to the seen and the unseen she studied closely, as fenced in by God. God kept him from seeing as far as his imagination might have allowed, she wrote: "So lively a curiosity deserved a better fate."[16] God often appears in her novels and essays as a "brutal old bully," "Milton's bogey," a "malignant torturer."

Because of language like this, atheism is sometimes offered as the key to her novels and the bench from which to judge her characters. Michael Lackey, for example, asserts that Mrs. Ramsay is "defiled" by a theological thought ("We are in the hands of the Lord") that slips into her mind as she sits and follows the beam of the lighthouse,[17] betraying an insistence on purity that Woolf herself resisted. Analysis that sorts her characters into "unbelievers" and "believers" who are either "sympathetic" or "unsympathetic," and whose ideas are either "positive" or "negative," depending on the strength of their expression of atheism, renders Woolf's agnosticism much more like her father's and other prominent agnostics of the time who put their intellectual energies into debunking philosophical arguments for the existence of God. But Woolf's work is not an allegory for logic problems about divinity. Nor did she create characters to illustrate abstract ideas. Analysis that reduces Woolf's writing to an argument and attempts to render Woolf logically consistent and systematic in her agnosticism misses Woolf's curiosity, her sense of humor, her ability to marshal powerful ideas like atheism in the shaping and exploration of a character. Such readings seem more committed to atheism than to understanding Virginia Woolf. "In a world where there is a God," Lackey writes, "there is no room for creative freedom."[18] This would have come as a surprise to Woolf, who loved the poems of Anon, who sings "because he adores some God"[19] and for whom engagement with the art of Perugino, Giotto, and Piero della Francesca was a source for a deeper consideration of her own aspirations as an artist. "We sit in the Italian room at the National Gallery picking up fragments," Bernard says in *The Waves*, looking for a way to assuage his grief over Percival's death, seeking "the influence of minds like mine outside the sequence" and pictures that "do not point" but that "expand my consciousness of him and bring him back to me differently."[20] Religious art, religious ideas, religious texts were some of the fragments with which Woolf worked to stay "outside the sequence" and create an art of new combinations that aroused both thought and love.

In Woolf's fiction, even the most committed atheists have a difficult time keeping their minds free of God and struggle against the incursion of God into their thoughts. In "A Simple Melody," one of eight stories Woolf wrote in the mid-1920s about the people who attended Clarissa Dalloway's party, George Carslake, unable to get into the flow of the gathering, gazes at a landscape painting and imagines how much more naturally he would relate to those around him if they were walking out on the heath together. He imagines what he would come across in such a landscape: a deserted farm, a man and a cart, shepherds, a windmill—sights that "had this power—again he trembled on the silly words,—'to reconcile differences—to make one believe in God.'" The thought of God disrupts his reverie and makes him feel he has been trapped by "the crazy and craven idiocy of such a saying!" He is alarmed by "his mind's instinct, when unguarded, to rise into clouds and Heaven, and rig up the old comfortable figure, the old flowing garments and mild eyes and cloud-like mantle." He resents the coercive power of religious language to shape our understanding of life's simplest pleasures.[21]

As he works to shake himself free of God, Mr. Carslake remains attuned to things unseen. Imagining himself walking on the heath with his fellow partygoers, he sees beyond their anxieties and oddities and finds them all uniquely beautiful. The simple melody of the title is the music that runs beneath everyday life—a melody beyond words that activates the "deep reservoir" hidden within each person, that "rippled it, liquefied it, made it start and turn and quiver in the depths of one's being, so that all the time ideas were rising from this pool and bubbling up into one's brain."[22]

Perhaps because of his compassionate attention to the people around him—"don't worry, my dear Stuart, about your soul, its extreme unlikeness to anyone else's," he thinks as he looks across the room at another guest behaving awkwardly—Mr. Carslake is soon joined by Miss Merewether, "who might easily have drifted off." While they exchange the usual small talk, Woolf opens a window onto their silent thoughts. Miss Merewether thinks how much she likes George Carslake. She imagines him as "a dark horse, a queer fish. There was no saying what he was after."[23] As he imagines walking in companionable silence with her on a heath, she sees him as he really is—dark, hidden, inexpressible: a mystery. Mr. Carslake has driven away thoughts of "the old comfortable figure" of God. But he himself retains these mystical qualities of divinity—indeed, for Miss Mereweather, he embodies them. Fourteen years after writing this story, Woolf would profess in her autobiography that "certainly and emphatically there is no God. We are the words, we are the music, we are the thing itself." George Carslake, with his hidden depths and his unsayable purpose, is that thing.

In *To the Lighthouse*, Woolf gives another account of a character who feels encroached on by thoughts of God that arise unbidden. Mrs. Ramsay sits alone for a moment and imagines her inner life as "a wedge-shaped core of darkness, something invisible to others."[24] As she rests in that darkness, she finds herself thinking, "We are in the hands of the Lord." Resenting this "insincerity slipping in among the truths," Mrs. Ramsay immediately begins scrubbing the thought from her mind, "purifying out of existence that lie." She runs through all the reasons it cannot be true: "Suffering, death, the poor."[25] As she sits with her knitting, contemplating the problem of evil, her husband passes, thinking of a story about the philosopher David Hume, who pondered the very problem with which Mrs. Ramsay is engaged, concluding, as she does, that the reality of evil makes it impossible to believe that a good and powerful God made this world. Mr. Ramsay is not thinking of Hume's exploration of the problem of evil, though; he is remembering an anecdote about Hume in which the philosopher gets stuck in a bog and is required by the woman who pulls him out to recite the Lord's Prayer—a small triumph of materiality over thought. But the sight of Mrs. Ramsay interrupts his amusement over the story. Seeing "the sternness at the heart of her beauty," he feels sad that he is unable to help her. In a moment of self-knowledge, he understands that he had been wrong to lose his temper earlier in the day over the trip to the lighthouse. He often made things worse for her, he knows, with his touchiness. As he stands there, regretting his behavior, he looks into the hedge, "into its intricacy, its darkness."[26]

The dark intricacy of the hedge holds the scene still for a beat. Mr. Ramsay looks into the hedge, as if for answers to the questions crowding the moment: the problem of evil, the problem of the distance between lovers, the problem of his temper, the problem of God. But no answers come back, only intricate darkness. This is where theological language and thought often lead for Woolf: into a complex darkness that silences language. Mr. Ramsay's hedge does not burst forth in hierophanic flame, like Moses's burning bush, or even like Clarissa Dalloway's "match burning in a crocus." It remains still, silent, dark: an embodiment of the darkness where God must be sought in the apophatic English mystical tradition. As the anonymous author of the fourteenth-century *Cloud of Unknowing* writes, "If you are ever to feel or see [God], so far as is possible in this life, it must always be in this cloud and this darkness."[27] This tradition, with its emphasis on the unknowability of God, is also part of Woolf's religious inheritance.

Having been interrupted by the thought of God, Mrs. Ramsay follows the beam of the lighthouse out of her solitude. The light is "steady," "pitiless," "remorseless"; the light is her, and it is not her. Contemplating it, a "mist" lifts "from the lake of her being" like "a bride to meet her lover." The light strokes something in her brain until "the ecstasy burst in her eyes and waves of pure delight raced over the floor of her mind and she felt, It is enough! It is enough!"[28] The thought of God has been effectively banished, replaced with Mrs. Ramsay's ecstatic, erotic experience of life itself—which, like the Song of Songs, the biblical book that Woolf's language echoes, does not need to speak of God. Like Mr. Carslake's simple melody, which activates the "deep reservoir" hidden in each person, allowing ideas—"impossible to analyse"—to rise from it and bubble into the brain, the lighthouse beam floods her mind with pleasure. These are the moments of being that make life worth living. She calls out to her husband and rises to join him, offering him the thing he had longed for but for which he had resolved not to ask: her presence, her companionship, her love. Having reached her own intricate darkness, she is able to reach out, once more, to him.

Woolf explores, from myriad angles, both the idea of God and the space that remains when God disappears, beginning with her first novel, *The Voyage Out*. Here, she approaches the question of God through an account of English people at worship as seen through the eyes of Rachel Vinrace, the young woman at the center of the novel. When asked whether she believes in "a personal God," Rachel responds, "I believe there are things we don't know about, and the world might change in a minute and anything appear."[29] Her atheist aunt Helen dismisses her answer as "nonsense" and suggests that there are other, better questions to ponder than whether one believes in God. But for Rachel, the idea of God leads, not to any particular answers, but toward the mystery and flux of existence itself.

A few chapters later, Rachel attends a worship service in the South American hotel where a group of English people are on holiday. English Christians, Woolf seems to say, can dampen a Sunday anywhere on earth. Even here, in the tropics, Sunday feels like "the mute black ghost or penitent spirit of the busy weekday."[30]

With this unpromising beginning, the tourists descend to an old chapel in the bottom of the hotel. The hotel had once been a monastery, and the monk's chapel has been transformed into a space for Protestant worship, complete with a lectern held up by a brass eagle and a harmonium on which one of the guests "struck emphatic chords with uncertain fingers."[31]

As the assembled congregation begins saying the liturgy together, a peaceful feeling of goodwill—shot through with self-congratulation—arises, only to be interrupted by Psalm 56, read by Mr. Bax, the minister. Calling on God to break the teeth of the psalmist's enemies, the psalm grates against the worshippers—except Susan Lushington, whose mind was so "occupied with praise of her own nature and praise of God" that the strangeness of the psalm cannot break through. As the psalmist curses his enemies, the men in the congregation "felt the inconvenience of the sudden intrusion of this old savage."[32] Far from home, in a hotel on the edge of the rainforest, even the familiar voice of the Bible sounds alien to these Englishmen. The assembled worshipers do not find the "sad and beautiful figure of Christ" who speaks in the reading from the New Testament any more comprehensible than the figure they conjure from the psalm, and they struggle to "fit his interpretation of life upon the lives they lived."[33] In the end, they adapt Christ's words in vastly different ways and let those words represent goodness for them in some vague sense.

But not Rachel. Her senses heightened by the unfamiliar surroundings and by having fallen in love, she, "for the first time in her life . . . listened critically to what was being said."[34] As she listens, she becomes more and more uncomfortable, as "when forced to sit through an unsatisfactory piece of music badly played." Feeling that Mr. Bax was putting "the stress in the wrong places" and that, worse, the members of the congregation were "pretending to feel what they did not feel," her discomfort turns to anger. She hates that the worshipers pretend to understand that "beautiful idea, an idea like a butterfly" that floated above her, present, yet out of reach. They were not, she felt, even trying to comprehend that elusive reality. She imagines all the churches of the world misunderstanding and misrepresenting the mystery at the heart of life. She sees them giving up, acquiescing to something far less than that ungraspable, beautiful idea. She tries to break through the film of acquiescence that envelops the service and "to conceive something to be worshipped"—to imagine God—but finds it "tiring and dispiriting." Looking closely at a woman worshipping near her, she concludes that the woman's satisfied look "was produced by no splendid conception of God within her." With the arrogance of the young and sheltered, she decides that no one "with a commonplace face" could possibly understand God. The woman was a limpet, Rachel concludes, "with the sensitive side of her stuck to a rock, for ever dead to the rush of fresh and beautiful things past her."[35] She suddenly understands why her aunt Helen and her friend St. John Hirst despise Christianity. Sitting among the self-satisfied worshippers, Rachel decides to despise it, too.

Woolf casts an amused eye on Rachel's youthful snobbery toward the nurse whom she dismisses as commonplace and unable to comprehend the grand idea of God. But she also sympathizes with Rachel's frustration. There is an echo of Rachel's scorn in Woolf's own critique of the bishop whose essay about heaven she found so inadequate. Ten years after Woolf published *The Voyage Out*, Alfred North Whitehead would write in *Science and the Modern World* that "the worship of God is not a rule of safety—it is an adventure of the spirit, a flight after the unattainable."[36] Those words might have been thought by Rachel Vinrace.

In *Mrs. Dalloway*, Woolf returns to how one person can view another as unworthy of her own religious faith in an encounter between Clarissa Dalloway and Miss Kilman, her daughter's tutor, a German-born historian who had lost her job as a teacher because of anti-German feeling during the First World War and struggled along in poverty ever since. The two women hold each other in contempt. Miss Kilman sees Clarissa as a pampered, privileged society woman who has wasted her life on trifles. Clarissa feels Miss Kilman's critique of her acutely and fears that she is seducing her daughter, Elizabeth, away from her. Like Helen Ambrose, who worries that her nanny may be teaching her children the Lord's Prayer in her absence, Clarissa fears that Miss Kilman and Elizabeth pray together behind closed doors. When Clarissa and Miss Kilman come face to face, and Clarissa feels Miss Kilman's hatred of her, she matches Miss Kilman's contempt with her own. "This is a Christian—this woman! This woman had taken her daughter from her! She in touch with invisible presences! Heavy, ugly, commonplace, without kindness or grace, she know the meaning of life!"[37]

Like Rachel Vinrace, Clarissa Dalloway despises the religion of this "ugly, commonplace" woman because it does not match her own lofty view of what religion points to—invisible presences, the meaning of life. Although she is an avowed atheist, Clarissa Dalloway does not fit Michael Lackey's view of Woolf's fiction that associates atheists with purity and reality and theists with errors and dreams. Both Rachel and Mrs. Dalloway take offense at expressions of explicit Christian worship and belief, but not on the grounds of atheism. They are offended because the believers seem, to them, to have missed the point—to have claimed access to a mystery that they are either too ordinary or too mean to understand. In *Three Guineas*, Woolf herself claimed a religious knowledge superior to that of religious people because she had not been "forced from childhood" to hear biblical texts "dismembered" and parceled out by a priest each week; she read them, instead, as literary wholes.[38] Mrs. Dalloway's critique of Miss Kilman is grounded in her faith in her own ability to diagnose such hypocrisy because of her profound sensitivity to and love of existence itself: "Life; London; this moment of June."[39]

Much has been made of Miss Kilman's hypocrisy and the "notably harsh authorial drubbing" Woolf seems to give her.[40] But even though Woolf presents Miss Kilman as full of internal violence, her portrait of Miss Kilman is not without sympathy.[41] Woolf could have left Miss Kilman behind in the tea shop, as Elizabeth does, mentally clutching her dogma for comfort. But instead she follows her out into the street, through the crowds on the sidewalk, and into Westminster Abbey where she observes Miss Kilman at prayer. Miss Kilman tents her face with her hands alongside other worshippers, and Woolf notes that the posture of prayer obscures their social rank and gender. The others around Miss Kilman eventually lower their hands, revealing themselves to be "reverent, middle class, English men and women," but Miss Kilman keeps her hands over her face and struggles to transcend "the vanities, the desires, the commodities, to rid herself both of hatred and of love" as other worshippers come and go around her.[42] When Mr. Fletcher, a retired Treasury employee, passes her in the pew (with difficulty—she does not make it easy), he notes with some distress her disordered appearance. But it is not just her messy hair that arrests him. He is impressed by her—by "her largeness, robustness, and power"—as Mrs. Dalloway has been, as the Reverend Edward Whittaker, who shepherded her through her conversion has been, as Elizabeth has been. Once seen, Miss Kilman was unforgettable—indeed, Woolf writes, Clarissa Dalloway had not been able to stop thinking about her all afternoon. As Woolf describes Miss Kilman shifting about on her knees and notes how "rough the approach to her God" was and how "tough her desires," it seems clear that Woolf has been impressed by her too. For other worshippers, "God was accessible and the path to Him smooth"; they pray for a while and then lean back in the pew to listen to the organ music. For Miss Kilman, the search for God is a journey into "double darkness," a struggle over rough terrain. Who is the God Miss Kilman seeks? He is not the "brutal old bully" Woolf so often references in her work but something less explicable—a God that is hidden, silent, inaccessible. The God who remains hidden in double darkness seems closer to the God of *The Cloud of Unknowing* than the God of the Reverend Mr. Whittaker.

In *Mrs. Dalloway*, it is the Christian Miss Kilman who struggles to find God while the atheist Clarissa Dalloway seems able to touch the mystery at the heart of life at will. But the two women are not polar opposites. One of the ways Woolf illuminates the connections between them is through how they respond to pain and anxiety. As explored in the previous chapter, Clarissa practices a kind of *lectio divina*, repeating lines she reads in the open book in Hatchards's window: "Fear no more the heat o' the sun, nor the furious winter's rages." This passage from Shakespeare's *Cymbeline* echoes throughout her day. When she is in pain—as when her exclusion from Lady Bruton's luncheon makes her feel "the dwindling of life"—she invokes the words as a way to steady herself: "'Fear no more,' said Clarissa."[43]

Miss Kilman also uses a repetitive phrase to try to replace chaotic feelings with steadier ones. But just as Miss Kilman's feelings are wilder—rage, fury—than Clarissa's, her phrase is also a less soothing one than Clarissa has chosen. "It is the flesh," Miss Kilman repeats as she leaves Clarissa's house, smarting from Clarissa's laughter. "'It is the flesh, it is the flesh,' she muttered (it being her habit to talk aloud) trying to subdue this turbulent and painful feeling as she walked down Victoria Street."[44] Clarissa repeats words of comfort that reground her in the present moment. Miss Kilman lacerates herself with words of punishment that further isolate her from those around her.

The two women also pray their portions differently: Miss Kilman mutters, while Clarissa murmurs. Miss Kilman seems nearly unhinged; Clarissa graceful and sane, if a bit fragile. Clarissa moves through the city on waves of "divine vitality," while Miss Kilman must battle her way through its noise and chaos. At the striking of the hour, Clarissa feels how Big Ben renders the moment solemn, its stroke "like a bar of gold on the sea," whereas the chime of the clock that sounds a beat later breaks over Miss Kilman "like the spray of an exhausted wave." Miss Kilman's prayer—"it is the flesh"—reflects the theology she learned from Mr. Whittaker, that "knowledge comes through suffering." Clarissa's prayer—"fear no more"—reflects her ecstatic experience of life. Is this simply because Miss Kilman is a Christian and Clarissa is an atheist? The differences between them seem to arise more from their vastly different economic and social situations than from their belief or unbelief. Woolf shows the ways in which social and economic privilege cushion one—not from everything; the snub from Lady Bruton still stings, and everyone dies—but from "the assault of carriages, the brutality of vans."[45] Even Clarissa understands that it is her servants who, by doing the work of her household, make it possible for her to be gracious—"to be what she wanted, gentle, generous-hearted."[46]

Clarissa worries that Miss Kilman is praying with her daughter behind closed doors. Elizabeth is "an inscrutable mystery"to her mother.[47] Woolf gives Elizabeth Dalloway the same "Chinese eyes" with which she will later endow Lily Briscoe, another modern young woman trying to break with the forms of the past.[48] Elizabeth's eyes and her capacity for perfect stillness render her something of a stranger; she is a pale, dark-haired girl in a family of blond, blue-eyed people. Clarissa mourns Elizabeth's loss of the sense of humor she possessed as a child and bemoans her newfound seriousness. She worries that Elizabeth is bored by men's attraction to her, that she does not care about clothes, that she has cultivated "this odd friendship" with her tutor. All of these things seem to pull Elizabeth out of her orbit and into Miss Kilman's. But Elizabeth herself exhibits none of Miss Kilman's Christian piety or religious ideas in the novel, not even when she is alone with Miss Kilman and out of Clarissa's sight.

When Woolf looks at Miss Kilman through Elizabeth's eyes, religion is not the main thing she sees. Miss Kilman exposes Elizabeth to "other points of view" in ways her mother does not: by introducing her to religious ideas, certainly, but more visibly in the novel by lending Elizabeth books, encouraging her to enter a profession, urging her not to be absorbed by parties, and educating her about the humiliations of poverty. Miss Kilman also loves Elizabeth with a kind of desperation. "If she could grasp her, if she could clasp her, if she could make her hers absolutely and forever and then die; that was all she wanted," Miss Kilman thinks as she sits with Elizabeth in a tea shop. But Elizabeth, although she sympathizes with her tutor, has no trouble slipping from her grasp. When Elizabeth leaves the tea shop, Miss Kilman feels their separation in "the very entrails of her body."[49] Elizabeth, by contrast, feels relief.

As Miss Kilman heads over to Westminster Abbey to make her rough approach to God, Elizabeth, "delighted to be free," boards an omnibus. Although she does think of Miss Kilman as she rides the bus—reflecting on how difficult it is to talk with her but also on how Miss Kilman encouraged her to consider entering a profession—she is, in this scene, very much her mother's daughter. The bustling life of the Strand enlivens her: "She liked the geniality, sisterhood, motherhood, brotherhood of this uproar." As if she were the creator in Genesis gazing on the newly made world, the life of the Strand "seemed to her good." More than the books she received from Miss Kilman or the clergymen to whom Miss Kilman introduced her, the crowds on the city streets "stimulate what lay slumberous, clumsy, and shy on the mind's sandy floor to break surface." What the third stroke of light from the lighthouse does for Mrs. Ramsay, the energy of the city does for Elizabeth: it awakens some dormant part of herself. As it does for Clarissa, the life of the city offers Elizabeth a "revelation, which has its effects for ever."[50]

Elizabeth imagines the uproar of the city as a voice, consoling in its indifference even the dying and the bereaved. If Miss Kilman searches in Westminster Abbey for a God who cares about her and her suffering, Elizabeth finds, near St. Paul's, an eternal voice whose indifference does not wound but rather gathers up "this vow; this van; this life; this procession . . . wrap[s] them all about and carr[ies] them on, as in the rough stream of a glacier the ice holds a splinter of bone, a blue petal, some oak trees, and rolls them on."[51] If Westminster is Miss Kilman's sacred space, the city itself is Elizabeth's. Whereas Miss Kilman's God is hidden from her, as "inscrutable" as Elizabeth herself, Elizabeth, like her mother, seems effortlessly to enter the divine life of the world. The God of Elizabeth's outdoor cathedral is a God of change and motion—even the clouds above the city, which "had all the appearance of settled habitations assembled for the conference of gods above the world," are constantly moving, casting light and shadow over everything below, indiscriminately. Elizabeth's God is not a king, nor a moralist, nor an unmoved mover. The God of the city is movement itself, life itself, an inclusive indifference that has room for everything. It is a divine indifference that appears throughout Woolf's work, bearing a comfort quite different from Christianity's consolations. It is the indifference of the "god of rain" that she imagines in *The Years* who sends rain "over the mitred and bareheaded," a god who says "let all breathing kind . . . share my bounty."[52]

Like Miss Kilman, Mr. Bax, the clergyman in *The Voyage Out* who leads the worship service in which Rachel Vinrace rejects the faith in which she was raised, also looks more complex close up. Rachel cannot see that he is "a man of much kindliness and simplicity though by no means clever" because "she was not in the mood to give any one credit for such qualities" and so dismisses him as "an epitome of all the vices of his service."[53] But Woolf devotes more than a page to Mr. Bax's sermon, a mix of uncritical support for the colonial enterprise, the vacant pieties that undergird that support, and one surprising insight. Mr. Bax rambles through a sermon that argues that the tourists "owed a duty to the natives" whose land they were visiting on holiday, because "all human beings are very much the same under their skins." Cluelessly, he asserts that English politeness to the natives led to successful British rule in India, "which led to the remark that small things were not necessarily small." Woolf notes that he seemed to be speaking particularly to women, exhorting them with his conviction that even "the humblest could help."[54]

Mr. Bax is oblivious to the violence of the colonial project, and he ignores the mysteries that Rachel feels religion should address. He also ignores the confounding scriptures that he has read aloud to the congregation. If he appeals to any authority, it is science. Rather than turning away, like Rachel, in disgust, though, Woolf follows Mr. Bax to the end of his sermon, just as she followed Miss Kilman into the pew at Westminster Abbey. And she writes a conclusion to it that contains an idea central to her own understanding of reality. The scientists teach us, Mr. Bax proclaims, that a drop of water can alter an ocean—"and by this means alters the configuration of the globe and the lives of millions of sea creatures, and finally the lives of the men and women who seek their living upon the shores." Mr. Bax proclaims this a "solemn thought," a religious one: what we say and do matters. No human action is inconsequential but rather changes the universe "for good or for evil, not for one instant, or in one vicinity, but throughout the entire race, and for all eternity."[55] Mr. Bax's assertion of the hidden connections between all the living might be grounded in what Woolf will call, decades later, her "philosophy": that we are all connected through the pattern hidden behind the cotton wool of nonbeing, all of us parts of the same work of art. This philosophy also animates Mrs. Dalloway's sense that she belonged to all she had encountered and was also "part of people she had never met,"[56] as well as Mr. Carslake's conviction that "we are all of us."[57] Mr. Bax has not made the connection between the ability of a drop of water to alter an ocean and the violent alterations wrought by British colonialism whose consequences ripple out across the globe. He does not realize that his conclusion has the power to shatter the entire sermon. But Woolf does.[58]

Mr. Bax does not speak of God in his sermon, and Woolf emphatically asserts in her autobiography that there is no God. But present as a possibility within both of their credos is something akin to Alfred North Whitehead's understanding of God as the "author of the play," the "poet of the world," the ground of the "eternal relatedness" that gives our actions their significance.[59] Woolf's philosophy was "that behind the cotton wool is hidden a pattern; that we—I mean all human beings—are connected with this; that the whole world is a work of art; that we are parts of the work of art."[60] Whitehead's understanding of God was as "the unconditioned actuality of conceptual feeling at the base of things," the nature of which he imagined as "that of a tender care that nothing be lost."[61] Both ways of imagining the world posit something hidden that unites, something hidden through which all the invisible connections that link us to each other run.

The idea of God that hovers in Woolf's work as a potential answer to questions she and her characters pose is not the brutal old bully whose heavy hand she felt throughout the losses of her childhood but a potential presence that both gives and receives. Mrs. Dalloway knows her party is an offering—"but to whom?" She offers herself, "drenched in fire," as does Mrs. Ramsay, who telegraphs to Lily Briscoe during her own party, "I am drowning, my dear, in seas of fire." Mrs. Ramsay also waits, as she assembles the offering of her dinner party, "for some one to answer her."[62] This is not the rigging up of the "old comfortable figure" that Mr. Carslake abhors, or an insincerity, as Mrs. Ramsay puts it, slipping in among the truths. It is a presence, or perhaps an absence, that is silent and hidden, a space in which one might wait with one's offering in one's hands, ready both to offer it up and to receive that which "seems given to me, not made by me," as Woolf put it in her autobiography.[63] Many of Woolf's characters long to give and receive, even though both the offering and the receiver remain obscure. As Mrs. Jarvis struggles to say in *Jacob's Room*: "If only some one could give me . . . if I could give some one . . ."[64] The idea of God lingers around the edges of these desires.

The idea of God also hovers as a potential answer to questions that arise again and again throughout Woolf's work. Like Mrs. Jarvis in *Jacob's Room*, like Clarissa Dalloway, like Mrs. Ramsay, Rhoda in *The Waves* longs to make an offering. Rhoda asks over and over the question repeated throughout Percy Bysshe Shelley's poem "The Question"—"Oh! to whom?": "To whom shall I give all that now flows through me, from my warm, my porous body? I will gather my flowers and present them—Oh! to whom?"[65] For whom is Rhoda's offering? A lover? A god? The world itself? "I will give," she says, as a girl in school; "I will enrich; I will return to the world this beauty." Rhoda's questions throughout the novel seek not only a Platonic reality behind appearances but also something akin to what the medieval German mystic Meister Eckhart once called the "God beyond God."[66] "'Like' and 'like' and 'like'—but what is the thing that lies beneath the semblance of the thing?" Rhoda asks. Julia Briggs hears in Rhoda's question a "search for an absent God."[67]

Woolf revisits these questions continually. In a diary entry on 4 January 1929, she describes a visit she and Leonard paid to their friend

S. S. Koteliansky, a Russian-born translator, on Christmas day. Living in Katherine Mansfield's former house, Koteliansky was full of talk about Mansfield and her husband—an old vein of gossip that both he and Woolf loved to mine—as well as opinions about books and writers. Woolf clearly respects his life of poverty, attention, and devotion—he's still concentrating, she notes, "upon say 5 objects which he has been staring at these 40 years." She was moved by the visit, could feel "some emotion was working in him."[68] She and Leonard were glad they had come.

Remembering the visit leads Woolf to reflect on life itself—is it "very solid," she asks, "or very shifting?" She feels both the permanence and the passing of the moment in which she stands. "Perhaps," she muses, "it may be that though we change; one flying after another, so quick so quick, yet we are somehow successive, & continuous—we human beings; & show the light through." As she experiments with the relationship between individual lives and the common life of human beings, a question arises: "But what is the light?"[69] What is it that shines through? What is it that the moment that is both eternal and transitory, the life that is both individual and communal, reveals?

These suggestive, unanswered questions turn up again and again in Woolf's diaries, sometimes in the form of questions, other times as ellipses or silences. Writing on 7 November 1928, she notes that her "temperament" leads her to experiment with many different styles and subjects. Being "very little persuaded of the truth of anything," she follows "blindly instinctively with a sense of leaping over a precipice—the call of—the call of—. . ."[70] A similar silence permeates her vision of the "fin passing far out" that she experienced in the depth of a depression. She both dreads those experiences but is also intellectually interested in them—what happens down there in depths without reading and writing? What answers emerge to the question of "what am I"? When she reflects on "the mystical side of this solitude," she says: "It is not oneself but something in the universe that one's left with," an excess presence, undefinable.[71] In an echo from the account of her dream of God that she wrote as a child, she asks herself, as she struggles to give shape to the form of the novel that would become *The Waves*: "Who thinks it? And am I outside the thinker? One wants some device which is not a trick."[72]

The God who haunts the desires and questions expressed throughout Woolf's writing resists definition and is shaped by a range of sources. The scholarship of Jane Ellen Harrison, Frazer's *Golden Bough*, the Bible, Dante, Renaissance art, the sermon collections she read, the hymns she knew, the "God in the process of change" about whom she wrote as a teenager, Caroline Emelia Stephen's God who communicates intermittently like a lighthouse, the "steady beat of the great Creator" she apprehended in her youth—all of these and more shape the images of divinity in her work.

A passage at the center of *Mrs. Dalloway* shows Woolf's brilliant interweaving of such sources to bring into view a layered and feminine divine presence. It begins with Peter Walsh dozing off in Regent's Park as a "grey nurse" in a "grey dress" sits beside him, knitting, a liminal figure at the threshold of waking and sleeping.[73] In her grey dress, she recalls Caroline Emelia Stephen, who called her house "The Porch" because she imagined it as an antechamber to heaven. Working quietly at her knitting, the grey nurse also evokes the many Great Mothers of ancient religions "weaving the web and pattern of life with the thread of destiny"[74] as well as the goddess Night, the nurse of both Sleep and Death.[75]

As Peter sinks into sleep, his identity begins to dissolve into a more generalized "solitary traveller" while the grey nurse points beyond herself to multiple forms of the feminine divine. This layered vision reflects Harrison's understanding of the constant flux that marks religion in which ritual figures and ghosts become, over time, gods to be worshipped. The grey nurse transforms into a spectral presence among the trees, then into the trees themselves, to sirens in the waves, to "this great figure who will, with a toss of her head . . . let me blow to nothingness," to "the mother whose sons have been killed in the battles of the world," back to an elderly woman knitting and finally to the landlady who conducts her own rituals "among ordinary things." It is a palimpsest of images, each one drawn on top of the others, with a divine female presence always showing through.

Like Clarissa, the solitary traveler is "by conviction an atheist perhaps" but is nonetheless vulnerable to "moments of extraordinary exaltation," like Marius's epiphany, like the solitary traveler's own experience in the woods. With a nod to G. E. Moore, the solitary traveler thinks to himself that "nothing exists outside us except a state of mind." The next sentence invokes, by contrast, Anselm of Canterbury's ontological argument for God, thinking that "if he can conceive of her, then in some sort she exists."[76] The trees around him reflect both the goddess's solace and her unpredictability as they shower down with their leaves "charity, comprehension, absolution" while at the same time upending "the piety of their aspect with a wild carouse,"[77] an echo of the ritual dances that Jane Ellen Harrison found at the origins of religion itself.

Such visions, writes Woolf, "ceaselessly float up, pace beside, put their faces in front of, the actual thing."[78] These visions are both given and conjured at once—conjured here from absences and lacks. Clarissa is not who Peter wants her to be—he wakes from his dream thinking of a memory from Bourton that seems to him to illustrate the death of her soul—and "nothing exists outside us except a state of mind." From the absence of an ideal Clarissa and the absence of God, a vision arises of a female presence who offers both "compassion, comprehension, absolution"[79] and who might also lift him from the earth and scatter him to the winds.

The solitary traveler emerges from the wood, and Peter begins to awaken. The voice of the landlady speaks, asking if there is anything else she can do for him, returning the traveler to the ordinary world of day and night, marmalade and cupboards. Woolf asks: "But to whom does the solitary traveller make reply?"[80] For the solitary traveler's vision has folded the landlady too into all that the absence and presence of a great goddess can hold: consolation, violence, ecstasy, grief. Another question haunts this passage as well: not only the question of to whom the solitary traveler would reply, but also, who would be making the reply? His encounter with the many-faceted, many-layered goddess has revealed hidden layers within Peter as well. He is himself, and yet he is more than himself. He is also the solitary traveler who encounters the divine in the woods, the waves, and the sorrows of the world.

Ideas of divinity often attach to characters in Woolf's novels, just as other invisible things—emotions, for example—often attach to material objects in her work. The picture of the refrigerator James Ramsay cuts out at the beginning of *To the Lighthouse* becomes "fringed with joy" because he associates it with the possibility of sailing to the lighthouse and with his mother. Lily Briscoe's excitement over her painting attaches to the salt cellar on the table during Mrs. Ramsay's dinner party, and every time Lily's eye falls on it, she remembers her painting and takes pleasure in thinking of how to solve its formal challenges.

In a similar way, certain characters take on aspects of the ideas of divinity that linger, unspoken, around them. The unknowable qualities of divinity attach to Mr. Carslake, even as he inwardly critiques the idea of God. Milly Pargiter, in *The Years*, attaches the idea of divinity to her sister, Eleanor. Wise, compassionate, powerful in her way, Eleanor is a "goddess" to whom Milly spontaneously prays: "Protect me, she thought, handing her a teacup, who am such a mousy, downtrodden, inefficient little chit, compared with Delia, who always gets her way, while I'm always snubbed by Papa, who was grumpy for some reason."[81]

The idea of divinity attaches even more powerfully to absent figures. After Jane Ellen Harrison's death, Woolf rendered her as a deity whose name is too holy to write out or pronounce in *A Room of One's Own*.[82] Woolf had spent time with Harrison during her last months and attended her funeral. Like Rose Pargiter in *The Years*, Woolf appreciated some part of the service—"the lovelier, more rational parts of the Bible" and "the beauty of the Come unto me all ye that are weary"—but felt "dulled & bothered" by "the obstacle of not believing." She loved the "gay indifference" of the bird who sang at the graveside and thought Harrison would have enjoyed it as well. But the theological questions generated by the liturgy intruded uncomfortably for Woolf, just as they had for her aunt Caroline: "Who is 'God' & what the Grace of Christ? &what did they mean to Jane?"[83]

As if writing about one of the resurrection-gods[84] who appear in Jane Ellen Harrison's scholarship, Woolf resurrects Harrison herself in the garden of her fictional women's college, Fernham, in *A Room of One's Own*. Woolf describes a spring evening animated by a wind blowing from some unknown quarter, recalling Jesus's words in the gospel of John about not knowing where the wind comes from or where it goes. She describes figures, dim as phantoms in the light—one in a hammock, another racing across the grass. "Would no one stop her?" Woolf writes, recalling her own encounter with the beadle policing the grass in the first pages and delighting in the fact that no one, at Fernham, will stop this young woman. And then, "as if popping out to breathe the air," a figure appears on the terrace. Woolf asks: "Could it be the famous scholar, could it be J____ H____ herself?" Her presence seems to tear the veil of twilight like "the flash of some terrible reality leaping, as its way is, out of the heart of the spring."[85]

Resurrected, Harrison is as mysterious as the wind and as powerful as the spring itself. Harrison had argued in *Ancient Art and Ritual* that the roots of tragedy could be found in the rituals of ancient spring festivals, a passage that Woolf had copied into her reading notebook. The rituals of that fertile season brought the communities from which they arose closer to that "terrible reality" that animates all the possibilities existence holds. Harrison seems to have emerged from her grave to breathe that same spring air in the heart of a college dedicated to the education of women who had the potential to "tear asunder" all that separated them from the college gardens beyond their walls. With her unpronounceable name, J____ H____ is both the ghost of the scholar of the spring rituals and the "terrible reality" they reveal.

In *To the Lighthouse*, Mr. Ramsay may "demand sacrifices" like a god, but it is Mrs. Ramsay whose spiritual power persists after her death. In life, she is the sacrifice itself, offering herself for others. "I am drowning, my dear, in seas of fire," she silently communicates to Lily Briscoe at dinner, urging her to draw out Mr. Tansley and help the dinner party gather momentum. After her death, she becomes an absent presence that makes a continuing claim on the living and exerts a transformative power. It is her absent presence that sends Mr. Ramsay off on his journey to the lighthouse, at last, in the reluctant company of Cam and James. She allows herself—"it was part of her perfect goodness"—to be resurrected by Lily's desire for her. And it is her generative ongoing presence that makes "of the moment something permanent (as in another sphere Lily herself tried to make of the moment something permanent)—this was of the nature of a revelation."[86] Lily marvels over the divine power incarnate within this woman and, potentially, in all of us: "But what a power was in the human soul!" Lily understood that "fifty pairs of eyes were not enough to get round that one woman with," as if Mrs. Ramsay were a goddess of many moods and faces. One needed "some secret sense, fine as air" to see her as she really is.[87] The mystery of human beings, throughout Woolf's work, requires the same kind of devoted attention that people have given to the gods.

Lily sees and honors Mrs. Ramsay's godlike absent presence in her abstract painting of Mrs. Ramsay and captures in it Mrs. Ramsay's own secret understanding of her innermost self, her "wedge-shaped core of darkness." But she also senses as she paints something more akin to the "God beyond God" sought by Meister Eckhart or the impersonal divinity that Elizabeth Dalloway senses in the crowds on the Strand than to the goddess presiding over St. Ives. When Lily finally picks up her brush and makes the first risky mark on the canvas, she quickly develops a "dancing rhythmical movement" between making strokes on the canvas and pausing between them, a movement that recalls the ritual dances from which Jane Ellen Harrison believed religion had been born. The marks define a space that Lily feels "looming out at her" from the canvas. Confronting that looming space draws her out "of gossip, out of living, out of community with people" and into the presence of "this truth, this reality, which suddenly laid hands on her, emerged stark at the back of appearances and commanded her attention."[88] This reality feels like a "formidable ancient enemy" that keeps calling her to the struggle with the canvas. Other "worshipful objects" only wanted her worship; this reality "roused one to perpetual combat." One could never wholly capture "the fluidity of life"; something real always escapes when that fluidity is exchanged for "the concentration of art." Like a worshipper who must walk past the gargoyles guarding the cathedral's entrance, Lily has to make her way past the "blasts of doubt" that collect at the threshold of the canvas: her fear that her effort is meaningless, the echo of Mr. Tansley's taunting voice saying "women can't paint, can't write."[89]

She finds the courage to pick up her brush, though, and falls in "with some rhythm which was dictated to her (she kept looking at the hedge, at the canvas) by what she saw."[90] Lily is not painting the hedge—she is painting her vision of Mrs. Ramsay—but she keeps looking from the hedge to the canvas, from the canvas to the hedge. What does she see there? Perhaps the same thing Mr. Ramsay saw when he gazed into the hedge earlier in the novel: intricacy and darkness. But

Lily recognizes what Mr. Ramsay does not, that the intricate darkness is an image of Mrs. Ramsay, a reflection of the way she understood the most hidden, private dimension of herself, her "wedge-shaped core of darkness." Mr. Ramsay can only "stand by and watch her" and regret the ways he "made things worse for her." Lily sees Mrs. Ramsay's hidden self and paints it.

Led into the rhythm between the hedge and the canvas, Lily becomes absorbed in the creation of her painting and "begins losing consciousness of outer things." As "her name and her personality and her appearance, and whether Mr. Carmichael was there or not" sink below what *The Cloud of Unknowing* calls "the cloud of forgetting,"[91] other things begin rising from the depths of her mind: "Scenes, and names, and sayings, and memories and ideas." In her absorption, a day she once spent with Mrs. Ramsay and Mr. Tansley comes back to her like an artifact created by Mrs. Ramsay, who, simply through her presence, gathered up the fragments of the moment and created something that would last, something that now affects Lily "like a work of art."[92] It is a match "struck unexpectedly in the dark," a revelation of the creative power of Mrs. Ramsay, who, like God, can bring shape to chaos, even in her absence.

Percival, in *The Waves*, affects those around him in a similar way, drawing them into community. Although much less vivid a character than Mrs. Ramsay, divinity attaches to him, too. Silent Percival seems to embody the dying-and-rising divinity studied by Harrison and the Cambridge ritualists—the "eniautos-daimon" who dies and out of whose ritual dismemberment the community is bound together.[93]

In *The Waves*, divinity first settles on Percival as the boys sit through a chapel service at school. Fastidious Louis—modeled in part on T. S. Eliot[94]—loves the dimness within the chapel, the "orderly progress" of the students filing in, the way the boys "put off our distinctions as we enter." He finds the headmaster's authority comforting and the crucifix he wears on his waistcoat grounding. Like Woolf's brother Thoby, who wrote a pamphlet arguing against compulsory chapel attendance at Cambridge on the grounds of religious and ethical liberty,[95] Neville feels his freedom threatened by the headmaster and his crucifix. The headmaster and his authority allow Louis to wrap his roots around "some hardness at the centre," but Neville feels the headmaster's words falling like paving-stones on his head. Christianity appears to him as a "sad religion"—too pathetic to be consoling. Bernard does not like the headmaster's performance in chapel either. He experiences it as intensely masculine—the headmaster's voice "rough and hairy" and violent, as if the headmaster had "minced the dance of the white butterflies at the door to powder." He notes the way the other teachers try to imitate the headmaster's walk and finds their attempts "pitiable." All of these things he treasures up to record in his notebook, and when he recalls the headmaster at the end of novel, he thinks, "I did not hate him like Neville, or revere him like Louis. I took notes as we sat together in the chapel."[96] Bernard is more interested in finding words for the experience than in judging it good or bad. Woolf believed that when she put experiences into words, she took away their "power to hurt me,"[97] and Bernard seems also to use words to keep from being overwhelmed positively or negatively by the combination of authority and piety that the headmaster wields.

The boys each have a different reaction to the compulsory religious ritual of their school. But they are united in one devotion: to Percival, sitting remote and indifferent in a "pagan universe." He flicks the back of his neck with his hand, and other boys try to imitate him. "For such gestures," Neville thinks, "one falls hopelessly in love for a lifetime." An aura of divinity gathers around Percival—he trails light in his wake, and the boys follow him. He possesses a careless, seductive, dangerous power, the kind those boys might one day follow into battle. Louis resents Percival's power but needs it, too: "It is Percival I need; for it is Percival who inspires poetry." Percival is the most god-like figure in the sacred space of the chapel. He exudes an erotic pull that draws the other boys to him. Even Louis, who would like to resist, cannot, because Percival is the source of his own creative energy.[98]

We see again how Percival gathers separate people into a community, giving it "solidity," when Louis, Neville, Rhoda, Susan, Jinny, and Bernard meet Percival for dinner to say good-bye before he leaves to take up a colonial appointment in India. Percival's name is associated with the quest for the Holy Grail, a story Woolf had written about in 1909 when she saw Wagner's *Parsifal* performed at the Beyreuth festival. She was fascinated by how the story did not revolve around love or war. "One feels vaguely for a crisis that never comes," she wrote in her essay on the festival, and "one is bewildered by a music that continues with the utmost calm and intensity independently of them."[99] This might serve as a description of *The Waves* itself, a novel that eschews the usual plots and through which the waves continually gather and break, no matter what is happening in the lives of the characters. Woolf described Parsifal to her sister as "a very mysterious emotional work" with "no love in it; it is more religious than anything." After seeing it, she studied the libretto, finding it "weak vague stuff, with the usual enormities," but some bits of it eventually made their way into her work.[100] The prophecy spoken by the voice from the Grail—"Enlightened through compassion, / the innocent fool; / wait for him / the appointed one"—echoes in the anticipation of the friends waiting for Percival to arrive.[101] Another version of the Grail story also resonates in the way Neville, in particular, awaits Percival. In the thirteenth-century *Queste del Saint Graal*, Arthur's knights await Galahad, who will sit in the Seat of Danger on which is written, "HERE SHALL SIT SUCH AN ONE."[102] Neville, who is in love with Percival, awaits him with a similar intensity: "This is the place to which he is coming. This is the table at which he will sit."[103] The red flowers on the table are Galahad's color, the red in which he was clothed. The story of Dionysius, the god who suffers and dies and rises again, is also layered into Percival's story. Known as "the god who comes," he sheds his divinity on Percival.

Percival's divine power precedes him. Even before he arrives, he "seems to pump into this room this prickly light, this intensity of being";[104] ordinary objects seem so saturated with the light of anticipation that they can no longer perform their uses. When he finally arrives, the others see him as "a hero." When he sits in his appointed place, "the occasion is crowned," just as the appearance of Mr. Carmichael as an "old pagan god" crowns the occasion of Lily Briscoe completing her painting in *To the Lighthouse*. But whereas Mr. Carmichael offers a blessing, violets falling from his hands, Percival is an impersonal, indifferent presence. He is there to be dismembered and reassembled by the community.

Seated among them, Percival seems to Rhoda "like a stone fallen into a pond round which minnows swarm"; for Louis, he is the one who makes them aware that they are not separate but rather one; for Bernard, he is "a God." For Jinny, the eucharistic Grail quest elements—"the chair, the cup, the table"—quiver and burn with the erotic energy she and Percival ignite when their hands touch. Rhoda sees Percival as the departure point for all pilgrimages. The religious rhythms of this gathering are even more ancient than the Christianized Celtic grail legends, but only Rhoda and Louis seem to sense them. In a section Woolf places in parentheses, Rhoda and Louis speak to one another of "dancing and drumming," of "the flames of the festival," of "the bleeding limbs which they have torn from the living body."[105] Rhoda and Louis's visionary images recall the dismemberment and consumption of Dionysius by the Titans and the rituals that commemorate his passion.[106] They alone seem to know what is coming: "'Death and again death.'"[107]

At the end of the evening, Bernard recognized that the moment has been "created by us from Percival." Neville is left asking religious questions, the kinds of questions asked in the wake of a mystical experience of God's presence: "What can we do to keep him? How bridge the distance between us? How fan the fire so that it blazes for ever?"[108] These are religious longings: to keep the divine close, to cross the distance between heaven and earth, "to make of the moment," in Woolf's words, "something permanent."[109] Or at least something that can be returned to, through ritual, again and again.

Along with Dionysius, Percival is also associated with England's colonial rule of India, which, at the time Woolf was writing *The Waves*, was under pressure from the nonviolent protests led by Gandhi and the growing calls for self-rule. When Percival dies in India, it is not a glorious death but a ridiculous accident: he is thrown from his horse. Neville, who was in love with him, feels Percival's death in his own body, just as Clarissa Dalloway felt the death of Septimus Warren Smith. Bernard feels that something of Percival remains and goes to look for it in Italian paintings, "picking up fragments." Rhoda feels that Percival has shown her, through his death, "the thing that lies behind the semblance of the thing." There is a political dimension to that hidden reality in the cruel absurdity that lies behind the colonial project, in which "time seems endless, ambition vain," an absurdity that can expect the "the Oriental problem" to be "solved" by Percival.[110] And there is a mystical dimension of "the thing that lies behind the semblance of the thing" that is less describable but points to Rhoda's vision of the festival dismemberment, the "terrible reality leaping, as its way is, out of the heart of the spring."[111]

The six friends meet once more later in life, carrying the vulnerabilities and desires of their youth in their elderly bodies. They gather at Hampton Court where, without Percival, they attempt to reassemble themselves as a community. Their childhoods remain present to them. Louis, in his Christian way, finds it "difficult to weep, calling ourselves little children, praying that God may keep us safe while we sleep." Neville's longing "to rejoin the body of our mother from whom we have been severed" invokes the goddesses studied by Jane Ellen Harrison. Just as he stood outside the judgments Louis and Neville made about the headmaster in chapel when they were children, Bernard does not look toward Louis's God or Neville's Great Mother. He knows that they themselves are the creators in this story, as does Jinny. The red flower that graced the table when they last dined with Percival has become "a six-sided flower, made of six lives." It was "'built up with much pain, many strokes,' said Jinny." Bernard wants to contemplate it. "Let us stop for a moment," he says; "let us behold what we have made. Let it blaze against the yew trees. One life."[112]

But the group cannot hold itself together. They break into couples—Susan and Bernard, Neville and Jinny, Louis and Rhoda. Rhoda and Louis "trust only in solitude and the violence of death and thus are divided." Louis prays, "Lord help us act our parts as we greet them returning—Susan and Bernard, Neville and Jinny." Neville regrets that, by pairing off, they have "torn the fabric." Susan feels something "has escaped me" that leaves her feeling "unsatisfied." Bernard wonders, looking back: Was this a death? Or a new combination? Or a glimpse of their future? Bernard feels not only the dissipation of the group but of each of them individually as well. "Little bits of ourselves are crumbling. . . . I cannot keep myself together."[113] Without Percival, the source of the inspiration to "put it together," they struggle to create their common life.

But that struggle to create is what they share; it is what their common life is made of. *The Waves* is a novel about creation, full of echoes of creation stories: the opening chapters of Genesis; the Song of Songs, made from the words exchanged by lovers; the stories of the dying-and-rising gods from whose bodies new communities come into being. And from these stories, the novel fashions its own narratives of creation. "In the beginning," as Bernard recounts, "there was the nursery, with windows opening on to a garden, and beyond that the sea."[114] There is the woman writing whom Susan and Bernard happen upon, who recalls Julia Stephen at her writing table, Caroline Stephen writing her books, and Woolf herself, writing Susan and Bernard into being. There is the moment Mrs. Constable squeezes water from a sponge onto Bernard's small back and awakens him to the life of his body. There is the community they create from Percival during their last supper with him. And there is the creation of the world in the opening passage. The novel begins and ends with a darkness that makes it impossible to tell the sea from the sky. In the beginning, the sun comes up like a woman's arm raising a lamp, gradually sharpening the line of the horizon, distinguishing one leaf from another. In an early draft of the novel, Woolf wrote, "I am telling myself the story of the world from the beginning."[115] This beginning recalls the first chapter of Genesis in which the voice of God distinguishes sea from sky, light from darkness, sun from moon. In Woolf's creation story, it is a woman raising a lantern with her arm that does the work of separating one thing from another.

But the woman does not create alone. Bernard, Susan, Rhoda, Neville, Jinny, and Louis are her partners. As the light illuminates the world, they respond, they describe, they continue speaking the world into being. "'I see a ring,' said Bernard, 'hanging above me. It quivers and hangs in a loop of light.'"[116] They speak of light and color, of sound and landscape, of beautiful things and of frightening things. They create the world through their words, and they enter it. Talking and eating together, they are creators. "We too have made something," Bernard writes, "that will join the innumerable congregations of past time."[117] They are the words, they are the music, they are the thing itself. There may be no Beethoven, no Shakespeare, and no God, but human beings have the capacity to create like them, to partake of that elusive creative power that surges "behind the outlines" of life.[118]

Is that power divine? Woolf and her characters cannot say. "What does the central shadow hold? Something? Nothing? I do not know," Bernard says.[119] In the fifth italicized section of *The Waves*, Woolf describes a "zone of shadow" in which a shape might be revealed when the shadow recedes. Or perhaps not. Perhaps there is, in that zone of shadow, "still denser depths of darkness."[120] From her childhood onward, Woolf never stopped lowering her net into those depths, bringing up the "quivering little fish" from which she might create something new.

5

OVERFLOWING BOUNDARIES

SACRED COMMUNITY AND THE COMMON LIFE

In *The Rock*, T.S. Eliot's 1934 pageant-play written to raise funds for new churches in the suburbs of London, he wrote, "There is no life that is not in community, / And no community not lived in praise of GOD."[1] Eliot's conviction that genuine community must be Christian at its core would shape his social criticism throughout the 1930s. In this, he was in agreement with the Protestant-led ecumenical movement that had begun to emerge from the establishment of the World Student Christian Federation in 1905 and the Edinburgh Conference of the International Missionary Council in 1910. In the 1930s, as totalitarian regimes gained strength in Europe, ecumenists began organizing with greater urgency and intensity on both sides of the Atlantic. Eliot became involved in this work—serving on committees, delivering papers, joining discussion groups, and participating in conversations about Britain's relationship to the nascent World Council of Churches.[2]

Although not a liberal Protestant like many of the leaders of the ecumenical movement, Eliot shared their concern over the weakening of community in the face of industrialization, secularization, and nationalism. In 1936, Eliot served on a committee to prepare for the 1937 Oxford Conference on Church, Community, and State, which would draw Christian leaders from all over the world. Although more than half of the delegates came from England and the United States, the Roman Catholics did not send any representatives, and German church leaders were forbidden to attend by the Nazis. The Oxford conference critiqued capitalism and the class divisions it generated and spoke forcefully against racism and nationalism. It argued for unity among Christians during times of war and for the primacy of Christian over national identity. "'Secularism,'" a report in the *Journal of Religion* claimed, "was a bugaboo of the whole conference which was never clearly examined, but served as a sort of Machiavellian external enemy to weld the group together."[3]

Eliot delivered a paper at the Oxford conference on "The Ecumenical Nature of the Church and Its Responsibility Towards the World" in which he counseled slow change. The *Journal of Religion* noted that "Mr. Eliot deprecated the attempt to cloak differences under formulas, or even to eradicate distinctions in a uniformity and pleaded instead for a slow, steady movement toward mutual understanding and common faith."[4] After the Oxford conference, Eliot was appointed to a subcommittee dealing with the economic order, bringing him into conversation with theologians like Paul Tillich and Reinhold Niebuhr. In January and March of 1938, he participated in discussions about the possibility of creating a British section of the World Council of Churches. And in September 1938, he attended a meeting of the Council on Christian Faith and the Common Life.[5]

In addition to this church-based organizing, Eliot also participated, from 1938 to 1943, in a discussion group of Christian intellectuals called "the Moot," convened by J. H. Oldham, a former missionary who had organized the Oxford conference and was a leading figure in the ecumenical movements of the first half of the twentieth century. The Moot brought Eliot into regular conversation with Karl Mannheim, John Baillie, John Middleton Murry, and other religious and political thinkers around questions of social and cultural order. These conversations shaped Eliot's sustained exploration of community, *The Idea of a Christian Society*, given as lectures in 1939 and published in 1940.

Eliot's vision of community arises from a critique of capitalism and the profit motive that he shared with Christian thinkers who were more theologically liberal than he was. He also shared with them a conviction that a "new Christendom" was needed to resist the destructive power of secular nationalism.[6] The Church and Community committee of the 1937 Oxford conference had argued that human life was being fractured "because it has tried to organize itself into unity on a secularistic and human basis without any reference to the divine Will and Power above and beyond itself."[7] Eliot affirmed this conviction in *The Idea of a Christian Society*, arguing that Europe had only two choices: "The formation of a new Christian culture" or "the acceptance of a pagan one."[8] No other foundation, he believed, was strong enough to sustain European civilization. He mistrusted democracy as too highly praised, too empty of content, and too easily appropriated by its enemies; he mistrusted liberalism for being too individualistic; and he deeply mistrusted liberal religion, which he believed would whittle Christianity down to nothing.

Eliot imagined a "Christian organisation of society," which, although "not the same thing as a society consisting exclusively of devout Christians," would nevertheless be shaped by them. He proposed a "Community of Christians," a kind of "Church within the Church."[9] This group of serious Christians, "especially those of intellectual and spiritual superiority," would develop a Christian framework for education capable of creating a unified culture, for "only a proper system of education can unify the active and the contemplative, action and speculation, politics and the arts."[10] There would be a mixture of believing instructors as well as indifferent and disbelieving ones (as long as they are "persons of exceptional ability") and "a proportion of other persons professing other faiths than Christianity." (Eliot does not specify what this proportion might be, but six years earlier, in *After Strange Gods*, he had written that "reasons of race and religion combine to make any large number of free-thinking Jews undesirable."[11]) From this education a Christian society would take shape that would be governed by a state that "is Christian only negatively; its Christianity is a reflection of the Christianity of the society which it governs."[12] Nevertheless, the only hope "for a society which would thrive and continue its creative activity in the arts of civilisation, is to become Christian," Eliot insisted. He readily admitted that the idea of a Christian society would not be "immediately attractive" to those who were not Christians; "even the majority of professing Christians," he wrote, "may shrink from it." The Christian society he imagined would demand "discipline, inconvenience and discomfort: but here as hereafter," he wrote, "the alternative to hell is purgatory."[13]

The project Eliot was involved in during the years leading up to England's involvement in the Second World War—that of arguing for a unified Christian culture that could resist secularism, fascism, and communism—was dominated by male theologians and churchmen. The *Journal of Religion*'s report on the 1937 Oxford conference noted that, not only were "too few laymen" present and young people "inadequately represented," women "were scarcely represented at all"—despite the fact that women "constitute so large a proportion of the most active membership of the churches and . . . share increasingly in the control of social policy in the several nations."[14] Eliot's *Idea of a Christian Society* does not address the role of women in such a society nor does it include the oppression of women in its catalogue of wrongs that a Christian society would address. He was not calling for a revolution in church or society, because he believed that revolution is "a denial of the permanent things."[15]

At the same time as T. S. Eliot was developing his idea of a Christian society, and in the face of the same challenges, Virginia Woolf was exploring her ideas about community, society, education, and religion in her own manifesto, *Three Guineas*, as well as in her last novel, *Between the Acts*. Like Eliot, her ideas were shaped by her engagement with organizations concerned with community, although the organizations in which she participated were political, rather than religious. But Woolf's ideas were also shaped by her lifetime as a female human being whose society seemed to regard the unequal status of women and men to be among Eliot's "permanent things." Eliot's conversations about community were conducted almost exclusively with other men. Those conversations are reflected in *The Idea of a Christian Society* in which women, and the challenges women face, are invisible. Eliot imagined a society guided by a "Church within the Church." Woolf imagined a Society of Outsiders critiquing and remaking the world in which we live.

Woolf's and Eliot's approaches to community had at least one thing in common: a conviction that ritual was needed to create it. In *Ancient Art and Ritual*, Harrison argued that the impulses that send people to the theater and to church are one and the same. Art and ritual have a "common root,"[16] she argued, that is at once social and moral. The ancient choral dance that so interested her is moral precisely because it is social; "that is," she writes, "it unites."[17] Ritual gives, as Clive Bell might say, significant form to the stuff of our days—eating and drinking, sowing and harvesting, birth and death, our experience of time.[18] It provides the bridge, Harrison wrote, "between actual life and that peculiar contemplation of our emotion towards life which we call art,"[19] a bridge that can be traveled in both directions. The impulse that sends us to church and to the theater is born of a desire to join with others, Harrison believed, in seeking a "fuller consciousness of life."[20]

There were many rituals Woolf mistrusted. She despised public rituals that kept gender hierarchies in place and fascists in power, rituals she analyzes in *Three Guineas*. But she was drawn to local, private rituals that bring people together to experience life more fully, the kinds of rituals that mark her novels. Joan Martyn's pilgrimage to the Marian shrine and Jacob's pilgrimage to Greece, Lily painting to a rhythm "dictated to her," Clarissa Dalloway's party, Mrs. Ramsay's dinner, the gatherings of Percival's friends in *The Waves*, the community play in *Between the Acts*—all of these rituals explore "the capacity of the human spirit to overflow boundaries and make unity out of multiplicity."[21] Critic James Wood has argued that, for Woolf, art "acts like ritual rather than doctrine: it cannot define truth, but it nicely ornaments what cannot be known."[22] But neither art nor ritual have an ornamental function for Woolf. They are both social and moral forms of engaging the real. For Woolf, as for the Greeks Harrison studied, ritual was "a thing done," an action that made an impact on the world.[23] Woolf was much more interested in the ritual actions from which new forms of community and social life might take shape than she was in doctrine or the protection of "the permanent things" that keep the status quo in place. Like her aunt Caroline Stephen, she found doctrine antagonizing. During her rare visits to church, she was sometimes moved by a hymn or a reading from the Bible. But she found much of the liturgy dissatisfying, promising more than it could deliver; it sounded, as Bernard says in *The Waves*, "too hearty to be true." The church's participation in Britain's colonial project, the flying of the Union Jack within the sanctuary, the church's refusal to ordain women, the platitudes she heard churchmen speak from pulpits and publish in newspapers all kept her, unlike Eliot, outside its doors. The impulse that Harrison believed sent people to church did not send Woolf there.

But if she did not feel an impulse to go to church, she did seek out new rituals and forms of community in "fresh chapels," places where the "common mind" she had apprehended as a young reader could be explored. She had learned the power of ritual in "that great Cathedral space which was childhood," where her mother had presided like a deity, sustaining the "common life of the family." Listening to her father read novels and recite poetry, she had experienced the ways in which a book or a poem could become a portable sacred space. Home is also where she experienced the failure of ritual to draw people below the surface into a deeper encounter with life. Virginia and Vanessa served, unhappily, at the "sacred spot" of the tea table, both when guests came and when they did not, for, according to the liturgy of the household, their father could not serve himself his tea.[24] Nor could he take a walk by himself, so afternoon walks with him became "a penance."[25] The sacred space within which Virginia Stephen became most fully herself—where she experienced rage, despair, ecstasy, where she "first heard those horrible voices," where she read herself "into a trance of perfect bliss"—was her own room.[26] There she established the rituals and practices—reading, writing—that would sustain her throughout her life.

When, after the death of their father, she and Vanessa were set free from the Kensington drawing rooms of their youth, they sought deliberately to transgress the liturgy of the tea table. Woolf acknowledged that the "game of Victorian society" had helped teach her how to make "something seemly out of raw odds and ends" and how to "slip in things that would be inaudible if one marched straight up and spoke out loud."[27] But she also knew that the conversation she had been required to make at the tea table left its mark in a kind of "sidelong approach" in her writing, especially in her early reviews.

Once free of those conventions, she and Vanessa began establishing forms of community based on fresh rituals and new sacred spaces. At 46 Gordon Square, the noise of London poured in through the windows, a startling change from the "muffled silence" of their childhood home in Hyde Park Gate. Virginia and her sister spread out into their new home's uncrowded spaces, no longer sharing a sitting room. They eradicated the red plush furniture and complicated wallpaper of their childhood and washed their walls with plain distemper. They no longer dressed for dinner or followed the rules about when to have their coffee. Having "lived under the sway of a society that was about fifty years too old for us," Virginia and Vanessa were set free to live as the "explorers and revolutionists" they both understood themselves to be.[28] "Everything was going to be new; everything was going to be different. Everything was on trial."[29]

Soon they were hosting Thursday evening parties, "the germ," Woolf wrote, from which Bloomsbury grew. Thoby's Cambridge friends began showing up late at night, and they all struggled awkwardly toward a new kind of conversation. Vanessa or Thoby or Clive would venture a question and receive a monosyllabic answer. But the silence, Virginia remembers, "was difficult, not dull," born of a sense that real conversation mattered.[30] Finally, someone would say something about beauty or the good or reality and ignite a conversation that would last into the early hours of the next day. Thinking back on those parties, Woolf remembered that no one ever said anything about her appearance, a welcome change from George Duckworth's critique of her hair, her clothes, and her behavior after an evening out. In Bloomsbury she was told "I must say you made your point rather well." Or, "I think you were talking rather through your hat."[31] For Virginia Stephen, this was a reassuring difference from the atmosphere of 22 Hyde Park Gate, so dominated by Victorian ideas about men and women and the relations between them. When Clive Bell did eventually propose marriage to Vanessa, Virginia and Thoby agreed that this was "the worst of Thursday evenings!"[32]

The early days of Bloomsbury possessed, according to Woolf, a "monastic character." Conversation focused on abstract ideas; the body was not spoken of, although they were all watching each other closely. One evening, Woolf writes in "Old Bloomsbury," Lytton Strachey entered the drawing room, pointed to a stain on Vanessa's dress, and asked, "Semen?" Everyone fell about laughing, and "all barriers of reticence and reserve went down. A flood of the sacred fluid seemed to overwhelm us." Sex became a topic of conversation, discussed "with the same excitement and openness that we had discussed the nature of good."[33] And with this, Virginia, Vanessa, and their friends set about rethinking and revolutionizing the ideas about sex and marriage with which they had been raised. Vanessa and Clive remained married, and often lived in the same house, but made lives with other lovers. Within her marriage to Leonard Woolf, Virginia conducted a love affair with Vita Sackville-West. Virginia's and Vanessa's marriages scandalized their parents' old friends and relatives, and Woolf imagined how furiously her father would have disapproved of it all. As Woolf put it, "the future of Bloomsbury was to prove that many variations can be played on the theme of sex."[34]

Virginia continued to participate in small communities within Bloomsbury for the rest of her life. At the end of 1907, Clive Bell initiated a play-reading society in which Virginia, Vanessa, their brother Adrian, Lytton Strachey, Clive Bell, Saxon Sydney-Turner, and others read aloud plays of Shakespeare, Dryden, Ibsen, and bawdy Restoration comedies. They kept minutes and analyzed each other's performances. Woolf was also an active member of the Memoir Club, organized by Molly MacCarthy in 1920 to regather the Bloomsbury group after the war. Vanessa, Clive, Leonard, Lytton, Virginia, E. M. Forster, Roger Fry, and other old friends met for dinner periodically and then, promising complete candor and frankness, read aloud autobiographical writing to each other. Woolf's earliest contributions, "22 Hyde Park Gate" and "Old Bloomsbury," were written in the early 1920s, and her latest, "Am I a Snob," in 1936. In 1940, she read aloud a piece on the Dreadnought hoax that she had originally written for the Rodmell Women's Institute. In her contributions, Woolf wrote openly about being sexually abused by her half-brothers. When she read her accounts aloud in the group, she sensed "a kind of uncomfortable boredom on the part of the males; to whose genial cheerful sense my revelations were at once mawkish

& distasteful."[35] Sometimes she felt overexposed after an evening at the Memoir Club; at other times she delighted in the brilliance of her performance. But the group remained important to her, and she kept participating until her death.

Bloomsbury, as Hermione Lee has noted, was full of such groups—Thursday evenings and Friday evenings, play-reading societies and memoir-writing ones.[36] But Woolf also participated in communities beyond the boundaries of her circle. As a young woman, she taught evening classes for working people at Morley College in London, a community of eager learners in whose company she worked out some of her ideas about English history and literature. Her students also taught her how educational opportunities were determined by social class, knowledge that helped shape *A Room of One's Own* and *Three Guineas*. She took her students to Westminster Abbey to try to make English history come alive for them, invited Vanessa to talk to them about paintings in the National Gallery, and tried to help at least one of her students—"a socialist, of a kind, and a poet"[37]—find a job. Hermione Lee sees in the relationship between Woolf and the socialist poet an inspiration for Septimus Warren Smith and his teacher, Miss Isabel Pole.[38] He might also have served as a model for the unemployed man who stands on the steps of St. Paul's with his bag of pamphlets in *Mrs. Dalloway*, wondering whether or not to go inside. All of her students were trying, she wrote, "to piece together what they heard; to seek reasons; to connect ideas"—a description that would appear again in her tribute to the common reader.[39]

Although she taught at Morley College for only two years, she drew on the experience throughout her life. In 1940, when Ben Nicholson, Vita Sackville-West's son, wrote to her criticizing the Bloomsbury group for not having used their considerable talents to turn the world from fascism, she defended herself in a draft of her reply by saying she had taught at Morley College. She also pointed to her work with the Women's Co-operative Guild, a movement of working class women. For four years, she chaired a weekly meeting of the guild in her home in Richmond.[40] A dozen women would gather for dinner and listen to a speaker, arranged by Woolf, who would address the group on some social question, labor issue, or other topic. A discussion followed, although most of the women remained quiet, and Woolf expressed puzzlement in her diary about what they got out of the meetings. The women occasionally frustrated her with their resistance to some of the topics she proposed, like venereal disease—although, in this case, she won them over, and they later asked for a session on sex education. When one woman opposed participating in a demonstration for peace on the Sabbath, Woolf worried over the "terrible grip Xtianity still has. . . . That I believe is still the chief enemy—the fear of God."[41] But she also admired their "good sense" and shared their desire for "something beyond the daily life." They were also wholeheartedly opposed to war, and the clarity of their position undergirds Woolf's own feminist embrace of pacifism in *Three Guineas*.

Woolf wrote in the draft of her reply to Ben Nicholson that, by participating in these communities, she had tried to reach beyond her "little private circle of exquisite and cultivated people."[42] She felt the distance, though, between herself and the working people with whom she read and studied and organized, and she was often tone-deaf to their interests. She more often saw herself as their teacher than they hers. She felt as "dulled and bothered" by their ceremonies as she did by being in church, describing the Women's Co-operative Guild Jubilee celebration as "windblown, gaseous, with elementary emotions." She wished she were home working on the novel that would become *The Years*; it felt to her "more real."[43] No doubt she felt more comfortable at the Thursday evenings in Gordon Square than she did in her classroom at Morley College or in the weekly meetings of the Women's Co-operative Guild. But her participation in these communities taught her something about both the possibilities and the limits of community, and the perspectives of those she encountered left their mark on her work. Even as she struggled to bridge the distance created by her privilege, she felt a kinship with those, like the student she tried to help, who loved poetry and with women who hated war. She felt a kinship to other "common readers" who, denied an education, were trying to create "some kind of whole" from the fragments of their reading.[44] The students of Morley College and the guild women had something in common with her that the Cambridge-educated men of the Memoir Club, who felt bored and discomfited by her account of being sexually abused as a child in her home, did not. And so she continued—through Morley College, through the Women's Co-operative Guild, through meetings of the Labour Party, through participation in the struggle for women's suffrage—to place herself in communities in which she did not feel wholly comfortable in order to cultivate relationships with people outside her circle and to work with them on matters of shared concern.

Andrew McNeillie, editor of Woolf's essays and assistant to the editor of Woolf's diaries, has described Woolf as someone who both "believed in community" and was also "an outsider, stranded" by "history, class and gender" and by "the tragic intensity of her vision."[45] But did her vision separate her from others, or draw her closer? Her vision illuminated the connections, however fragile, between people, and her experience of community stretched not only across the boundary of class and education but also across time. Thinking back on how she felt as a little girl being sexually abused by an older Gerald Duckworth, she describes how her instinctive revulsion connected her to thousands of years of "ancestresses" who had passed that instinct down through the ages. Certain characters—Lucy Swithin in *Between the Acts*, the unnamed woman who sings in Regent's Park in *Mrs. Dalloway*—illuminate the hidden connections between human beings from prehistory all the way through to an unknown future. Woolf located herself within several overlapping communities: women, artists, pacifists, common readers. The intensity of her vision helped her see connections that would otherwise remain invisible.

Rather than imagining Woolf stranded, it might be more accurate to think of her, as she imagined herself in *A Room of One's Own*, seeking new forms of community in the space between revelation and exile. In its opening pages, Woolf describes herself, a woman thinking, sitting on the banks of a river: "To the right and left bushes of some sort, golden and crimson, glowed with the colour, even it seemed burnt with the heat, of fire. On the further bank the willows wept in perpetual lamentation, their hair about their shoulders. . . . Thought—to call it by a prouder name than it deserved—had let its line down into the stream."[46] The image of the burning bush—drawn from the story of Moses encountering God in a burning bush in the third chapter of the book of Exodus—often appears in Woolf's writing. The revelation Clarissa Dalloway experiences when Sally Seton kisses her is "an illumination; a match burning in a crocus; an inner meaning almost expressed."[47] The hedge in *To the Lighthouse*, to which Lily keeps turning as she paints, trying to achieve her vision, recalls the revelatory bush in the Exodus story, as does Woolf's image of "matches struck unexpectedly in the dark." In her last novel, *Between the Acts*, a "megaphonic, anonymous" voice speaks from the bushes. "*Let's talk in words of one syllable*,"[48] it says, recalling, perhaps, the words Moses heard from the bush: I am who I am. At the novel's end, one character reflects: "Surely it was time someone invented a new plot, or that the author came out from the bushes."[49]

On the riverbank in *A Room of One's Own*, the bushes glow so powerfully they seem almost burnt, reflecting both the possibility and the risk of revelation. But on the other side of the river grow, not bushes lit up by the late afternoon sun, but the weeping willows of Psalm 137, a lament in which the people of Israel, in exile from their holy city, hang their harps in the willows rather than sing for their captors and dream violent dreams of revenge. The woman on the bank is trying to think her way toward a new understanding of fiction and of community. An undergraduate in a boat oars through the reflections of the burning bush and the willows weeping "in perpetual lamentation," and then they close behind him "as if he had never been." But for the woman thinking on the bank, neither revelation nor lamentation can be serenely oared through. She must lower the line of her thought through both. She is an outsider, an exile who could choose to hang her harp in the branches of the willow and be silenced by her exile from the university. But she is also alive to a revelation, a burning bush, a match struck in the dark and so draws up her fish through water that reflects her position as an outsider whose perspective reveals what is blazing beneath the surface.

Woolf may not have been stranded, but McNeillie is right that "history, class and gender" blocked her at many turns. After the woman brings the flashing fish of her thought to the surface, her mind becomes so active that she can no longer sit still. She walks across the grass of the university, only to be intercepted by a beadle who points out that only fellows and scholars are allowed to walk where she is walking; women emphatically are not. Woolf will go on to enumerate many other gendered exclusions in *Three Guineas*: "Both the Army and the Navy are closed to our sex," she writes. "Nor again are we allowed to be members of the Stock Exchange. . . . We cannot preach sermons or negotiate treaties."[50] The exclusion that she most resents, though, is the one at the center of *A Room of One's Own*: her exclusion from the university. A brilliant, intellectually alive young woman who was kept at home as her brothers were sent off to Cambridge, Woolf cultivated an outsider's view. Men may look at Eton or Harrow, Oxford or Cambridge as "the source of memories and of traditions innumerable," she writes. But women look at the monastic buildings of England's great universities and see the sacrifices they were forced to make so that family funds could support their brothers' educations. When the daughters of educated men gaze on the "noble courts and quadrangles" of the colleges, they see only "petticoats with holes in them, cold legs of mutton, and the boat train starting for abroad while the guard slams the door in their faces."[51]

The outsiders' perspective cultivated by the daughters of educated men—and by those who are excluded "because you are Jews, because you are democrats, because of race, because of religion"[52]—is an indispensable characteristic of the new community Woolf seeks because those who have been excluded from a community are free to reimagine it all the way down to Eliot's "permanent things" and beyond. We must ask ourselves, she writes in *Three Guineas*, whether or not we want to join "the procession of educated men" or to create something new. Looking not to replicate the rituals and communities that men have created to advertise their worth and advance their careers, she experiments instead with alternative rituals and ideas of community that could prevent war—ideas that "a different training and a different tradition put more easily within" the reach of women than men.[53]

Woolf imagines in the first chapter of *Three Guineas* what the university might look like if it could be reimagined by those kept outside of it. Composing a response to an imaginary appeal to send a guinea to support a struggling college for women, Woolf insists that she will support only a university that would "produce the kind of society, the kind of people that will help to prevent war."[54] Unlike Cambridge or Oxford, it should be built, not of stone, but of "some cheap, easily combustible material that does not hoard dust and perpetuate traditions." It would offer no degrees nor would it require lectures or sermons or ceremonies. Such things "breed competition and jealousy"; they separate people into "the miserable distinctions of rich and poor, of clever and stupid." The ideal university would have no chapels or museums or "libraries with chained books and first editions under glass cases." The books and art should be "new and always changing."[55] No doubt inspired by how Vanessa and her family had made the Charleston farmhouse their constantly evolving canvas,[56] Woolf imagined all decoration in this ideal college being done by hand by each new generation.

The ideal college would be poor and its curriculum centered around "the arts that can be taught cheaply and practiced by poor people," among which she counted the arts of medicine, mathematics, music, painting, and literature. Rather than learning "the arts of ruling, of killing, of acquiring land and capital," students should be taught how to engage with others, how to cultivate curiosity about "other people's lives and minds." The teachers should be drawn from the ranks of "good livers" as well as "good thinkers" and the students encouraged to seek learning for its own sake, rather than for examinations and degrees.[57]

A college that would cultivate a passion for liberty and a hatred of war would not replicate the academic life practiced at Oxford and Cambridge but be "an experimental college, an adventurous college," the central practices of which would not be specialization or competition but rather combination and cooperation. Echoing Lily Briscoe's vision of the artist's vocation, Woolf's new college would also seek to "discover what new combinations made good wholes in human life" and create from fragments new wholes over which "thought lingers and love plays."[58]

This lively, angry thought experiment, which ends with Woolf earmarking her guinea for the rags, petrol, and matches needed to burn the existing school to the ground, provides the groundwork for an imagined Society of Outsiders that could critique, rethink, and reimagine not only education but also the professions of law and politics and the institutions of religion. Woolf knows this is a tricky business for women. "The very word 'society,'" she writes, "sets tolling in memory the dismal bells of a harsh music: shall not, shall not, shall not. You shall not learn; you shall not earn; you shall not own; you shall not—. . ."[59] This is the kind of harsh music—women can't write, women can't paint—that plays in Lily Briscoe's mind as she struggles to find the courage to make the first mark on her canvas. It is the harsh music of the churchmen of Woolf's day, men like Lord Hugh Cecil, who described the idea of a woman priest as "flagrantly repulsive," echoing earlier male voices, like the nineteenth-century theologian Henry Lidden, who found female choristers "grotesque."[60]

But rather than remaining an "outsider, stranded," Woolf imagines a community of outsiders that would reimagine and remake the universities, the professions, and the church. This society would be pacifist, anonymous, elastic, and agile, characterized by "freedom from unreal loyalties."[61] It would move forward the work Woolf discussed in *A Room of One's One* of preparing for Shakespeare's sister by cultivating communities within which women could thrive and create. Does it matter that her Society of Outsiders did not exist in the way that the Labour Party or the Women's Co-operative Guild existed? Woolf saw signs of it everywhere, in acts of resistance large and small, past and present. She found it in the life of Mr. Leigh Smith, who believed, in the mid-nineteenth century, in educating his sons and daughters equally. She also found it in the "outsiders' school" founded by his daughter, Barbara, who used her allowance to open a school that welcomed "different sexes and different classes . . . different creeds, Roman Catholics, Jews and 'pupils from families of advanced free thought.'"[62] And she saw it in young women of her own day who did not attend church but rather experimented with the power of their absence from the pews.[63]

As in the university, with its beadles and dons and fathers who educate their sons but not their daughters, the gatekeepers of the Church of England of Woolf's day were men. Woolf employs the word "sacred" in *Three Guineas* to describe, not religious institutions, but "the sacred year 1919,"[64] in which the Sex Disqualification (Removal) Act was passed by Parliament, stipulating that no one could "be disqualified by sex or marriage from the exercise of any public function, or from being appointed to or holding any civil or judicial office or post, or from entering or assuming or carrying on any civil profession or vocation, or for admission to any incorporated society."[65] The act applied to the civil service, the courts, and the universities, although women continued to be excluded from these institutions. The Church of England, however, was untouched by this monumental change and continued to exclude women from ministerial vocations and leadership positions. Between 1910, the year in which, as Woolf famously wrote, "human character changed," and 1935, when a commission established by the archbishops of Canterbury and York produced a report on the ministry of women, there had been a vigorous movement for the ordination of women to the priesthood.[66] Once the Church League for Women's Suffrage began to turn its attention to sex discrimination in the church itself and to consider "the deep religious significance of the women's movement,"[67] the campaign to ordain women to the priesthood began gathering momentum. Woolf followed the debates and read closely the 1935 report of the Archbishops' Commission on the Ministry of Women, which she analyzes in *Three Guineas*. When women said they wished to enter the priesthood, Woolf writes, the commission was "forced to consult the New Testament," only to find that the founder of their religion did not require his followers to have a particular training or identify with a particular gender: "[Christ] chose his disciples from the working class from which he sprang himself. The prime qualification was some rare gift which in those early days was bestowed capriciously upon carpenters and fishermen, and upon women also."[68] Even St. Paul, at whose feet Woolf lays the church's policing of women's bodies and silencing of their voices, instructs women to be veiled when speaking in church, she notes. If he must instruct them, she argues, they must have been preaching.

How, then, is it possible that the commission's report concludes that women must continue to be excluded from the priesthood? Simple, Woolf explains: the commission chose the mind of the church, with its entrenched gender hierarchy, over the mind of the founder and his egalitarian vision. The report appeals to "the author of the Pastoral Epistles, be he St. Paul or another" who "regarded women as being debarred on the ground of her sex from the position of an official 'teacher' in the Church, or from any office involving the exercise of a governmental authority over a man." Sounding very like her Clapham Sect ancestors who argued that slavery overturned every law of Christ, Woolf notes that by excluding women from positions of leadership and teaching, the Church of England had overridden "the ruling of Christ himself." Apparently ensuring that women do not exercise "governmental authority over a man" trumps even Christ's own practice and teaching.[69]

She finds in an Anglo-Catholic response to the commission's report a gloss on that decision that makes plain the fear of women and their bodies that undergirds it. The authors of *Women and the Ministry, Some Considerations on the Report of the Archbishops' Commission on the Ministry of Women* (1936) argue that a woman in the pulpit will result in the "lowering of the spiritual tone of Christian worship" because, although women's "thoughts and desires" do not become aroused by male ministers, it would be impossible for men to witness the ministry of women without arousing feelings "which should be quiescent during the times of the adoration of almighty God." Woolf sums up the argument thus: "In the opinion of the Commissioners, therefore, Christian women are more spiritually minded than Christian men—a remarkable, but no doubt adequate, reason for excluding them from the priesthood."[70]

With the church putting forward misogynistic arguments for excluding women from ministry, religion was ripe to be questioned, critiqued, and reimagined by the Society of Outsiders. Members of the society, she imagined, would cultivate knowledge of the Bible and the history of Christianity; they would attend services and analyze "the spiritual and intellectual value of sermons." They would bring "the opinions of men whose profession is religion" under the same kind of critique they bring to the opinions of men in the universities and the professions. Their critique would be not only critical but creative, intended "to free the religious spirit from its present servitude" and "if need be, to create a new religion based, it might well be, upon the New Testament, but, it might well be, very different from the religion now erected upon that basis."[71]

Many of Woolf's close friends remained silent about *Three Guineas*. Leonard defended its "impeccable feminism," but other men in their circle—Forster, Keynes—did not take it seriously.[72] Vita found its arguments "misleading,"[73] an unsigned review in *Time and Tide* called it "indecent, and almost obscene,"[74] and Q. D. Leavis attacked it in *Scrutiny* as full of "preposterous claims and some nasty attitudes . . . the art of living as conceived by a social parasite."[75] But the book elicited a lively and appreciative response from a wide range of common readers, many of which, as Brenda R. Silver has shown, responded to Woolf's ideas about religion, ideas that reviews of the book had mostly ignored. Some correspondents wrote with criticisms—two clergymen objected to her description of the working-class origins of Jesus and his disciples, and a few other correspondents wanted to correct her implication that the salaries of Church of England clergy derived from taxpayer funds—but many other writers, mostly women, wrote to her because her discussion of religion resonated with them. Amelia Forbes Emerson, wife of Ralph Waldo Emerson's grandson, wrote to say that she detected the influence of Caroline Emelia Stephen in the book and believed that the Society of Outsiders contained a great deal of the spirit of the Society of Friends. A member of a Roman Catholic society of laypeople who, as she put it, "hate snobbery and love honest work," wrote to say she loved the book and only worried that Woolf's discussions of sex and her critique of St. Paul might keep those who most needed to read it from doing so. Very much of one mind with Woolf about the working-class origins of Jesus and his disciples, this correspondent signed her letters "Yrs. sincerely in Christ the Worker." Another letter, from a woman in the Scottish Episcopal Church, wrote to ask if Woolf knew of any "non-sectarian movement of Christians" pressing for change from the outside. Woolf imagined her Society of Outsiders so richly that many of her readers, including her religious readers, wanted to join.[76] The responses of these readers do not appeal to divisions between the religious and the secular, believers and unbelievers. They seem, instead, to assume with Woolf that a "common interest unites us; it is one world, one life."[77]

The vision of religious community reimagined by a Society of Outsiders is very like that of the new college: it is formed by the perspective of the outsider who, having been excluded by the rituals and ceremonies and the structures of the church, is free to imagine new ones. It would be a community shaped by experimentation, just as the new college and the reimagined professions would be marked by an experimentality grounded in "the interests of research and for love of the work itself."[78] Its experiments would be "not with public means in public but with private means in private," exchanging the beauty of the pageantry "in which only one sex takes an active part" for attention to natural beauty and "the scattered beauty which needs only to be combined by artists in order to become visible to all."[79] The fascists, Woolf writes, have hypnotized Europe with their pageantry, and "it must be our aim not to submit ourselves to such hypnotism" but rather help each other see new possibilities for life in community.

Woolf found inspiration in the courageous private experimentation she saw happening around her: the mayoress of Woolrich's statement that she "would not even do as much as darn a sock to help in a war," the women's sports teams whose membership increased each year despite offering no trophies or awards, and the decline in church attendance by young women. All of these outsider experiments, Woolf believed, supported the creation of a society that refused to wage war. That the newspapers have reported on these, Woolf believed, meant that there were many more "private and submerged experiments of which there is no public proof,"[80] the kinds of "unhistoric acts," as George Eliot put it in *Middlemarch*, that although unremembered make life better for those who will follow. Such obscurity was crucial, she believed, to the cultivation of new rituals and communities. Like the apophatic English mystics who believed God must be sought in darkness,[81] Woolf believed the creative power of the Society of Outsiders would need to shelter in obscurity. For "if we wish to help the human mind to create," she wrote, "and to prevent it from scoring the same rut repeatedly, we must do what we can to shroud it in darkness."[82] Secrecy also protects, and outsiders need protection, especially when jobs are scarce and salaries low.

Woolf's interest in the community that private, local rituals could create and sustain appears in her work from the beginning. In "The Journal of Mistress Joan Martyn," written when she was twenty-four years old, she lovingly describes the domestic rituals of Joan's medieval household that keep the violence of the time at bay: her mother swinging the bells up and down the road, calling the workers in for the night, and then locking the door with her keys to keep everyone safe;

Joan herself reading aloud to the household until it becomes too dark for her to see; Joan's prayer that the gates will hold and that robbers and murderers will pass by.

Joan, like Woolf, also ventured beyond the community of her household. If the domestic rituals of the household keep Joan safe, the local ritual of the pilgrimage to the shrine of Our Lady of Walsingham opens her life to the lives of strangers. Holding hands as they approach the shrine, "humbly as human beings,"[83] Joan realizes that the people she has been taught to fear and to oppress are human beings with their own lives and their own stories to tell.

In all of Woolf's novels, people struggle toward experiences of community that "overflow boundaries and make unity out of multiplicity."[84] They go to church, make pilgrimages, share meals, plan and attend parties, read together, gaze at views and paintings and bowls of fruit together, walk together, put on plays together, mourn together. Their experiments are private and local and not always successful. When they are successful, they are only temporarily so—moments of being that begin to vanish almost as soon as they have happened. But they all contain the hope that new ways of being and relating to each other might be found—ways of being together that reflect "the recurring dream that has haunted the human mind since the beginning of time; the dream of peace, the dream of freedom."[85]

In many of Woolf's novels, as in her life, artmaking and the creation of community go hand in hand. In *To the Lighthouse*, Mrs. Ramsay's creation of her dinner party and Lily Briscoe's creation of her painting follow a similar pattern. Both begin with each artist having to confront her deepest questions about her own life, questions that create a weariness that each artist must overcome in order to take the first steps toward creation. As she sits down at the head of the table and "wearily" begins trying to seat her guests, Mrs. Ramsay asks herself what she has done with her life. Returning to the Ramsay house after the war, Lily confronts a similar question and a similar weariness. "What does it mean then, what can it all mean?" Lily asks as she struggles to feel something for the past. Both artists know they have the fragments they need to create their art but feel unsure of how to combine them. "And the whole effort of merging and flowing and creating rested on her,"

Mrs. Ramsay thinks.[86] "Such were some of the parts," Lily thinks as she considers her memories, the light on the wall, the absences in the house, "but how bring them together?"[87] Men get in the way of both artists' efforts—Mrs. Ramsay feels Mr. Ramsay's anger before the dinner even begins and bemoans "the sterility of men," their inability to shoulder a portion of this creative work. Lily is interrupted by a needy Mr. Ramsay and hears Charles Tansley's words, spoken before the war, still running in her mind after the war has ended—"women can't write, women can't paint." Lily's emotions run from blankness as she confronts this place she had once loved to anger about the emotional labor Mr. Ramsay demands of the women around him. Sitting down with her guests at the table, Mrs. Ramsay feels like a sailor who "not without weariness sees the wind fill his sail and yet hardly wants to be off again," imagining the rest that would come with sinking to the bottom of the sea.[88]

Woolf described writing *The Waves* as "writing to a rhythm not to a plot."[89] Both Mrs. Ramsay and Lily have to find their rhythm in order to achieve their vision. Mrs. Ramsay gives herself a shake like "the little shake that one gives a watch that has stopped" and feels, faintly, the "old familiar pulse" begin, a pulse she has to guard like the weak flame of a candle. Lily sets her easel at the right angle and makes the first stroke of her brush, bringing herself into "a dancing rhythmical movement." Both suffer as they struggle to find the flow—"I am drowning, my dear, in seas of fire," Mrs. Ramsay telegraphs silently to Lily at the dinner table, urging her to say something soothing to Mr. Tansley so that his foul mood will not make it impossible for her to achieve her vision. Lily enters into combat with "this formidable ancient enemy of hers—this other thing, this truth, this reality" to which she strives to respond truthfully on her canvas.

Eventually, both artists find their way to the heart of their work through rituals that help them "overflow boundaries and make unity out of multiplicity." When the candles are lit on Mrs. Ramsay's table, those sitting around it are drawn closer together. Mrs. Ramsay finds herself looking at the bowl of fruit on the table with Mr. Carmichael, who does not like her and who has a different way of looking. "But looking together," Woolf writes, "united them."[90] The candlelight brings the people around the table closer to one another and changes them from people sitting separately into a party making "common cause against the fluidity out there."[91] The Swiss maid brings the *boeuf en daube* to the table and, as its delicious scent rises, Mrs. Ramsay has the feeling of "celebrating a festival," a feeling that gathers up both the glittery illusion of love and the way love carries "in its bosom the seeds of death." Mrs. Ramsay feels herself hovering like a hawk over the proceedings, unfurling like a flag in "an element of joy" that rises from "husband and children and friends" gathered together around this meal. "Of such moments, she thought, the thing is made that endures."[92]

Woolf seeds her description of Mrs. Ramsay's dinner party with religious imagery. Invoking the "festival" recalls the scholarship of Jane Ellen Harrison on the ancient spring festivals that renew the life of the community through rituals of rebirth. Mrs. Ramsay's successful matchmaking of Paul and Minta is a sign of that renewal, and she imagines them "danced round with mockery, decorated with garlands."[93] As many readers have noted, there are also many allusions to the Christian eucharist in this scene. Pericles Lewis and Jane de Gay, for example, both read Mrs. Ramsay's dinner party as a "female communion" in which Mrs. Ramsay, like Jesus at the Last Supper, distributes helpings of the *boeuf en daube* as sacred food[94] and feeds her guests "spiritually as well as physically."[95] Toward the end of the dinner, Mrs. Ramsay hears the voices around the table "as if they were voices at a service in the cathedral, for she did not listen to the words." This way of listening becomes a way of reading in the scene following the dinner party, when Mrs. Ramsay reads poetry without seeking the meaning, letting the sound of the words wash from side to side in her mind, attending to the colors of the poetry more than the meanings of the words themselves. While listening to her husband recite Charles Elton's poem "Luriana Lurilee" at the end of the dinner, she hears the words "like music," in "her own voice, outside her self, saying quite easily and naturally what had been in her mind the whole evening while she said different things."[96] Like scripture, the recited poem gathers up her unexpressed thoughts, gives them a voice, and a sound, if not an agreed-upon meaning.

The evening ends with Mr. Carmichael, holding his napkin before him so that he looks like a white-robed priest, offering Mrs. Ramsay a verse of "Luriana Lurilee." Mr. Carmichael bows to Mrs. Ramsay as she passes, laying the verse down like an offering, and she returns his gesture "with a feeling of relief and gratitude." She thinks he likes her better than he did at the beginning of the evening; something has been healed, made better, through her art. From the liminal space of the threshold, she turns to inhabit "a moment longer" the scene she created "which was vanishing even as she looked." Her art, made of fragments of conversation and silence, food and light, poetry and the unspoken feelings that poetry expresses, is ephemeral. But it has brought into being a community that "partook," for a moment, "of eternity."[97] Mrs. Ramsay has had her vision, just as Lily will at the end of the novel.

Mrs. Ramsay finds her creative flow in the rituals of the table—lighting the candles, serving the food, making conversation—while Lily finds hers in the rhythmic dance of the brush on the canvas. Woolf describes this rhythm as dictated to Lily—a notion that will reappear years later in "A Sketch of the Past" when she describes her understanding of the world as a work of art as "so instinctive that it seems given to me, not made by me."[98] The idea of something outside her that draws her into its rhythms also reaches back to her diary entry of 1906 when she describes feeling "the steady beat of the great Creator as I write."[99] As Lily gives herself over to this rhythm, other things fall away: her name, her personality, her appearance. Her mind becomes like a fountain—an image Woolf uses to describe Mrs. Ramsay in the first part of the novel—overflowing with memories and ideas.

As she paints, a new community begins to come into view, a community of the living and the dead, the present and the absent. She begins to recall Mrs. Ramsay's artmaking powers. Even in memory, Mrs. Ramsay "resolved everything into simplicity; made these angers, irritations fall off like old rags; she brought together this and that and then this and so made out of that miserable silliness and spite (she and Charles squabbling, sparring, had been silly and spiteful) something . . . which survived . . . , affecting one almost like a work of art."[100] The intersection of Mrs. Ramsay's artmaking with her own raises the question with which Lily began: What is the meaning of life? She sees that "Mrs. Ramsay making of the moment something permanent" is a revelation that comes close to an answer. And the answer is that the "great revelation perhaps never did come. Instead there were little daily miracles, illuminations, matches struck unexpectedly in the dark."[101] Mrs. Ramsay sitting on the beach, her presence easing the tension between Lily and Charles Tansley was one; her dinner party was another. These moments of being are not God's voice speaking from the burning bush, but they are akin to it—moments when something eternal is unexpectedly revealed.

Like Mrs. Ramsay's dinner party, Lily's art is also ephemeral: her painting "would be hung in the attics, she thought; it would be rolled up and flung under a sofa."[102] As she paints, she confronts the unknowability of others and the mysteries that would never resolve. "Could it be, even for elderly people, that this was life?—startling, unexpected, unknown?"[103] And for a moment, she has "a sense of some one there, of Mrs. Ramsay," a consoling vision that, like all visions, would have to be "perpetually remade." Her vision will be made and remade through art: creating from fragments "one of those globed, compacted things over which thought lingers and love plays," feeling her way along by "some secret sense, fine as air," finding the miracle, the ecstasy in the ordinary stuff of the world.

Lily's experience of the creation of her painting not only brings her into communion with the dead Mrs. Ramsay and the absent Charles Tansley; it also makes her long for community with the living and the present. She looks out over the water for the boat carrying Mr. Ramsay, Cam, and James to the lighthouse, feeling "she had something she must share."[104]

Echoing the words of Christ on the cross in the gospel of John, Lily says, "It is finished." Mr. Carmichael, "looking like an old pagan god," joins her to look out over the water. Lily feels they are thinking the same things and so need not speak. Like Mrs. Ramsay and Mr. Carmichael gazing appreciatively at a bowl of fruit years before, looking together united them. Mr. Carmichael appears to her to be offering a blessing, crowning the occasion of the arrival at the lighthouse and the completion of the painting at once.[105]

The vision of sacred community in *To the Lighthouse* is deeply associated with creativity and creation. Art has the power to knit people into such a community—not only by gazing together, as Mrs. Ramsay and Mr. Carmichael did, at something outside themselves, but by being part of the work of art, being, as Woolf writes in her autobiography, "the thing itself." The war that separates the day in which Mrs. Ramsay creates her dinner party from the day in which Lily creates her painting works in the opposite direction, separating loved ones from each other, rendering fragments from wholes. In the creation of their art, Mrs. Ramsay and Lily point the way toward the community Woolf will imagine in *Three Guineas*—ephemeral, yet transformative; nurtured in obscurity; shaped by creative experimentation—a community that expresses the dream of peace and freedom for which it longs.

In Woolf's novels of the late 1930s, that dream seems more elusive than in the earlier novels. The limits of the practices by which she believed the world could be changed—reading, writing, artmaking—become more visible, as in the scene with North and Sara reading Marvell in *The Years*, published in 1937. Partygoers in *The Years* do not depart invigorated by their shared experience as they do in *Mrs. Dalloway* and *To the Lighthouse*, but rather full of questions and unfulfilled longings. Unlike the faces brought closer to one another in the candlelight of Mrs. Ramsay's dinner party, Eleanor Pargiter looks around at her family and friends at the end of a party at the end of the novel, and they look pale and wan, their conversations broken and trailing. "There must be another life, she thought, sinking back into her chair, exasperated. Not in dreams; but here and now, in this room, with living people." Existence itself seems "too short, too broken," and Eleanor holds her hands hollow in her lap, a gesture akin to prayer: "She held her hands hollowed; she felt that she wanted to enclose the present moment; to make it stay; to fill it fuller and fuller, with the past, the present, and the future, until it shone, whole, bright, deep with understanding."[106] But understanding eludes her, and so does communication. She tries to speak to Edward, but he's telling North "some old college story"—a story that excludes her because, like Woolf, she was not given a college education. She lets her hands drop and thinks of death—"the endless night; the endless dark"[107]—even as the morning light begins to fill the windows.

Woolf will be searching for new forms of sacred community—another life, "here and now"—until her death in 1941. Her credo in "A

Sketch of the Past," written in April 1939, imagines the "whole world as a work of art" and we as parts of it, the thing itself. Later that year, on September 3, the day the prime minister announced that Great Britain was at war with Germany and Woolf felt "the unreality of force" muffling everything, a thought about religious community appears in her diary. "Question: if we had a church? The relief of having some common outside interest or belief. If it were a belief . . ."[108] This question rises up from her reverie. She follows her thoughts as they move: the church bells are ringing, someone has sent beautiful flowers to the church, and then "Question: if we had a church?" Like the phrase "we are in the hands of the Lord" that arises in Mrs. Ramsay's reverie, this question floats up, she writes it down, and it trails off, unanswered, into an ellipsis. Would "some outside interest or belief" bring relief in the dark times through which she was living? She wonders for a moment and then moves on to think about work and sugar rations, the Hogarth Press, and making sure she and Leonard have enough gasoline. It is not any particular answer but the question itself that is revealing: it reflects the deepening of her concern with community as the war intensifies.

Although she did not live to see the end of the Second World War, she did look beyond it. In a talk she gave to the Workers' Educational Association in Brighton in April 1940, she imagines the kind of community that could emerge in the war's wake: a society in which income tax would undermine distinctions between classes and the public libraries make the whole of literature available to the common reader, a society in which "we are all to have equal opportunities, equal chances of developing whatever gifts we may possess." Just as society would change, literature would also change. "Literature," she says without anxiety, "is always ending, and beginning again."[109]

Woolf imagines her vision for a new community through the lens of literature. Through the nineteenth century down to the beginning of the First World War, she writes, novelists sat securely in a tower of privilege created from education, family rank, and parental wealth. The wars of their day did not impinge on their lives as the wars of the twentieth century did on hers. News of the battles of the Napoleonic Wars took time to arrive on the shores of England. Jane Austen and Sir Walter Scott did not hear Napoleon's voice "as we hear Hitler's voice as we sit at home of an evening."[110] These writers did not question the "limited vision" of their life in their secure tower. They may have wished to make the tower more accessible to more people, but they did not want to destroy it or come down from it.

After the First World War, though, the tower began to lean. Once a tower leans, Woolf says, we become aware that we are in one. Writers in their leaning towers became more conscious "of their middle-class birth; of their expensive educations." With the knowledge of the suffering of the First World War and the threat of another war hovering, writers began to see that the towers in which they were living and writing were "founded upon injustice and tyranny." They began to long to come down and join the common life of humanity. What Woolf finds in the literature created in the years leading up to the Second World War is the writer's desire "to be closer to their kind, to write the common speech of their kind, to share the emotions of their kind, no longer to be isolated and exalted in solitary state upon their tower, but to be down on the ground with the mass of human kind."[111] This passage echoes in both language and rhythm the first chapter of Genesis, in which God creates animals and fish and birds "after their kind." This echo emphasizes that the new postwar society Woolf imagines, in which writers make their art within the human community rather than from towers of privilege, will have to be a deliberate act of creation.

Silver has shown how Woolf's image of being "down on the ground with the mass of human kind" picks up an echo of the Elizabethan playhouse, in which the audience shares in the work of creation—doing, in Woolf's words, "half the work of the dramatists."[112] Woolf had, in 1927, bemoaned the state of the poetic play, which she feared could not be revived. She did not believe T. S. Eliot's plays had succeeded, and she would particularly dislike *The Rock* when it was published in 1934. She wrote to Stephen Spender that she worried that Eliot was "petrifying into a priest." The dogmatism of *The Rock* hit one "too full in the face" and was "rather like an old ship swaying in the same track as the Waste Land."[113] Woolf had imagined, in 1927, a new literary form that would "be dramatic, and yet not a play," a work that would be "read, not acted."[114] Her last novel, *Between the Acts*, reflects something of that vision as well as her love of the communal artmaking that happened in

Elizabethan playhouses. It offers her most sustained attempt in fiction to explore how a community facing a war might be drawn together.

In the year before her death, Woolf became an active member of the Rodmell Women's Institute, and they asked her to write and produce a play for the village. Although she did not accept that invitation, she did write a novel about such a play, written and produced by Miss La Trobe, a quintessential Outsider. Miss La Trobe is queer, she is critical, she is an artist. She belongs to the village but does not fit in; she describes herself as an "outcast." On a summer evening only months before England declares war on Germany, she puts on a play she has written about the history of England, performed by people who live in the village. It recalls the commemorative rituals studied by Harrison and ancient spring festivals of renewal and rebirth. On the verge of war, a community gathers to remember and enact their history, awakening the "unacted parts" of actors and audience members alike. A mosaic of forms reveals the rhythms and patterns that have shaped the community, critiques and cherishes what has gone before, and offers the community a chance to reconnect with the land and with each other.

Stories of trauma murmur through the novel. The ancient Greek story of Philomela, who is turned into a swallow after being raped by her sister's husband, echoes throughout the day. Audience members ask each other, "'And what about the Jews? The refugees . . . the Jews . . . People like ourselves, beginning life again.'"[115] It is not only the war with Germany that threatens to shatter community, however. As she does in *Three Guineas*, Woolf has her eye on homegrown threats to human community as well. At the beginning of the novel, Isa reads a newspaper account of a rape in the Whitehall military barracks. Some soldiers lured a girl inside with a story about a horse with a green tail and, once inside, turned on her. "That was real," Isa thinks as she sets the newspaper down. Like Clarissa Dalloway, who feels Septimus Warren Smith's death in her body, the rape appears before Isa's eyes as if it is happening in her own home. In the rhythms of a nursery rhyme, Isa's imagination leads her closer and closer to the rape itself: "On the mahogany door panels she saw the Arch in Whitehall; through the Arch the barrack room; in the barrack room the bed, and on the bed the girl was screaming and hitting about the face."[116] Throughout the day, the rape haunts her: she hears the girl's screams running beneath her conversations, and phrases from the newspaper account repeat in various ways throughout the novel. Down to the last page of the book, the rape remains in Isa's mind: "The girl had gone skylarking with the troopers. She had screamed. She had hit him. . . . What then?"[117]

This is one of the central questions of *Between the Acts*: What then? How does a community move forward when human bodies have been violated and human bonds trespassed? Woolf sets her novel two months before war is declared, but she writes it with bombs falling from the sky. Her novel asks: How will humanity survive? How, in the midst of war, do we live toward a future beyond it?

In one of Woolf's first fictional efforts, "The Journal of Mistress Joan Martyn," the answer is found in the daily work of women, in storytelling and ritual-making, in remembering the past and imagining the future. Her last novel retains faith in these same practices. As in all of her novels, women's work is creative work, embodied in *Between the Acts* not by a hostess like Clarissa Dalloway, or a mother and wife like Mrs. Ramsay, or a painter like Lily Briscoe, but a playwright. Miss La Trobe is in many ways the opposite of Mrs. Dalloway and Mrs. Ramsay: whereas they operate within marriages shaped by Victorian understandings of men and women, Miss La Trobe is a lesbian whose lover, an actress, has recently walked out on her. Whereas Mrs. Dalloway and Mrs. Ramsay stand at the center of their community, drawing others to them through their beauty and their sympathy, Miss La Trobe lives on the margins of hers. Whereas their physical presence pulses at the heart of their creations, Miss La Trobe deliberately makes herself hidden, standing behind trees and bushes to watch her play unfold, making her the most godlike of Woolf's creators.

Like Mrs. Dalloway and Mrs. Ramsay, though, Miss La Trobe suffers when the play does not, at the beginning, take hold of the audience—when the first actor forgets her lines and audience members arrive late, disrupting the fragile beginnings of the audience's absorption as they find their way to a seat. Like Mrs. Dalloway and Mrs. Ramsay, she has to rely on others for her work of art to come to life. Like them, she creates her work both from and for the community itself. As Harrison might say, the boundary between actor and spectator is fluid: "All are actors, all are doing the thing done."[118]

But whereas Mrs. Dalloway and Mrs. Ramsay create their art from the present moment, Miss La Trobe's work invokes the past, the present, and the future. Miss La Trobe's play leads her audience through the eras of Queen Elizabeth I, Queen Anne, and Queen Victoria and into the present day. The play embeds critiques among its comedy and is especially critical of Victorian pieties, leading some to deride the play as "cheap and nasty" and others to ignore the critique in order to enjoy nostalgia for "the lamplit room; the ruby curtains; and Papa reading aloud."[119]

Even more striking than the scenes from history is the way Miss La Trobe attempts to invoke the present moment, to reveal the audience as also actors within history. After the Victorian scenes, Miss La Trobe lets the music fall silent and keeps the actors off-stage so that the audience can experience the present moment in its fullness as part of the unfolding history. "She wanted to expose them, as it were," Woolf writes, "to douche them, with present-time reality."[120] Miss La Trobe can feel the audience slipping away, not understanding what she is trying to achieve. But then a shower begins to fall, "like all the people in the world weeping." That intervention by Nature herself pulls them all into Miss La Trobe's vision for a moment, and they hear "the other voice speaking, the voice that was no one's voice . . . the voice that wept for human pain unending" speaking first in the tune of a nursery rhyme and then in jazz. Isa feels for a moment that she could give this voice "all her treasure," lay it down "on the altar of the rain-soaked earth."[121]

In the present moment, swallows—or perhaps "the temple-haunting martins"—dance among the trees, which appear in this saturated moment like "the spaced pillars of some cathedral church" that "prevented what was fluid from overflowing." And as the jazz plays on the gramophone, the actors come out from the bushes holding mirrors and reflect the audience back to themselves in fragments. As the audience shifts uncomfortably, trying to evade its reflection, a voice begins speaking from the bushes urging the audience not to hide, to consider how no one is innocent, to ask how civilization can be built by "orts, scraps and fragments like ourselves?"[122] The voice urges them to "talk in words of one syllable," just as the anonymous author of the fourteenth-century English mystical text *The Cloud of Unknowing* urges its readers to use "a short word of one syllable" to "beat on the cloud and the darkness" in which God is hidden.[123] As they listen to this voice, "the distracted [became] united," recalling the "high and strenuous religious attention" that Harrison described ancient Athenians bringing to the theater.[124] Some enjoyed the beauty on the surface; others descended "to wrestle with the meaning." But all are pulled in. All "crashed; solved; united." And then, the play is over.

But before the audience scatters, there is a final word from the Reverend G. W. Streatfield, whose church will receive electricity from the proceeds of the play. He is ridiculous in the way of all the clergymen who appear in Woolf's novels, and members of the audience brace themselves to have the unity they just experienced reduced to some religious platitude. But like Mr. Bax in the *The Voyage Out*, Mr. Streatfield says something insightful.[125] He looks around for Miss La Trobe, but, like God, she is "invisible." He speaks, he says, as one of the audience, one who also caught himself reflected in Miss La Trobe's mirrors, and wonders if what the play meant is that "we act different parts; but are the same," a gesturing toward I Corinthians 12:12, where Paul writes of the community of Christians as one body made up of many members who, inspired by the same spirit, act, as it were, different parts. Noting also the role of nature in Miss La Trobe's play, Mr. Streatfield pushes beyond a vision of community that is made up only of human beings. "'Dare we, I asked myself, limit life to ourselves? May we not hold that there is a spirit that inspires, pervades. . . . Scraps, orts and fragments! Surely, we should unite?'"[126]

Mr. Streatfield quickly transitions from that moment of insight to the mundane task of raising the remaining funds for "the illumination of our dear old church." But as he is speaking, the sound of what the villagers thought was some sort of distant music resolves into the sound of war planes flying in formation overhead. Above them, the future looks violent and bleak. Below, on the ground, a small community reflects on the meaning of a play and pools its resources toward a common goal. Will these practices ensure survival? The play has reached them, as Lucy Swithin says to Miss La Trobe, in their unacted parts and revealed them not only to be scraps, orts, and fragments, but also as more than they knew themselves to be. Later that evening, Lucy asks Isa if she agreed with Mr. Streatfield, that "we act different parts but are the same?" "'Yes,' Isa answered. 'No,' she added. It was Yes, No, Yes, yes, yes, the tide rushed out embracing. No, no, no, it contracted."[127] Can we survive? Can we rebuild? Can we create a whole out of fragments? Yes yes yes, no no no is the rhythm on which these questions rock in Woolf's last novel. The answer shifts, but the fluidity between the options is where hope lies. As long as we can move back and forth, the possibility for survival, rebuilding, creating exists.

Sometime during the days leading up to her death, Woolf wrote to John Lehman, the managing director of the Hogarth Press, and told him that she believed *Between the Acts* too "silly and trivial" to publish. I'll revise it, she told him, and we can publish it next autumn. Leonard mailed her letter to Lehman on March 27 with a note attached saying that "Virginia was on the verge of a complete nervous breakdown."[128]

The next day, Woolf drowned herself in the river Ouse, a slash of water that flows through the Sussex countryside. She left two notes for Leonard, assuring him that he had given her "the greatest possible happiness," that he had done all he could for her and could not have done more. She left a note for Vanessa asking her to reassure Leonard that he was not to blame for her death. She writes to both of them that she is hearing voices and "I know I shant get over it now." In all three letters, she speaks of being unable to read, or write, or think; the spiritual practices from which she had crafted her life and her work had become inaccessible to her. Her diary records her struggle to hold onto them. Working with ideas is "what one's made for. And the only contribution one can make," she writes in 1939. "Thinking is my fighting," she writes the following year.[129] She writes in her last letter to Vanessa of trying to fight against her illness, "but I cant any longer."[130]

Unspoken in her letters but surely also at work is her despair over the war. Vanessa had written to her on March 20 to please "be sensible" and "rest a little" so that if Hitler invades England, she is not "a helpless invalid."[131] Virginia and Leonard, fearing arrest by the Nazis should such an invasion happen, made a plan to kill themselves in the garage if need be. In a letter to the writer May Sarton in April 1941, the

Woolfs' friend S. S. Koteliansky, a Jewish emigrant from Russia whose translations the Hogarth Press published, described Woolf as "a victim of the war as made by the Germans."[132]

This is surely true. But the reasons Woolf offers in her final letters for her suicide are more personal—the loss of "the things that made her who she was," as Phyllis Rose has put it,[133] and the desire not to be a burden to those she loved. Indeed, as she did in "The Leaning Tower" and *Between the Acts*, she seems in those last letters to look beyond the war into the future—a future in which Leonard does all the work he was meant to do.

As richly as Woolf saturates the present moment with attention in her work, she also, like Miss La Trobe, frequently stretches the present moment to include the past and the future. On the last page of *A Room of One's Own*, she offers a stirring homily on what she calls "the common life which is the real life and not . . . the little separate lives which we live as individuals." Woolf writes in this passage about what it will take to bring Shakespeare's sister to life in the future. Though she is "buried at the crossroads," Shakespeare's sister also lives in women whose ability to write is constrained by "washing up the dishes and putting the children to bed." If we want Shakespeare's sister to become incarnate among us, to "put on the body which she has often laid down," we will have to work for her, Woolf tells us. But the "we" in this sentence does not refer only to her, or to us, who read her in the present moment. It refers to the common life, a life to which we contribute, but which stretches far beyond the boundaries of our own lives.

> For my belief is that if we live another century or so—I am talking of the common life which is the real life and not of the little separate lives which we live as individuals—and have five hundred a year each of us and rooms of our own; if we have the habit of freedom and the courage to write exactly what we think; if we escape a little from the common sitting-room and see human beings not always in their relation to each other but in relation to reality; and the sky, too, and the trees or whatever it may be in themselves; if we look past Milton's bogey, for no human being

> should shut out the view; if we face the fact, for it is a fact, that there is no arm to cling to, but that we go alone and that our relation is to the world of reality and not only to the world of men and women, then the opportunity will come and the dead poet who was Shakespeare's sister will put on the body which she has so often laid down. Drawing her life from the lives of the unknown who were her forerunners, as her brother did before her, she will be born.[134]

Rejecting both the patriarchal structures of society, including the religion of "Milton's bogey," and the religious consolations of an imagined "arm to cling to," this passage anticipates the credo Woolf will write ten years later: "There is no Shakespeare; there is no Beethoven; certainly and emphatically there is no God. We are the words; we are the music; we are the thing itself." And yet there is something beyond "the world of men and women" for Woolf, something that she captures in a scene at the end of *Between the Acts*, when Miss La Trobe sits alone in a pub, upheld by the people around her, receiving the first words of a new play as they rise up into her mind from some primordial creative source. Woolf captures in this scene the other life Eleanor longs for in *The Years*, "another life . . . here and now." Woolf glimpses this "world of reality" in moments of being and in the "invisible presences" that stretch behind and before us, with whom we are gathered into "the common life which is the real life." Woolf herself was and is and always will be part of that common life, working to resurrect Shakespeare's sister in a future she did not live to see but that would be impossible without her and the many anonymous artists whose hidden lives she honors in her work.

Woolf agreed with her friend T. S. Eliot that "there is no life that is not in community," even if she did not like the play for which he wrote those words. But while Eliot believed that true community must be built from a common faith, Woolf worked for a community grounded in a greater consciousness of the "common life which is the real life." She could not agree with Eliot that there is "no community not lived in praise of GOD," at least not the way he meant it. And yet her vision of the common life we share across time and space, shaped by the spiritual practices of reading and writing, possesses an experimental religious quality. Until the very end of her life, she explored the repeated revelation of "some real thing behind appearances" by discovering, through writing, "what belongs to what."[135] For Woolf, literature was the common ground, even the sacred ground, of this common life. Literature "is not cut up into nations; there are no wars there," she wrote in 1940, a few months before she died. It is a place where we can meet one another on equal footing and "find our own way for ourselves."[136]

NOTES

INTRODUCTION

1. T. S. Eliot, *Selected Essays*, 347.
2. Although she was never baptized, Woolf did have a godfather in the American poet James Russell Lowell. She referred to Lowell throughout her life as her godfather, but Leslie Stephen preferred to call him her "sponsor." See Annan, *Leslie Stephen*, 56.
3. *Letters*, 3:458.
4. Q. Bell, *Virginia Woolf*, 2:136.
5. Zaleski and Zaleski, *Prayer*, 288.
6. Spender, "Remembering Eliot," 79.
7. Noble, *Recollections*, 184.
8. Quoted in David Bowman, "Read It Again, Sam," 75.
9. *Room of One's Own*, 71.
10. Harris, *Virginia Woolf*, 9.
11. Hussey, *Singing of the Real World*, xiv.
12. *Essays*, 2:60.
13. Marcus, "Liberty, Sorority, Misogyny," 71.
14. Marcus, "Niece of a Nun," 27.
15. See, for example, Moore, *Short Season*.
16. *Room of One's Own*, 75.
17. See, for example, Moore, *Short Season*; Haller, "Isis Unveiled"; Shattuck, "Stage of Scholarship"; Carpentier, *Ritual, Myth, and the Modernist Text*.
18. Lewis, *Religious Experience*.
19. Wood, *Broken Estate*, 105–18.
20. Lazenby, *Mystical Philosophy*.
21. Lackey, "Gender of Atheism"; "Atheism and Sadism"; and "Virginia Woolf and T. S. Eliot."
22. De Gay, *Virginia Woolf and Christian Culture*.
23. See, for example, the volume on Virginia Woolf in Oxford University Press's "Authors in Context" series: Whitworth, *Virginia Woolf*.
24. See, for example, Lazenby, *Mystical Philosophy*; Moore, *Short Season*; Paulsell, "Writing and Mystical Experience"; Gough, "'That Razor Edge of Balance'"; and Wood, *Broken Estate*, 105–18.

25. McNeillie, "Bloomsbury," 17.
26. Wood, *Broken Estate*, 111.
27. Marcus, "Niece of a Nun," 10.
28. *Diary*, 3:181.
29. *Essays*, 4:50–51.
30. Harrison, *Epilegomena*, 5.
31. *Moments of Being*, 80.
32. *Essays*, 3:426.
33. *Three Guineas*, 122.
34. Ibid.
35. See Woolf's discussion of the influence of St. Paul in *Three Guineas*, 166–69.
36. *Diary*, 5:135.
37. *Essays*, 4:323.
38. *Moments of Being*, 73.
39. *Diary*, 1:186.
40. *Essays*, 5:46.
41. Ibid., 5:79.
42. *Diary*, 3:196.
43. Arnold, *Selected Prose*, 340.
44. *Essays*, 4:429.
45. Ibid., 4:439.
46. See Froula, "Mrs. Dalloway's Postwar Elegy" and Graham and Lewis, "Private Religion, Public Mourning."
47. *Mrs. Dalloway*, 26–28.
48. Wood, *Broken Estate*, 114.
49. *Diary*, 2:263.
50. *Waves*, 208.
51. For a discussion of the complex ways Christian missionary activity functioned in relation to British society, see Williams, "British Religion and the Wider World."
52. *Complete Shorter Fiction*, 202.
53. *Jacob's Room*, 27.
54. *Years*, 263.
55. *Mrs. Dalloway*, 27.
56. Teresa of Avila, *Interior Castle*, 195.
57. Lambert, "'And Darwin Says,'" 18.
58. *Essays*, 4:429.
59. *Mrs. Dalloway*, 27–28.
60. Ibid., 23, 15.
61. *Essays*, 3:153.
62. Herbert, *Complete English Poems*, 6.
63. *Three Guineas*, 119.
64. Graham and Lewis, "Private Religion, Public Mourning," 89.
65. *Essays*, 4:19.
66. *Passionate Apprentice*, 392.

67. *Waves*, 197.
68. *Essays*, 5:316.
69. *Three Guineas*, 34.
70. Graham and Lewis, "Private Religion, Public Mourning," 95.

CHAPTER 1

1. *Night and Day*, 36.
2. *Moments of Being*, 65.
3. The phrase was coined by Woolf's cousin J. K. Stephen (1859–1892) and used by Leonard Woolf to describe the Stephen and Strachey families in *Sowing*, 186. See also Annan, "Intellectual Aristocracy," 243–87.
4. *Night and Day*, 36.
5. Ibid., 37.
6. J. Stephen, *Essays*, 2:202.
7. Taylor, *Secular Age*, 322, 377, 394–95.
8. *Between the Acts*, 111.
9. Gilley, "Church of England in the Nineteenth Century," 294–95.
10. Tomkins, *Clapham Sect*, 11.
11. Lee, *Virginia Woolf*, 58–60.
12. *Passionate Apprentice*, 46.
13. Ibid., 51.
14. *To the Lighthouse*, 29.
15. J. Stephen, *Essays*, 2:244. John Bowdler, the son of the social reformer of the same name, was a lawyer and a poet who died at a young age of tuberculosis.
16. *Essays*, 4:435.
17. Ibid., 4:162.
18. Altick, *Victorian People*, 191.
19. J. Stephen, *Essays*, 2:190.
20. *Three Guineas*, 152.
21. J. Stephen, *Essays*, 2:197–98.
22. Ibid., 219.
23. Ibid., 223.
24. *To the Lighthouse*, 192.
25. *Moments of Being*, 80.
26. Ibid., 68.
27. *Letters*, 5:351.
28. Quoted in Annan, *Leslie Stephen*, 17.
29. *Essays*, 5:588.
30. Law, *Serious Call*, 49.
31. *Diary*, 4:208.
32. *Moments of Being*, 73.
33. *Letters*, 6:372.
34. *Diary*, 2:94.

35. J. Stephen, *Letters*, 105.
36. Lewis, *Religious Experience*, 3.
37. Hempton, "Religious Life in Industrial Britain," 306–7.
38. J. Stephen, *Essays*, 2:245.
39. Annan, *Leslie Stephen*, 2.
40. Taylor, *Sources of the Self*, 402.
41. L. Stephen, *Some Early Impressions*, 16.
42. Altick, *Victorian People*, 209.
43. Ibid., 254.
44. L. Stephen, *Some Early Impressions*, 75.
45. Ibid., 10.
46. Ibid., 13–14.
47. Ibid., 34.
48. Annan, *Leslie Stephen*, 42.
49. L. Stephen, *Some Early Impressions*, 43.
50. Annan, *Leslie Stephen*, 45.
51. *Moments of Being*, 108.
52. L. Stephen, *Some Early Impressions*, 68.
53. L. Stephen, *Mausoleum Book*, 6.
54. *Years*, 146.
55. L. Stephen, *Some Early Impressions*, 69.
56. Ibid., 70.
57. Quoted in Maitland, *Life and Letters of Leslie Stephen*, 264.
58. Ibid., 98.
59. Annan, *Leslie Stephen*, 51.
60. *Essays*, 5:585.
61. Maitland, *Life and Letters of Leslie Stephen*, 107.
62. Quoted in ibid., 112.
63. Quoted in McNeillie, "Bloomsbury," 25.
64. Maitland, *Life and Letters of Leslie Stephen*, 124.
65. Quoted in ibid.
66. Annan, *Leslie Stephen*, 54.
67. *Diary*, 4:77.
68. Maitland, *Life and Letters of Leslie Stephen*, 129.
69. Annan, *Leslie Stephen*, 56.
70. Lowell, *Letters*, 2:168.
71. MacCarthy, *Leslie Stephen*, 11.
72. L. Stephen, *Men, Books, and Mountains*, 18.
73. S. A. O. Ullman, introduction to L. Stephen, *Men, Books, and Mountains*, 13.
74. L. Woolf, "Note," 8.
75. *Moments of Being*, 115.
76. Arnold, *Selected Prose*, 341.
77. On religion as a form of critique, see Hollywood, *Melancholia*, 7–19.
78. L. Stephen, *Hours in Library*, 3:224.
79. *Essays*, 4:435.
80. Grosskurth, *Leslie Stephen*, 33.

81. *Essays*, 5:585.
82. Annan, *Leslie Stephen*, 2.
83. MacCarthy, *Leslie Stephen*, 7.
84. Wood, *Broken Estate*, 256.
85. Ibid., 264.
86. L. Stephen, *Agnostic's Apology*, 10.
87. L. Stephen, *Some Early Impressions*, 67.
88. L. Stephen, *Agnostic's Apology*, 116.
89. Maitland, *Life and Letters of Leslie Stephen*, 142.
90. L. Stephen, *Hours in a Library*, 3:220.
91. L. Stephen, *Agnostic's Apology*, 3–4.
92. Ibid., 2, 90, 366.
93. *Moments of Being*, 72.
94. L. Stephen, *Agnostic's Apology*, 37, 111, 126; V. Woolf, *Moments of Being*, 72.
95. L. Stephen, *Agnostic's Apology*, 148.
96. *Moments of Being*, 72.
97. *To the Lighthouse*, 207.
98. Quoted in Annan, *Leslie Stephen*, 304.
99. *Moments of Being*, 115.
100. Quoted in Taylor, *Secular Age*, 396.
101. *Moments of Being*, 115.
102. Taylor, *Secular Age*, 396.
103. Tomkins, *Clapham Sect*, 139.
104. G. Eliot, *Middlemarch*, 58.
105. *Moments of Being*, 148.
106. *Passionate Apprentice*, 111, 36, 95.
107. *Diary*, 3:208.
108. *Moments of Being*, 144.
109. Ibid., 133.
110. *Essays*, 6:480.
111. Ibid., 6:480–81.
112. Ibid., 6:481.
113. "An Appeal Against Female Suffrage," signed by 104 women, including the novelist Mrs. Humphrey Ward, was published in *Nineteenth Century* in June 1889 and in the *New York Times* in August 1889.
114. *Letters*, 6:419.
115. *To the Lighthouse*, 198.
116. J. D. Stephen, *Julia Duckworth Stephen*, 241.
117. Ibid.
118. *Moments of Being*, 33.
119. Ibid., 32.
120. J. D. Stephen, *Julia Duckworth Stephen*, 243.
121. Annan, *Leslie Stephen*, 135.
122. *Essays*, 5:588.
123. Ibid.
124. *Moments of Being*, 45–46.

125. Ibid., 95.
126. *To the Lighthouse*, 161.
127. Lee, *Virginia Woolf*, 57.
128. Biographical note by C. Stephen in J. Stephen, *Letters*, 296.
129. Ibid., 291.
130. Ibid., 300.
131. Ibid., 294.
132. C. Stephen, *Light Arising*, 5.
133. Ibid., 33.
134. C. Stephen, *Quaker Strongholds*, 54.
135. Ibid., 4.
136. C. Stephen, *Vision of Faith*, lxii.
137. *Moments of Being*, 81.
138. *Room of One's Own*, 39.
139. R. Jones, *Quakerism*, 1:437.
140. Ibid., 1:277–81.
141. Ibid., 1:307.
142. Dandelion, *Quakerism*, 85–86.
143. Quoted in R. Jones, *Quakerism*, 1:492.
144. Chadwick, *Victorian Church*, 1:432.
145. Quoted in R. Jones, *Quakerism*, 1:496.
146. Ibid., 1:500.
147. R. Jones, *Quakerism*, 2:967.
148. *Library of Leonard and Virginia Woolf*, 213–14.
149. R. Jones, *Quakerism*, 2:969.
150. C. Stephen, *Vision of Faith*, ciii.
151. Ibid., lxxii.
152. C. Stephen, *Light Arising*, 20.
153. C. Stephen, *Quaker Strongholds*, 189.
154. Ibid., 190.
155. C. Stephen, *Light Arising*, 61.
156. Ibid., 28.
157. C. Stephen, *Vision of Faith*, cxi.
158. *Moments of Being*, 115.
159. *Letters*, 1:146.
160. Ibid., 1:163.
161. Ibid., 1:144.
162. Ibid.
163. Ibid., 1:229.
164. Ibid., 1:285–86.
165. Ibid., 1:229.
166. Ibid., 1:147–48.
167. Ibid., 1:148.
168. See Marcus, "Tintinnabulations"; Bell, "'Radiant' Friendship"; Marcus, "Quentin's Bogey"; Bell, "Reply to Jane Marcus."
169. Bell, "Reply to Jane Marcus," 500.

170. G. Eliot, *Middlemarch*, 182.
171. *Moments of Being*, 72.
172. C. Stephen, *Light Arising*, 5.
173. C. Stephen, *Vision of Faith*, 49. Jane Marcus has argued that Woolf used her aunt's image for the central image of *To the Lighthouse*. Marcus, "Niece of a Nun," 24.
174. C. Stephen, *Vision of Faith*, 11–12.
175. *Moments of Being*, 72.
176. G. Eliot, *Middlemarch*, 182.
177. *Moments of Being*, 72.
178. Ibid.
179. C. Stephen, *Vision of Faith*, cxxiii.
180. Lee, 66; Marcus, "Niece of a Nun," 7–8, 17.
181. C. Stephen, *Light Arising*, 117.
182. Ibid., 21.
183. *Letters*, 2:499.
184. *To the Lighthouse*, 62.
185. C. Stephen, *Quaker Strongholds*, 175.
186. *Moments of Being*, 72.

CHAPTER 2

1. Tolley, *Domestic Biography*, 6.
2. *Passionate Apprentice*, 311.
3. Cowper wrote "God Moves in a Mysterious Way" in 1773.
4. *Passionate Apprentice*, 296.
5. Ibid., 141.
6. Ibid.
7. Quoted in De Gay, *Virginia Woolf and Christian Culture*, 33.
8. Quoted in Tolley, *Domestic Biography*, 37.
9. D. Stephen, *Studies in Early Indian Thought*, 172.
10. Tolley, *Domestic Biography*, 251.
11. *Passionate Apprentice*, 107.
12. *Letters*, 1:11.
13. Ibid., 1:43.
14. Ibid., 1:85.
15. Ibid., 1:87.
16. Ibid., 1:193.
17. Ibid., 2:488–89.
18. Ibid., 2:492.
19. Ibid. Julie Kane offers a different reading of this letter. She sees in it a disdain on Woolf's part for Buddhism and criticizes Woolf for not being more interested in Dorothea Stephen's book. See Kane, "Varieties of Mystical Experience," 331.
20. *Diary*, 2:140.

21. *Orlando*, 128.
22. *Mrs. Dalloway*, 180.
23. *Letters*, 4:333.
24. *Moments of Being*, 69.
25. *Passionate Apprentice*, 138.
26. *Essays*, 4:119.
27. *Passionate Apprentice*, 177.
28. Ibid., 178.
29. *Three Guineas*, 180.
30. *Moments of Being*, 181.
31. "The Light of World" did not begin its tour of the empire until 1905. When it returned to England in 1907, it was hung in St. Paul's Cathedral, where it remains today. For more on Holman Hunt's painting, its tour of the British Empire, and the response to it in the colonies, see Potter, "British Art and Empire."
32. Ibid., 10. As Potter has shown, the press in several colonies resisted this mandate by critiquing the painting.
33. *Moments of Being*, 182.
34. Hafley, "Walter Pater's 'Marius,'" 99, 104.
35. Bloom, *Genius*, 441.
36. Wright, "'His Own Nearer Household Gods.'"
37. Pater, *Marius*, 235.
38. From Pater's review of Mrs. Humphrey Ward's *Robert Elsmere*, quoted in Knoepflmacher, *Religious Humanism*, 3.
39. Pater, *Marius*, 37.
40. Levey, introduction to Pater, *Marius*, 25.
41. Pater, *Marius*, 45.
42. Ibid., 65–66.
43. *Essays*, 3:172–73.
44. Knoepflmacher, *Religious Humanism*, 168.
45. Meisel, *Absent Father*, 46–47.
46. Fletcher, *Walter Pater*, 35.
47. Pater, *Appreciations*, 14.
48. *Passionate Apprentice*, 392.
49. Ibid., 251.
50. Yeats, *Autobiographies*, 372–73.
51. Potolsky, "Fear of Falling," 701.
52. *Passionate Apprentice*, 274.
53. Pater, *Renaissance*, 252.
54. L. Stephen, "Art and Morality," 101.
55. Ibid., 93.
56. Fraser, *Beauty and Belief*, 201.
57. Fletcher, *Walter Pater*, 9.
58. T. S. Eliot, *Selected Essays*, 6.
59. Pater, *Marius*, 137.

60. Ibid., 136.
61. Ibid.
62. Ibid., 38.
63. Hafley, "Walter Pater's 'Marius,'" 103.
64. *Diary*, 3:271.
65. Pater, *Marius*, 89.
66. Ibid., 136.
67. *Essays*, 3:33.
68. Pater, *Marius*, 275.
69. *Passionate Apprentice*, 384.
70. Pater, *Marius*, 44–49.
71. *Orlando*, 24–25.
72. *Letters*, 1:146.
73. Pater, *Marius*, 275.
74. Ibid., 208.
75. Ibid., 210.
76. Ibid., 210–11.
77. Ibid., 213.
78. Ibid., 212.
79. *Complete Shorter Fiction*, 53.
80. Ibid., 59.
81. Ibid., 46.
82. Ibid., 62.
83. See Desalvo, "As 'Miss Jan Says,'" 96–124.
84. Beard, "My Hero."
85. Harrison, *Ancient Art and Ritual*, vi.
86. *Letters*, 1:145.
87. Ibid., 3:58.
88. Briggs, *Reading Virginia Woolf*, 91–92.
89. *Letters*, 2:384–85.
90. Briggs, *Reading Virginia Woolf*, 89.
91. Silver, *Virginia Woolf's Reading Notebooks*, 103.
92. *Letters*, 2:58–59.
93. Harrison, *Epilegomena*, 33.
94. *Diary*, 2:136.
95. Harrison, preface to *Epilegomena*.
96. Harrison, *Epilegomena*, 6.
97. Harrison, *Ancient Art and Ritual*, 1.
98. Ibid., 5.
99. *Essays*, 3:422.
100. Tolley, *Domestic Biography*, 39.
101. *Passionate Apprentice*, 204.
102. Ibid., 294.
103. *Mrs. Dalloway*, 55–57.
104. *Passionate Apprentice*, 193.

105. Ibid., 376.
106. Ibid., 205.
107. Ibid., 316.
108. Ibid., 319.
109. Ibid., 322.
110. *Complete Shorter Fiction*, 68.
111. *Passionate Apprentice*, 348.
112. Ibid., 350.
113. Ibid., 353.
114. Ibid., 355.
115. *Orlando*, 91.
116. *Passionate Apprentice*, 356.
117. Ibid., 386.
118. Ibid., 391.
119. Ibid., 392.
120. Ibid., 392.
121. *To the Lighthouse*, 177.
122. *Passionate Apprentice*, 392–93.
123. For a rich account of Vanessa Bell's life and work, see Spalding, *Vanessa Bell*.
124. Spalding, *Vanessa Bell*, 124, and Tickner, "Vanessa Bell," 77–78.
125. Spalding, *Vanessa Bell*, 104–5.
126. Quoted in Tickner, "Vanessa Bell," 90.
127. Ibid., 75.
128. *Moments of Being*, 81.
129. *To the Lighthouse*, 196.
130. Quoted in Tickner, "Vanessa Bell," 68.
131. C. Bell, *Art*, 8.
132. Ibid., 44.
133. Ibid., 279.
134. Ibid., 82.
135. Ibid., 280.
136. Ibid., 282.
137. Ibid., 292.
138. Ibid., 291–92.
139. Spalding, *Vanessa Bell*, 126.
140. C. Bell, *Art*, 247.
141. *To the Lighthouse*, 53.
142. Ibid., 29.
143. Ibid., 209.
144. *Letters*, 3:572.
145. *Letters*, 3:572–73.
146. Santayana, *Life of Reason*, 180.
147. C. Bell, *Art*, 82.
148. *Roger Fry*, 174.
149. Ibid., 152.

150. Ibid., 153–54.
151. Quoted in ibid., 155.
152. Ibid., 156.
153. Quoted in ibid., 157.
154. Quoted in ibid.
155. See *Second Post-Impressionist Exhibition, Oct. 5–Dec. 31, 1012, Illustrated Catalogue*.
156. Quoted in Stansky, *On or About December 1910*, 7.
157. *Essays*, 3:421.
158. Dorrien, *Kantian Reason and Hegelian Spirit*, 555.
159. *Essays*, 3:421–22.
160. Fry, *Vision and Design*, 203–4. See also Virginia Woolf's discussion of Fry's analysis of the resistance to the First Post-Impressionist Exhibition in *Roger Fry*, 158–59.
161. *To the Lighthouse*, 91.
162. See *Hilma af Klint: Paintings for the Future*.
163. C. Bell, *Art*, 26.
164. Kandinsky, *Concerning the Spiritual in Art*, 4.
165. Ibid., 1–2.
166. Ibid., 29.
167. Ibid., 6.
168. Ibid., 9.
169. Ibid., 31.
170. Ibid., 29, 44–45.
171. Ibid., 54.
172. Edel, *Bloomsbury*, 53.
173. Levy, *Moore*, 298.
174. Quoted in Regan, *Bloomsbury's Prophet*, 17.
175. Goodwin, "Art of an Ethical Life," 220.
176. Keynes, "My Early Beliefs," 435.
177. Regan, *Bloomsbury's Prophet*, 28.
178. Quoted in ibid., 168.
179. Quoted in Levy, *Moore*, 4–5.
180. Hutchinson, *G. E. Moore's Ethical Theory*, 172–98.
181. Keynes, "My Early Beliefs," 436.
182. MacIntyre, *After Virtue*, 14–19.
183. Ibid., 19.
184. Keynes, "My Early Beliefs," 444.
185. Quoted in Levy, *Moore*, 1.
186. Quoted in Regan, *Bloomsbury's Prophet*, 21.
187. Spalding, *Vanessa Bell*, 125.
188. Levy, *Moore*, 3.
189. *Letters*, 1:340.
190. Ibid., 1:364.
191. Levy, *Moore*, 7.

192. *Letters*, 2:120.
193. *Diary*, 1:155.
194. Ibid., 2:49.
195. *Letters*, 6:400.
196. *Complete Shorter Fiction*, 27.
197. *Voyage Out*, 74.
198. *Diary*, 5:168–69.
199. Ibid., 1:265.
200. Keynes, "My Early Beliefs," 442.
201. *Diary*, 2:49.
202. Keynes, "My Early Beliefs," 442.
203. Hutchinson, *G. E. Moore's Ethical Theory*, 193.
204. Lewis, *Cambridge Introduction to Modernism*, xx.
205. Kandinsky, *Concerning the Spiritual in Art*, 42.

CHAPTER 3

1. *Passionate Apprentice*, 77.
2. Ibid., 79.
3. Ibid., 107.
4. *Letters*, 1:147.
5. *Diary*, 5:234–35.
6. Ibid., 5:355.
7. For a discussion of Woolf's concentration, see See, "Comedy of Nature."
8. *Letters*, 6:481.
9. *Essays*, 4:xxi.
10. *Essays*, 5:274.
11. Griffiths, *Religious Reading*, 40.
12. *Passionate Apprentice*, 178–79.
13. *Moments of Being*, 72.
14. *Passionate Apprentice*, 384.
15. Quoted in Tolley, *Domestic Biography*, 12.
16. Ibid., 24.
17. Ibid., 52.
18. Annan, *Leslie Stephen*, 330.
19. Tolley, *Domestic Biography*, 13.
20. Robertson, *Lectio Divina*, xv.
21. *Essays*, 1:128.
22. L. Stephen, *Studies of a Biographer*, 4:119.
23. *Essays*, 1:129.
24. Robertson, *Lectio Divina*, xix.
25. *Essays*, 4:62.
26. Leclercq, *Love of Learning*, 73.
27. Guigo II, *Ladder of Monks*, 80.

28. Quoted in Robertson, *Lectio Divina*, 43, 118.
29. Ibid., 15.
30. *Essays*, 2:55.
31. Quoted in Leclercq, *Love of Learning*, 73.
32. Robertson, *Lectio Divina*, 15.
33. L. Stephen, *Hours in a Library*, 3:139.
34. *Essays*, 5:573.
35. Ibid., 5:574.
36. Ibid., 4:320 and L. Stephen, *Agnostic's Apology*, 148.
37. *Letters*, 5:293.
38. Ibid., 5:320.
39. Griffiths, *Religious Reading*, 41. For another example of reading in eternity, see Augustine's discussion of angels reading the face of God in *Confessions*, 327.
40. *Letters*, 5:319.
41. Flint, "Reading Uncommonly," 187.
42. *Essays*, 5:588.
43. Ibid., 5:573.
44. L. Stephen, "Study of English Literature," 508.
45. *Waves*, 146–48.
46. *Essays*, 4:389.
47. *Orlando*, 55.
48. *Essays*, 6:278.
49. Ibid., 4:398–99.
50. *Orlando*, 128.
51. *Essays*, 6:277–78.
52. Ibid., 3:479.
53. Ibid., 3:153.
54. See ibid., 3:482 and 4:19.
55. Ibid., 4:390.
56. Ibid., 3:84.
57. Ibid., 4:395.
58. Ibid., 4:393.
59. Ibid., 4:19.
60. Ibid., 5:41.
61. Griffiths, *Religious Reading*, 44.
62. See Marguerite d'Oingt, *Writings*, John of the Cross, *Collected Works*, and Paulsell, "Writing and Mystical Experience."
63. Robertson, *Lectio Divina*, 105.
64. Ibid., 40.
65. *Letters*, 3:385.
66. *Essays*, 6:94.
67. Ibid., 6:92, 95.
68. Ibid., 4:367.
69. Griffiths, *Religious Reading*, 41.
70. Robertson, *Lectio Divina*, 149.

71. Teresa of Avila, *Collected Works*, 215.
72. *Voyage Out*, 229.
73. *Years*, 80.
74. John 11:25–26, Authorized Version. Leonard and Virginia Woolf owned many Bibles. Except for one Revised Standard Version of the Old Testament, all of their English Bibles were the Authorized Version. They also owned a Latin Bible, a Tamil Bible, two Greek New Testaments, and a Hebrew New Testament. See *Library of Leonard and Virginia Woolf*, 20–22. For a discussion of Woolf's study of the Bible, see De Gay, *Virginia Woolf and Christian Culture*, 186–218.
75. *Years*, 80–81.
76. 1 Corinthians 15:34, Authorized Version.
77. *Years*, 82.
78. Ibid.
79. Ibid., 146.
80. Ibid., 47.
81. Ibid.
82. Ibid., 48.
83. Ibid., 322.
84. For an insightful discussion of Woolf's anti-Semitism and the critical literature on the anti-Semitic passages in *The Years*, see Linett, "Jew in the Bath."
85. Ibid., 345.
86. *Essays*, 4:398–99.
87. Marcus, "Niece of a Nun," 10.
88. Harvena Richter proposed in 1982 that the structure of *Mrs. Dalloway* took its shape from the eight canonical hours of the Divine Office (although Richter examined only seven). Woolf's original title for the novel, *The Hours*, may reflect this. See Richter, "Canonical Hours."
89. *Mrs. Dalloway*, 79.
90. Schidel, "Lauds," 531.
91. See, for example, Hildegard, *Symphonia*, 150. For more on Hildegard of Bingen and *viriditas*, see Newman, *Sister of Wisdom*.
92. *Hours of the Divine Office*, 7.
93. *Mrs. Dalloway*, 14–16.
94. Ibid., 18.
95. Ibid., 35.
96. Ibid., 119.
97. Ibid., 163.
98. Ibid., 167.
99. Ibid., 146.
100. Ibid., 182.
101. Ibid., 190.
102. Ibid., 30.
103. Teresa of Avila, *Interior Castle*, 35.
104. Sackville-West, *The Eagle and the Dove*.
105. *Mrs. Dalloway*, 35.

106. Ibid., 36.
107. Ibid., 8.
108. Ibid., 119.
109. Ibid., 76.
110. Ibid., 8.
111. Ibid., 9.
112. Ibid., 29–30.
113. Ibid., 31.
114. Ibid., 39.
115. Childs, "Mrs. Dalloway's Unexpected Guests," 69–70.
116. *Moments of Being*, 64–65.
117. *Mrs. Dalloway*, 136.
118. *To the Lighthouse*, 97.
119. Ibid., 105.
120. Ibid., 120.
121. Ibid., 83.
122. Ibid., 117.
123. Ibid., 118.
124. Ibid., 119.
125. *Diary*, 2:133.
126. *To the Lighthouse*, 121.
127. *Essays*, 5:577.
128. Flint, "Reading Uncommonly," 190.
129. Co-operative Working Women, *Life as We Have Known It*, xxxvi.
130. Ibid., xxxxi.
131. Ibid., 76.
132. Ibid., 73.
133. Ibid., xxxxi.
134. Ibid., 78.
135. For a discussion of *scriptio divina*, see Paulsell, "*Scriptio divina*: Women, Writing and God" and Paulsell, "*Scriptio divina*: Writing and the Experience of God in the Works of Marguerite d'Oingt."
136. For a more detailed comparison of Marguerite d'Oingt and Virginia Woolf, see Paulsell, "Writing and Mystical Experience."
137. Marguerite d'Oingt, *Writings*, 26.
138. Ibid.
139. *Moments of Being*, 72.
140. Ibid., 73.
141. *Years*, 388.
142. *Orlando*, 54–60.
143. Briggs, *Virginia Woolf*, 263.
144. *Waves*, 145.
145. *Years*, 45.
146. *To the Lighthouse*, 198.
147. Luke 5:4, Authorized Version.

CHAPTER 4

1. Lee, *Virginia Woolf*, 217.
2. *To the Lighthouse*, 207.
3. *Moments of Being*, 72.
4. Virginia's cousins, Rosamond and Dorothea Stephen, also produced a family newspaper during their childhood.
5. *Hyde Park Gate News*, 179–80.
6. *To the Lighthouse*, 75.
7. Ibid., 75–76.
8. *Diary*, 3:271.
9. See Whitehead, *Science and the Modern World*; Whitehead, *Religion in the Making*; and Whitehead, *Process and Reality*. See also Faber, *God as Poet*; Hartshorne and Reese, *Philosophers Speak of God*.
10. L. Woolf, *Letters*, 540.
11. *Moments of Being*, 200–201.
12. The relationship between Whitehead's ideas and Woolf's is discussed in Banfield, *Phantom Table*; Carver, "'Behind the Cotton Wool'"; and Olson, *Authorial Divinity*.
13. *Letters*, 1:85.
14. *Passionate Apprentice*, 311.
15. Olson, *Authorial Divinity*, 64.
16. *Essays*, 3:155.
17. Lackey, "Gender of Atheism," 60.
18. Lackey, "Virginia Woolf and T. S. Eliot," 83.
19. *Essays*, 6:581–82.
20. *Waves*, 112–13.
21. *Complete Shorter Fiction*, 203–4.
22. Ibid., 205–6.
23. Ibid., 207.
24. *To the Lighthouse*, 62.
25. Ibid., 63–64.
26. Ibid., 64.
27. *Cloud of Unknowing*, 22.
28. *To the Lighthouse*, 65.
29. *Voyage Out*, 145.
30. Ibid., 225.
31. Ibid., 226.
32. Ibid., 227.
33. Ibid.
34. Ibid., 228.
35. Ibid., 229.
36. Whitehead, *Science and the Modern World*, 192.
37. *Mrs. Dalloway*, 122.

38. *Three Guineas*, 180.
39. *Mrs. Dalloway*, 4.
40. Knight, "'God of Love Is Full of Tricks,'" 28.
41. On this point, see Griesinger, "Religious Belief in a Secular Age," 449.
42. *Mrs. Dalloway*, 130.
43. Ibid., 29.
44. Ibid., 125.
45. Ibid.
46. Ibid., 38.
47. Ibid., 128.
48. See Laurence, *Lily Briscoe's Chinese Eyes*.
49. *Mrs. Dalloway*, 129.
50. Ibid., 134.
51. *Mrs. Dalloway*, 135.
52. *Years*, 45.
53. *Voyage Out*, 229.
54. Ibid., 231.
55. Ibid., 232.
56. *Mrs. Dalloway*, 9.
57. *Complete Shorter Fiction*, 205.
58. For another discussion of Mr. Bax's sermon, see Pecora, *Secularization and Cultural Criticism*, 181–85.
59. Whitehead, *Process and Reality*, 346.
60. *Moments of Being*, 72.
61. *Process and Reality*, 522, 525.
62. *To the Lighthouse*, 83.
63. *Moments of Being*, 72.
64. *Jacob's Room*, 27.
65. *Waves*, 40.
66. McGinn, "God Beyond God."
67. Briggs, *Virginia Woolf*, 250.
68. *Diary*, 3:218.
69. Ibid.
70. Ibid., 3:203.
71. Ibid., 3:113.
72. Ibid., 3:257.
73. Viola, "'Buds on the Tree of Life,'" 241.
74. Quoted in ibid., 242.
75. Harrison, *Prolegomena*, 268–69.
76. *Mrs. Dalloway*, 55–56.
77. Ibid., 56.
78. Ibid.
79. Ibid.
80. Ibid., 57.

81. *Years*, 13–14.
82. Julia Briggs suggests that Woolf does not write out Harrison's name "as if to emphasize her spiritual power." Briggs, *Virginia Woolf*, 461.
83. *Diary*, 3:181.
84. Harrison, *Ancient Art and Ritual*, 4.
85. *Room of One's Own*, 17.
86. *To the Lighthouse*, 161.
87. Ibid., 198.
88. Ibid, 158.
89. Ibid., 159.
90. Ibid.
91. *Cloud of Unknowing*, 29.
92. *To the Lighthouse*, 160.
93. See, for example, Cramer, "Jane Harrison and Lesbian Plots," and Briggs, *Virginia Woolf*, 254. Jean Mills reads *Jacob's Room*, *Mrs. Dalloway*, and *The Waves* as a trilogy featuring three "Dionysian Young Gods"—Jacob, Septimus, and Percival—in *Virginia Woolf, Jane Ellen Harrison, and the Spirit of Modernist Classicism*, 86–114.
94. Briggs, *Virginia Woolf*, 250–51.
95. De Gay, *Virginia Woolf and Christian Culture*, 58.
96. *Waves*, 179.
97. *Moments of Being*, 72.
98. *Waves*, 23–27.
99. *Essays*, 1:289.
100. *Letters*, 1:404.
101. Richard Wagner, *Parsifal*, http://www.operafolio.com/libretto.asp?n=Parsifal&language=UK.
102. *Quest of the Holy Grail*, 33.
103. *Waves*, 85.
104. Ibid., 86.
105. Ibid., 101–2.
106. Frazer, *Golden Bough*, 398–99.
107. *Waves*, 102.
108. Ibid., 106.
109. *To the Lighthouse*, 161.
110. *Waves*, 98.
111. *Room of One's Own*, 17.
112. *Waves*, 168.
113. Ibid., 172–73.
114. Ibid., 177.
115. *Waves: The Two Holograph Drafts*, Draft 1, 6.
116. *Waves*, 4.
117. Ibid., 106.
118. Ibid., 184.

119. Ibid., 216.
120. Ibid., 108.

CHAPTER 5

1. Quoted in Marshall, "'England and Nowhere,'" 103. For more on T. S. Eliot's play, see Atkins, "Raising the Rock."
2. The World Council of Churches would not be fully established until after the war.
3. Aubrey, "Oxford Conference," 385–86.
4. Ibid., 387.
5. Ackroyd, *T. S. Eliot*, 242–43.
6. Edwards, "'God's Totalitarianism,'" 285.
7. Quoted in ibid., 289.
8. T. S. Eliot, *Christianity and Culture*, 10.
9. Ibid., 28.
10. Ibid., 33.
11. T. S. Eliot, *After Strange Gods*, 20.
12. Eliot, *Christianity and Culture*, 35.
13. Ibid., 18–19.
14. Aubrey, "Oxford Conference," 395.
15. Eliot, *Christianity and Culture*, 76.
16. Harrison, *Ancient Art and Ritual*, 1.
17. Ibid., 119.
18. Ibid., x.
19. Ibid., 113.
20. Ibid., 113.
21. *Three Guineas*, 143.
22. Wood, *Broken Estate*, 116.
23. Harrison, *Ancient Art and Ritual*, 10.
24. *Moments of Being*, 148.
25. Ibid., 133.
26. Ibid., 123.
27. Ibid., 150.
28. Ibid., 147.
29. Ibid., 185.
30. Ibid., 189.
31. Ibid., 191.
32. Ibid., 192.
33. Ibid., 195–96.
34. Ibid., 196–97.
35. *Diary*, 2:26.
36. Lee, *Virginia Woolf*, 259.

37. *Letters*, 1:321.
38. Lee, *Virginia Woolf*, 219.
39. Quoted in ibid., 220.
40. Ibid., 355. See also Black, "Virginia Woolf and the Women's Movement."
41. *Diary*, 1:165.
42. *Letters*, 6:420.
43. *Diary*, 4:165.
44. *Essays*, 4:19.
45. McNeillie, "Bloomsbury," 14.
46. *Room of One's Own*, 5.
47. *Mrs. Dalloway*, 31.
48. *Between the Acts*, 127.
49. Ibid., 146.
50. *Three Guineas*, 12.
51. Ibid., 5.
52. Ibid., 103.
53. Ibid., 21.
54. Ibid., 33.
55. Ibid., 34.
56. See Bell and Nicolson, *Charleston*.
57. *Three Guineas*, 34.
58. *To the Lighthouse*, 192.
59. *Three Guineas*, 105.
60. T. W. Jones, "'Unduly Conscious of Her Sex,'" 645, 647.
61. *Three Guineas*, 113.
62. Ibid., 136.
63. Ibid., 118.
64. Ibid., 22.
65. Ibid., 114.
66. T. W. Jones , "'Unduly Conscious of Her Sex,'" 639.
67. Ibid., 641–42.
68. *Three Guineas*, 122.
69. Ibid., 123.
70. Ibid., 161.
71. Ibid., 112–13.
72. Glendinning, *Leonard Woolf*, 295.
73. *Letters*, 6:243.
74. Ibid., 6:251.
75. Ibid., 6:271.
76. Silver, "*Three Guineas* Before and After," 266–67. See also Staveley, "Marketing Virginia Woolf."
77. *Three Guineas*, 142.
78. Ibid., 112.
79. Ibid., 113–14.
80. Ibid., 119.

81. See, for example, *Cloud of Unknowing*.
82. *Three Guineas*, 114.
83. *Complete Shorter Fiction*, 58.
84. *Three Guineas*, 143.
85. Ibid.
86. *To the Lighthouse*, 83.
87. Ibid., 147.
88. Ibid., 84.
89. *Diary*, 3:316.
90. *To the Lighthouse*, 97.
91. Ibid.
92. Ibid., 105.
93. Ibid., 100.
94. Lewis, *Religious Experience*, 164–65.
95. De Gay, *Virginia Woolf and Christian Culture*, 101.
96. *To the Lighthouse*, 111.
97. Ibid., 105.
98. *Moments of Being*, 72.
99. *Passionate Apprentice*, 311.
100. *To the Lighthouse*, 160.
101. Ibid., 161.
102. Ibid., 179.
103. Ibid., 180.
104. Ibid., 202.
105. Ibid., 208.
106. *Years*, 406.
107. Ibid., 405–6.
108. *Diary*, 5:234.
109. *Essays*, 6:275.
110. Ibid., 6:261.
111. Ibid., 6:273.
112. Ibid., 4:64. See Silver, "Virginia Woolf and the Concept of Community."
113. *Letters*, 5:315.
114. *Essays*, 4:435.
115. *Between the Acts*, 84.
116. Ibid., 14–15.
117. Ibid., 147.
118. Harrison, *Ancient Art and Ritual*, 66.
119. *Between the Acts*, 117–18.
120. Ibid., 122.
121. Ibid., 123.
122. Ibid., 127.
123. *Cloud of Unknowing*, 29.
124. Harrison, *Ancient Art and Ritual*, 2.

125. Jane de Gay argues that Mr. Streatfield is the most insightful of Woolf's ministers, the one who is best able to apply "biblical ideas to the world around him." See De Gay, *Virginia Woolf and Christian Culture*, 110–11.
126. *Between the Acts*, 131.
127. Ibid., 146.
128. *Letters*, 6:486.
129. *Diary*, 5:235, 285.
130. *Letters*, 6:485.
131. Ibid., 6:485.
132. Quoted in Diment, *Russian Jew of Bloomsbury*, 266.
133. Rose, *Woman of Letters*, 244.
134. *Room of One's Own*, 112.
135. *Moments of Being*, 72.
136. *Essays*, 6:278.

BIBLIOGRAPHY

Ackroyd, Peter. *T. S. Eliot: A Life*. New York: Simon and Schuster, 1984.

Altick, Richard D. *Victorian People and Ideas: A Companion for the Modern Reader of Victorian Literature*. New York: W. W. Norton, 1973.

Annan, Noel. "The Intellectual Aristocracy." In *Studies in Social History: A Tribute to G. M. Trevelyan*, edited by J. H. Plumb, 243–87. London: Longmans, Green, 1955.

——. *Leslie Stephen: The Godless Victorian*. New York: Random House, 1984.

"An Appeal Against Women's Suffrage." *Nineteenth Century*, 25 June 1889, 781–88, and *New York Times*, 4 August 1889, 10.

Arnold, Matthew. *Selected Prose*. Harmondsworth: Penguin Books, 1970.

Atkins, Hazel. "Raising *The Rock*: The Importance of T. S. Eliot's Pageant-Play." *Christianity and Literature* 62, no. 2 (Winter 2013): 261–82.

Aubrey, Edwin Ewart. "The Oxford Conference, 1937." *Journal of Religion* 17, no. 4 (October 1937): 379–96.

Augustine of Hippo. *The Confessions of Saint Augustine*. Translated by Rex Warner. New York: Mentor, 1963.

Banfield, Ann. *The Phantom Table: Woolf, Fry, Russell, and the Epistemology of Modernism*. Cambridge: Cambridge University Press, 2000.

Beard, Mary. "My Hero: Jane Ellen Harrison." *Guardian*, 3 September 2010.

Beer, Gillian. *Virginia Woolf: The Common Ground*. Ann Arbor: University of Michigan Press, 1996.

Bell, Clive. *Art*. Oxford: Oxford University Press, 1987.

Bell, Quentin. "A 'Radiant' Friendship." *Critical Inquiry* 10, no. 4 (June 1984): 557–66.

——. "Reply to Jane Marcus." *Critical Inquiry* 11, no. 3 (March 1985): 498–501.

——. *Virginia Woolf: A Biography*. 2 vols. San Diego: Harcourt Brace Jovanovich, 1977.

Bell, Quentin, and Virginia Nicholson. *Charleston: A Bloomsbury House and Garden*. London: Frances Lincoln, 1997.

Black, Naomi. "Virginia Woolf and the Women's Movement." In *Virginia Woolf: A Feminist Slant*, edited by Jane Marcus, 180–97. Lincoln: University of Nebraska Press, 1983.

Bloom, Harold. *Genius*. New York: Warner Books, 2003.

Bowman, David. "Read It Again, Sam." *New York Times Book Review*, 4 December 2011, 75.

Briggs, Julia. *Reading Virginia Woolf*. Edinburgh: Edinburgh University Press, 2006.

———. *Virginia Woolf: An Inner Life*. Orlando: Harcourt, 2005.

Carpentier, Martha C. *Ritual, Myth, and the Modernist Text: The Influence of Jane Ellen Harrison on Joyce, Eliot, and Woolf*. Amsterdam: Gordon and Breach Publishers, 1998.

Carver, Katelynn. "'Behind the Cotton Wool': Process Philosophy in the Works of Virginia Woolf." *Graduate Journal of Harvard Divinity School* (Spring 2013). http://projects.iq.harvard.edu/hdsjournal/book/behindcottonwool.

Chadwick, Owen. *The Victorian Church*, parts 1–2. New York: Oxford University Press, 1966.

Childs, Donald J. "Mrs. Dalloway's Unexpected Guests: Virginia Woolf, T. S. Eliot, and Matthew Arnold." *Modern Language Quarterly* 58, no. 1 (1997): 63–82.

The Cloud of Unknowing and Other Works. Translated by A. C. Spearing. London: Penguin, 2001.

Co-operative Working Women. *Life as We Have Known It*. Edited by Margaret Llewelyn Davies with an introductory letter by Virginia Woolf. London: Virago, 1977.

Cramer, Patricia. "Jane Harrison and Lesbian Plots: The Absent Lover in Virginia Woolf's *The Waves*." *Studies in the Novel* 37, no. 4 (Winter 2005): 443–63.

Dandelion, Pink. *An Introduction to Quakerism*. Cambridge: Cambridge University Press, 2007.

De Gay, Jane. *Virginia Woolf and Christian Culture*. Edinburgh: Edinburgh University Press, 2018.

Desalvo, Louise A. "As 'Miss Jan Says': Virginia Woolf's Early Journals." In *Virginia Woolf and Bloomsbury: A Centenary Celebration*, edited by Jane Marcus, 96–124. Bloomington: Indiana University Press, 1987.

Diment, Galya. *A Russian Jew of Bloomsbury: The Life and Times of Samuel Koteliansky*. Montreal: McGill-Queen's University Press, 2011.

Dorrien, Gary. *Kantian Reason and Hegelian Spirit: The Idealistic Logic of Modern Theology*. Malden, Mass.: Wiley-Blackwell, 2015.

Edel, Leon. *Bloomsbury: A House of Lions*. Philadelphia: J. B. Lippincott, 1970.

Edwards, Mark Thomas. "'God's Totalitarianism': Ecumenical Protestant Discourse During the Good War, 1941–45." *Politics, Religion and Ideology* 10, nos. 3–4 (2009): 285–302.

Eliot, George. *Middlemarch: A Study in Provincial Life*. Oxford: Oxford University Press, 1996.

Eliot, T. S. *After Strange Gods: A Primer of Modern Heresy*. New York: Harcourt, Brace, 1934.

———. *Christianity and Culture*. New York: Harcourt, Brace, 1940.

———. *Selected Essays of T. S. Eliot*. New York: Harcourt, Brace & World, 1936.

Faber, Roland. *God as Poet of the World: Exploring Process Theologies*. Translated by Douglas W. Stott. Louisville: Westminster John Knox Press, 2004.

Fletcher, Ian. *Walter Pater*. London: Longmans, Green, 1959.
Flint, Kate. "Reading Uncommonly: Virginia Woolf and the Practice of Reading." *Yearbook of English Studies* 26 (1996): 187–98.
Fraser, Hilary. *Beauty and Belief: Aesthetics and Religion in Victorian Literature*. Cambridge: Cambridge University Press, 2008.
Frazer, James George. *The Golden Bough: A Study in Magic and Religion*. London: Oxford University Press, 1994.
Froula, Christine. "*Mrs. Dalloway*'s Postwar Elegy: Women, War, and the Art of Mourning." *Modernism/Modernity* 9, no. 1 (January 2002): 125–63.
Fry, Roger. *Vision and Design*. Edited by J. B. Bullen. Mineola, N.Y.: Dover Publications, 1998.
Gilley, Sheridan. "The Church of England in the Nineteenth Century." In *A History of Religion in Great Britain: Practice and Belief from Pre-Roman Times to the Present*, edited by Sheridan Gilley and W. J. Sheils, 291–305. Oxford: Blackwell, 1994.
Glendinning, Victoria. *Leonard Woolf: A Biography*. New York: Free Press, 2006.
Goodwin, Craufurd D. "The Art of an Ethical Life: Keynes and Bloomsbury." In *The Cambridge Companion to Keynes*, edited by Roger E. Backhouse and Bradley W. Bateman, 217–36. Cambridge: Cambridge University Press, 2006.
Gordon, Lyndall. *Virginia Woolf: A Writer's Life*. New York: W. W. Norton, 1985.
Gough, Val. "'That Razor Edge of Balance': Virginia Woolf and Mysticism." *Woolf Studies Annual* 5 (1999): 57–77.
Graham, Elyse, and Pericles Lewis. "Private Religion, Public Mourning, and *Mrs. Dalloway*." *Modern Philology* 111, no. 1 (August 2013): 88–106.
Griesinger, Emily. "Religious Belief in a Secular Age: Literary Modernism and Virginia Woolf's *Mrs. Dalloway*." *Christianity and Literature* 64, no. 4 (2015): 438–64.
Griffiths, Paul J. *Religious Reading: The Place of Reading in the Practice of Religion*. New York: Oxford University Press, 1999.
Grosskurth, Phyllis. *Leslie Stephen*. London: Longmans, Green, 1968.
Guigo II. *The Ladder of Monks and Twelve Meditations*. Translated by Edmund Colledge, OSA, and James Walsh, SJ. Kalamazoo, Mich.: Cistercian Publications, 1979.
Hafley, James. "Walter Pater's 'Marius' and the Technique of Modern Fiction." *Modern Fiction Studies* 3, no. 2 (Summer 1957): 99–109.
Haller, Evelyn. "Isis Unveiled: Virginia Woolf's Use of Egyptian Myth." In *Virginia Woolf: A Feminist Slant*, edited by Jane Marcus, 109–31. Lincoln: University of Nebraska Press, 1983.
Harris, Alexandra. *Virginia Woolf*. New York: Thames & Hudson, 2011.
Harrison, Jane Ellen. *Ancient Art and Ritual*. Bradford-on-Avon: Moonraker Press, 1913.
———. *Epilegomena to the Study of Greek Religion*. Cambridge: Cambridge University Press, 1921.
———. *Prolegomena to the Study of Greek Religion*. 3rd ed. Cambridge: Cambridge University Press, 1922.

Hartshorne, Charles, and William L. Reese. *Philosophers Speak of God*. Chicago: University of Chicago Press, 1953.

Hempton, David. "Religious Life in Industrial Britain, 1830–1914." In *A History of Religion in Great Britain*, edited by Sheridan Gilley and W. J. Sheils, 306–21. Oxford: Blackwell, 1994.

Herbert, George. *The Complete English Poems*. Edited by John Tobin. London: Penguin Books, 1991.

Hildegard of Bingen. *Symphonia armonia celestium relevationum*. 2nd ed. Translated and edited by Barbara Newman. Ithaca: Cornell University Press, 1998.

Hilma af Klint: Paintings for the Future. Edited by Tracey Bashkoff. New York: Guggenheim Museum Publications, 2018.

Hollywood, Amy. *Acute Melancholia and Other Essays: Mysticism, History, and the Study of Religion*. New York: Columbia University Press, 2016.

The Hours of the Divine Office in English and Latin, vol. 3. Collegeville, Minn.: The Liturgical Press, 1964.

Hussey, Mark. *The Singing of the Real World: The Philosophy of Virginia Woolf's Fiction*. Columbus: Ohio State University Press, 1986.

Hutchinson, Brian. *G. E. Moore's Ethical Theory: Resistance and Reconciliation*. New York: Cambridge University Press, 2001.

John of the Cross. *The Collected Works of St. John of the Cross*. 3rd ed. Translated by Kieran Kavanaugh, OCD, and Otilio Rodriguez, OCD. Washington, D.C.: ICS Publications, 2017.

Jones, Rufus. *The Later Periods of Quakerism*. 2 vols. London: Macmillan, 1921.

Jones, Timothy Willem. "'Unduly Conscious of Her Sex': Priesthood, Female Bodies, and Sacred Space in the Church of England." *Women's History Review* 21, no. 4 (2012): 639–55.

Kandinsky, Wassily. *Concerning the Spiritual in Art*. Translated by M. T. H. Sadler. New York: Dover Publications, 1977.

Kane, Julie. "Varieties of Mystical Experience in the Writings of Virginia Woolf." *Twentieth Century Literature* 41, no. 4 (Winter 1995): 328–49.

Keynes, John Maynard. "My Early Beliefs." In *The Collected Writings of John Maynard Keynes*, vol. 10, *Essays in Biography*, 433–51. London: Macmillan, 1972.

Knight, Christopher J. "'The God of Love Is Full of Tricks': Virginia Woolf's Vexed Relation to the Tradition of Christianity." *Religion and Literature* 39, no. 1 (Spring 2007): 27–46.

Knoepflmacher, U. C. *Religious Humanism and the Victorian Novel: George Eliot, Walter Pater, and Samuel Butler*. Princeton: Princeton University Press, 1965.

Lackey, Michael. "Atheism and Sadism: Nietzsche and Woolf on Post-God Discourse." *Philosophy and Literature* 24, no. 2 (October 2000): 346–63.

——. "The Gender of Atheism in Virginia Woolf's 'A Simple Melody.'" *Studies in Short Fiction* 35 (1998): 49–63.

——. "Virginia Woolf and T. S. Eliot: An Atheist's Commentary on the Epistemology of Belief." *Woolf Studies Annual* 8 (2002): 62–87.

Lambert, Elizabeth G. "'and Darwin says they are nearer the cow': Evolutionary Discourse in *Melymbrosia* and *The Voyage Out*." *Twentieth Century Literature* 37, no. 1 (Spring 1991): 1–21.

Laurence, Patricia. *Lily Briscoe's Chinese Eyes: Bloomsbury, Modernism, and China*. Columbia: University of South Carolina Press, 2013.
Law, William. *A Serious Call to a Devout and Holy Life*. ReadaClassic.com, 2010.
Lazenby, Donna J. *A Mystical Philosophy: Transcendence and Immanence in the Works of Virginia Woolf and Iris Murdoch*. London: Bloomsbury, 2014.
Leclercq, Jean. *The Love of Learning and the Desire for God: A Study of Monastic Culture*. Translated by Catharine Misrahi. New York: Fordham University Press, 1961.
Lee, Hermione. *Virginia Woolf*. New York: Knopf, 1998.
Levy, Paul. *Moore: G. E. Moore and the Cambridge Apostles*. London: Weidenfeld and Nicolson, 1979.
Lewis, Pericles. *The Cambridge Introduction to Modernism*. Cambridge: Cambridge University Press, 2007.
——. *Religious Experience and the Modernist Novel*. Cambridge: Cambridge University Press, 2010.
The Library of Leonard and Virginia Woolf: A Short-Title Catalogue. Compiled and edited by Julia King and Laila Miletic-Vejzovic. Pullman: Washington State University Press, 2003.
Linett, Maren. "The Jew in the Bath: Imperiled Imagination in Woolf's *The Years*." *Modern Fiction Studies* 48, no. 2 (Summer 2002): 341–60.
Lowell, James Russell. *Letters of James Russell Lowell*, vol. 2. Edited by Charles Eliot Norton. New York: Harper and Brothers, Publishers, 1893.
MacCarthy, Desmond. *Leslie Stephen*. Folcroft, Pa.: Folcroft Library Editions, 1937.
MacIntyre, Alasdair. *After Virtue: A Study in Moral Theory*. Notre Dame: University of Notre Dame Press, 1981.
Maitland, Frederic William. *The Life and Letters of Leslie Stephen*. London: Duckworth, 1906.
Marcus, Jane. "Liberty, Sorority, Misogyny." In *The Representation of Women in Fiction*, edited by Carolyn G. Heilbrun and Margaret R. Higonnet, 60–97. Baltimore: Johns Hopkins University Press, 1983.
——. "The Niece of a Nun: Virginia Woolf, Caroline Stephen, and the Cloistered Imagination." In *Virginia Woolf: A Feminist Slant*, edited by Jane Marcus, 7–36. Lincoln: University of Nebraska Press, 1983.
——. "Quentin's Bogey." *Critical Inquiry* 11, no. 3 (March 1985): 486–97.
——. "Tintinnabulations." *Marxist Perspectives* 2 (Spring 1979): 144–67.
Marguerite d'Oingt. *The Writings of Margaret of Oingt: Medieval Prioress and Mystic*. Translated by Renate Blumenfeld-Kosinski. Newburyport, Mass.: Focus Information Group, 1990.
Marshall, Alan. "'England and Nowhere.'" In *The Cambridge Companion to T. S. Eliot*, edited by A. David Moody, 94–107. Cambridge: Cambridge University Press, 1984.
McGinn, Bernard. "The God Beyond God: Theology and Mysticism in the Thought of Meister Eckhart." *Journal of Religion* 61, no. 1 (January 1981): 1–19.
McNeillie, Andrew. "Bloomsbury." In *The Cambridge Companion to Virginia Woolf*, edited by Susan Sellers, 1–28. 2nd ed. Cambridge: Cambridge University Press, 2010.

Meisel, Perry. *The Absent Father: Virginia Woolf and Walter Pater*. New Haven: Yale University Press, 1980.
Mills, Jean. *Virginia Woolf, Jane Ellen Harrison, and the Spirit of Modernist Classicism*. Columbus: Ohio State University Press, 2014.
Moore, Madeline. *The Short Season Between Two Silences: The Mystical and the Political in the Novels of Virginia Woolf*. Boston: George Allen & Unwin, 1984.
Newman, Barbara. *Sister of Wisdom: St. Hildegard's Theology of the Feminine*. Berkeley: University of California Press, 1987.
Noble, Joan Russell, ed. *Recollections of Virginia Woolf by Her Contemporaries*. London: Peter Owen, 1972.
Olson, Barbara K. *Authorial Divinity in the Twentieth Century: Omniscient Narration in Woolf, Hemingway, and Others*. London: Associated University Presses, 1997.
Pater, Walter. *Appreciations: With an Essay on Style*. London: Macmillan, 1924.
———. *Marius the Epicurean: His Sensations and Ideas*. Introduction by Michael Levey. Middlesex, England: Penguin, 1985.
———. *The Renaissance: Studies in Art and Poetry*. New York: Macmillan, 1899.
Paulsell, Stephanie. "*Scriptio divina*: Women, Writing and God." *Spire* 26, no. 1 (Fall 2005): 10–17.
———. "*Scriptio divina*: Writing and the Experience of God in the Works of Marguerite d'Oingt." Ph.D. diss., University of Chicago, 1993.
———. "Writing and Mystical Experience in the Works of Marguerite d'Oingt and Virginia Woolf." *Comparative Literature* 44, no. 3 (Summer 1992): 249–67.
Pecora, Vincent P. *Secularization and Cultural Criticism: Religion, Nation, and Modernity*. Chicago: University of Chicago Press, 2006.
Potolsky, Matthew. "Fear of Falling: Walter Pater's *Marius the Epicurean* as a Dangerous Influence." *ELH* 65, no. 3 (1998): 701–29.
Potter, Matthew C. "British Art and Empire: Holman Hunt's *The Light of the Word* Reflected in the Mirror of the Colonial Press." *Media History* 13, no. 1 (2007): 1–23.
The Quest of the Holy Grail. Translated by P. M. Matarasso. New York: Penguin, 1969.
Regan, Tom. *Bloomsbury's Prophet: G. E. Moore and the Development of His Moral Philosophy*. Philadelphia: Temple University Press, 1986.
Richter, Harvena. "The Canonical Hours in *Mrs. Dalloway*." *Modern Fiction Studies* 28, no. 2 (Summer 1982): 236–40.
Robertson, Duncan. *Lectio Divina: The Medieval Experience of Reading*. Collegeville, Minn.: Cistercian Publications, 2011.
Rose, Phyllis. *Woman of Letters: A Life of Virginia Woolf*. New York: Oxford University Press, 1978.
Sackville-West, Vita. *The Eagle and the Dove*. London: Michael Joseph, 1943.
Santayana, George. *The Life of Reason*. One-volume edition. New York: Charles Scribner's Sons, 1954.
Schidel, G. E. "Lauds." In *New Catholic Encyclopedia*, 8:379–80. 2nd ed. Detroit: Thomson, Gale, 2003.

Second Post-Impressionist Exhibition, Oct 5–Dec 31, 1912, Illustrated Catalogue. London: Ballantyne, 1912.

See, Sam. "The Comedy of Nature: Darwinian Feminism in Virginia Woolf's *Between the Acts*." *Modernism/Modernity* 17, no. 3 (September 2010): 639–67.

Shattuck, Sandra D. "The Stage of Scholarship: Crossing the Bridge from Harrison to Woolf." In *Virginia Woolf and Bloomsbury: A Centenary Celebration*, edited by Jane Marcus, 278–98. Bloomington: Indiana University Press, 1987.

Silver, Brenda R. "*Three Guineas* Before and After: Further Answers to Correspondents." In *Virginia Woolf: A Feminist Slant*, edited by Jane Marcus, 254–76. Lincoln: University of Nebraska Press, 1983.

——. "Virginia Woolf and the Concept of Community: The Elizabethan Playhouse." *Women's Studies* 4, nos. 2-3: 291-98.

——. *Virginia Woolf's Reading Notebooks*. Princeton: Princeton University Press, 1983.

Spalding, Frances. *Vanessa Bell*. New Haven: Ticknor & Fields, 1983.

Spender, Stephen. "Remembering Eliot." *Sewanee Review* 74, no. 1 (Winter 1966): 58–84.

Stansky, Peter. *On or About December 1910: Early Bloomsbury and Its Intimate World*. Cambridge: Harvard University Press, 1996.

Staveley, Alice. "Marketing Virginia Woolf: Women, War, and Public Relations in *Three Guineas*." *Book History* 12 (2009): 295–339.

Stephen, Caroline Emelia. *Light Arising: Thoughts on the Central Radiance*. Cambridge: W. Heffer & Sons, 1908.

——. *Quaker Strongholds*. London: Kegan Paul, Trench, Trübner, 1890.

——. *The Vision of Faith and Other Essays*. Cambridge: W. Heffer & Sons, 1911.

Stephen, Dorothea Jane. *Studies in Early Indian Thought*. London: Cambridge University Press, 1918.

Stephen, James, Sir. *Essays in Ecclesiastical Biography*. 2 vols. New York: Longmans, Green, 1907.

——. *Letters: With Biographical Notes by His Daughter, Caroline Emelia Stephen*. Gloucester: J. Bellows, 1906.

Stephen, Julia Duckworth. *Julia Duckworth Stephen: Stories for Children, Essays for Adults*. Syracuse: Syracuse University Press, 1987.

Stephen, Leslie. *An Agnostic's Apology and Other Essays*. London: Smith, Elder, 1903.

——. "Art and Morality." *Cornhill Magazine* 32, no. 187 (July 1875): 91–101.

——. *Hours in a Library*, vol. 3. London: Smith, Elder, 1892.

——. *Men, Books, and Mountains: Essays by Leslie Stephen*. Edited by S. A. O. Ullman. London: The Hogarth Press, 1956.

——. *Sir Leslie Stephen's Mausoleum Book*. Oxford: Clarendon Press, 1977.

——. *Some Early Impressions*. London: The Hogarth Press, 1924.

——. *Studies of a Biographer*, vols. 1–4. London: Smith, Elder / Duckworth, 1907.

——. "The Study of English Literature." *Cornhill Magazine* 8, no. 47 (May 1887): 486–508.

Taylor, Charles. *A Secular Age*. Cambridge, Mass.: Belknap Press, 2007.
——. *Sources of the Self: The Making of Modern Identity*. Cambridge: Harvard University Press, 1989.
Teresa of Avila. *The Collected Works of St. Teresa of Avila*, vol. 2. Translated by Kieran Kavanaugh, OCD, and Otilio Rodriguez, OCD. Washington, D.C.: ICS Publications, 1980.
——. *Interior Castle*. Translated by Kieran Kavanaugh, OCD, and Otilio Rodriguez, OCD. Mahwah, N.J.: Paulist Press, 1979.
Tickner, Lisa. "Vanessa Bell: *Studland Beach*, Domesticity, and 'Significant Form.'" *Representations* 65 (Winter 1999): 63–92.
Tolley, Christopher. *Domestic Biography: The Legacy of Evangelicalism in Four Nineteenth-Century Families*. Oxford: Clarendon Press, 1997.
Tomkins, Stephen. *The Clapham Sect: How Wilberforce's Circle Transformed Britain*. Oxford: Lion Hudson, 2010.
Viola, André. "'Buds on the Tree of Life': A Recurrent Mythological Image in Virginia Woolf's *Mrs. Dalloway*." *Journal of Modern Literature* 20, no. 2 (Winter 1996): 239–47.
Whitehead, Alfred North. *Process and Reality*. New York: Macmillan, 1929.
——. *Religion in the Making*. New York: Macmillan, 1926.
——. *Science and the Modern World*. New York: Macmillan, 1925.
Whitworth, Michael. *Virginia Woolf*. Oxford: Oxford University Press, 2005.
Williams, C. Peter. "British Religion and the Wider World: Mission and Empire, 1800–1940." In *A History of Religion in Britain: Practice and Belief from Pre-Roman Times to the Present*, edited by Sheridan Gilley and W. J. Sheils, 381–405. Oxford: Blackwell, 1994.
Wood, James. *The Broken Estate: Essays on Literature and Belief*. New York: Picador, 1999.
Woolf, Leonard. *Letters of Leonard Woolf*. Edited by Frederic Spotts. London: Weidenfeld and Nicolson, 1989.
——. "A Note by Leonard Woolf." In Virginia Woolf, *Hours in a Library*, 7–9. New York: Harcourt, Brace, 1957.
——. *Sowing: An Autobiography of the Years 1880 to 1904*. London: The Hogarth Press, 1967.
Woolf, Virginia. *Between the Acts*. Annotated and with an introduction by Melba Cuddy-Keane. Orlando: Harcourt, 1941.
——. *The Complete Shorter Fiction of Virginia Woolf*. Edited by Susan Dick. San Diego: Harcourt Brace Jovanovich, 1985.
——. *The Diary of Virginia Woolf*. Edited by Anne Olivier Bell. 5 vols. New York: Harcourt Brace Jovanovich, 1977–1984.
——. *The Essays of Virginia Woolf*, vols. 1–4. Edited by Andrew McNeillie. San Diego: Harcourt Brace Jovanovich, 1986–1994.
——. *The Essays of Virginia Woolf*, vol. 5. Edited by Stuart N. Clarke. Boston: Houghton Mifflin Harcourt, 2010.
——. *The Essays of Virginia Woolf*, vol. 6. Edited by Stuart N. Clarke. London: The Hogarth Press, 2011.

———. *Jacob's Room*. San Diego: Harcourt Brace Jovanovich, 1922.
———. *The Letters of Virginia Woolf*. Edited by Nigel Nicholson and Joanne Trautmann Banks. 6 vols. New York: Harcourt Brace Jovanovich, 1975–1980.
———. *Moments of Being*. 2nd ed. Edited by Jeanne Schulkind. San Diego: Harcourt Brace Jovanovich, 1985.
———. *Mrs. Dalloway*. Annotated and with an introduction by Bonnie Kime Scott. Orlando: Harvest, 1925.
———. *Night and Day*. New York: George H. Doran, 1920.
———. *Orlando: A Biography*. Annotated and with an introduction by Maria DiBattista. Orlando: Harcourt, 1928.
———. *A Passionate Apprentice: The Early Journals, 1897–1909*. Edited by Mitchell A. Leaska. San Diego: Harcourt Brace Jovanovich, 1990.
———. *Roger Fry: A Biography*. New York: Harcourt Brace Jovanovich, 1940.
———. *A Room of One's Own*. Annotated and with an introduction by Susan Gubar. Orlando: Harcourt, 1929.
———. *Three Guineas*. Orlando: Harcourt, 1938.
———. *To the Lighthouse*. Orlando: Harcourt, 1927.
———. *The Voyage Out*. Orlando: Harcourt, 1920.
———. *The Waves*. Annotated and with an introduction by Molly Hite. Orlando: Harcourt, 1931.
———. *The Waves: The Two Holograph Drafts*. Edited by J. W. Graham. Toronto: University of Toronto Press, 1976.
———. *The Years*. Annotated and with an introduction by Eleanor McNees. Orlando: Harcourt, 1939.
Woolf, Virginia, and Vanessa Bell with Thoby Stephen. *Hyde Park Gate News: The Stephen Family Newspaper*. Edited by Gill Lowe. London: Hesperus Press, 2005.
Wright, Jude. "'His Own Nearer Household Gods': Pagans, Christians, and *Marius the Epicurean*'s Religious Hermeneutics." *Cahiers victoriens et édouardiens* 80 (Autumn 2014): 2–11.
Yeats, William Butler. *Autobiographies*. New York: Macmillan, 1927.
Zaleski, Philip, and Carol Zaleski. *Prayer: A History*. New York: Houghton Mifflin, 2005.

INDEX

BOOKS IN THE SERIES:

VOLUME 1
Religion Around Shakespeare
Peter Iver Kaufman

VOLUME 2
Religion Around Emily Dickinson
W. Clark Gilpin

VOLUME 3
Religion Around Billie Holiday
Tracy Fessenden

VOLUME 4
Religion Around John Donne
Joshua Eckhardt

VOLUME 5
Religion Around Mary Shelley
Jennifer L. Airey